Ethics for Social Care in Ireland: Philosophy and Practice

SECOND EDITION

Manus Charleton

GILL & MACMILLAN

Gill & Macmillan
Hume Avenue
Park West
Dublin 12
www.gillmacmillan.ie

© Manus Charleton 2014

978 07171 5977 2

Print origination by O'K Graphic Design, Dublin
Index compiled by Eileen O'Neil
Printed by GraphyCems, Spain

The paper used in this book is made from the wood pulp of managed forests. For every tree felled, at least one tree is planted, thereby renewing natural resources.

A CIP catalogue record is available for this book from the British Library.

To my wife, Barbara,
daughters Oonagh, Medb and Muireann,
and grandchildren Ben, Josh and Eva

Contents

Acknowledgments

I would like to thank the students in the Institute of Technology, Sligo with whom I have discussed ethics over the years. They were the students of the degree course in Applied Social Care, the Certificate in Social Care Advocacy, and the Masters in Business Administration. Their interest in the theory and practice of ethics has been a source of great encouragement. I would also like to thank Dr Perry Share, Head of the Department of Human Sciences in the Institute, together with my former colleagues. I have learned a lot from their experience, knowledge and understanding of social care education while working alongside them in developing course programmes. I would also like to thank the publisher Gill & Macmillan for giving me the opportunity to write a second edition. I would especially like to thank my family for their support and encouragement in writing the book. I am also grateful to family and friends for many lively discussions about ethical and social issues. In particular, I would like to thank my good friend Gerard McCarthy. His experience and understanding of social work, together with his knowledge of philosophy and wise judgment have been of immense help and support.

Preface

What gives ethics its importance? And how is its importance to be understood? In recent years in Ireland, the need to ask these questions and try and answer them has become clearer. The need to explore the questions follows on from public criticism of much that has gone wrong in Irish society.

In 2008 the country suffered an economic collapse, due in part to negligent banking practices, which has led to austerity and much hardship for many. We have also seen the publication of reports into abuse of children. Notably, in 2009, the Ryan report found that in the past many children suffered physical, sexual and emotional abuse in residential institutions run by Catholic religious orders, while the Murphy report found that church and state authorities failed to handle properly allegations of child sexual abuse against clerics in the Dublin Archdiocese.

More recently, in 2011 and 2013, there have been filmed reports by RTÉ's Prime Time of lapses in basic standards of care in home help services for the elderly and in care of children in some private crèches. Also in 2013, the long-running tribunal of enquiry into planning matters and payments among some politicians and business people issued its final report, which included findings of corruption and improper behaviour.

These and other examples show that there is a wider ethical dimension to social care than directly helping people to meet their individual needs. They show that how people behave in general, and in particular in their work, has implications for the well-being of others, especially for those who are vulnerable. In social care, the main public response to ensure better care has been through policy and regulation. Examples have included the setting up a new child and family services agency, and a referendum to strengthen children's rights in the Constitution. There has also been an emphasis on setting care standards and providing for inspections to try to ensure compliance, notably through the work of the Health Information and Quality Authority. Also, the social professions are now regulated by the national Heath & Social Care Professionals Council, and it has developed a code of professional conduct and ethics for social workers.

Policy responses that include tighter regulation are necessary and essential to try to ensure better observance of ethical values and principles. However, there is a risk of ethics becoming associated with nothing more than requirements for compliance. Ethics is first and foremost about behaving in the right way for its own sake, and this is underpinned by knowledge and understanding of what gives ethics its importance. In a speech in 2013, entitled 'Toward an Ethical Economy', President Michael D. Higgins called for philosophical understanding of ethical sources to inform ethical consciousness in public discourse and action, and for philosophy to be made a formal subject in secondary schools.

The President also made the point that codes of ethics are of limited use unless there is also understanding of their purpose, which is to give effect to human values. Values that are understood and shared can help to ensure a deeper human response to treating people who have need of care in contrast to a response based merely on following requirements in a code. Also, it is from understanding values that the best way can be found to respond to people whose need is set in complicated circumstances, such as where it might be met in different but conflicting ways and where a choice has to be made.

Philosophers regard ethics as a radical subject which explores ideas about how we should live, or how to have a fulfilling life, on the basis of understanding what is ultimately of value for the individual and society. As a subject, ethics is about ideas. But ideas have more influence on what happens in practice than they are often given credit for. Kant is an example of a philosopher whose ideas have had particular practical effect. Kant's arguments for the ideas that all people are equal in worth and deserving of respect contributed to these ideas having practical effect in society and legislation in the modern period. They can be seen, for example, as one of the influences behind the United Nations Declaration of Human Rights. It is also in Kant's ideas that we find there is a duty of care.

Perhaps more than any other factor there is the need to see our sense of ethics as a core dimension of the person we are and would like to be for ourselves and others, and not merely something that arises for us on occasions of particular moral challenge. Ethics is not something we engage with only when a moral issue arises for us and then leave aside. Some sense of ethics is central to how we get on with our daily life; it is part of our prevailing outlook. We have what Taylor calls a 'moral orientation' or framework (1989: 99), which characterises our responses. We use our ethical sensibility to evaluate our way through situations and issues, but it is not always clear to us that our responses contain information about the place that values have in our lives. This is because values are so closely bound up with how we engage with our experiences. For Iris Murdoch, our values show in 'what we see things as, what we let, or make, ourselves think about'. Things, people, situations we encounter everyday have 'moral colour'; this may be black or white, but usually it is one of a large number of subtle shades of grey (1992: 215; 265). This makes it important to know what values are and how they are understood, along with the ways in which they are expressed, ignored or disregarded.

In one way or another we use moral language all the time, often investing it with strong emotional conviction, especially when we feel we have been wronged. However, what people mean by ethical and moral and related terms can sometimes come across as assertion which may, or may not, be well-founded. Whether done intentionally or not, moral language is sometimes used to manipulate others where it disguises self-interest, such as a need to exercise authority or for some material or emotional gain. For example, we can notice when people and governments have double standards, that is, they criticise others for behaving in ways which they themselves behave. From experience we know, too, how our own sense of values can become clouded by the pressure of circumstances and that we fall short of standards we expect of ourselves.

Philosophers have provided an understanding of the gap between values that are held up for us to follow and our actual behaviour. Spinoza points to the power of underlying causes which affect our emotions and behaviour to an extent that means we are never fully in charge. Also, recent findings in neuroscience about how the brain works suggest we may not have the kind of freedom to control how we behave as we once thought.

Ethics arising from philosophical understanding is quite different from moralising or being judgmental – it is not about taking the high moral ground; it is about acquiring understanding as a basis for good living. Philosophical understanding also enables us to recognise a range of possible ethical standpoints, and that there are limits to human knowledge and understanding of ethics.

Asked what he thought of Western civilisation, Ghandi is reported to have said that 'it would be a good idea'. In other words, he appreciated the values on which Western civilisation is based but recognised that they existed more in theory than in practice. This book is about some of the values that Ghandi recognised. In light of them we can, in Montaigne's phrase, 'hope for the better and desire the better' (2003: 924). It is based on the belief that understanding sources for values can contribute to living up to them in practice.

More particularly, this book aims to enable people who work in social care to have confidence in knowing that there is a body of theory about values which can be considered to inform, support and provide justification for their work in caring for others. It is a book in which values and principles are explored to enable students to have a deeper understanding of the ethical basis of care work, and to draw from this understanding in solving problems and making decisions as part of their reflective practice.

I'm conscious that there is much more relevant material available for the understanding of values, principles and issues than I have included. The main aim has been to provide an introductory textbook which will give students an understanding of some of the basic insights that have proved influential, and from which they can take their direction for further study and exploration.

REFERENCES

Higgins, M. D. (2013) 'Toward an Ethical Economy', speech available on the website for the Office of the President (accessed 22 September 2013).

Montaigne, M. de (2003) 'Of Vanity' in *The Complete Works*, Everyman Library.

Murdoch, I. (1992) *Metaphysics as a Guide to Morals*, Chatto & Windus.

Taylor, C. (1989) *Sources of the Self: The Making of the Modern Identity*, Cambridge University Press.

1

Introduction

OVERALL AIM

To introduce ethics as a subject of study in relation to providing social care.

LEARNING OBJECTIVES

At the end of this chapter you should be able to:

- Connect ethics with behaviour relating to values and principles.
- Distinguish ethics as a subject from its relation to religion, law and politics.
- Relate ethics to a professional code for guiding best practice.
- Begin to engage with the book's overall aim of exploring the understanding of values and principles to guide best social care practice.

BASIC TERMS

Values and Principles

Ethical and *unethical* are broad terms people use when discussing and judging desirable and undesirable behaviour or issues, such as poverty in the developing world. The terms imply that the behaviour or the response to an issue is either in accordance with, or breaches, a particular value or principle. More specifically, sentences containing the verbs *should* and *ought* to are used on the basis of some value or principle. For example, we might say to a friend with whom we are sharing accommodation, 'You should clean up the kitchen after you use it and not leave it for me to do.' Here we are appealing to a principle of fairness. Or, to take a social care example, we might say, 'Home help services for older people should not be reduced to save money.' In saying this, we are implying that it is not right morally to save money by reducing services for people who need help in meeting their basic needs, such as cooking or shopping. We are implying that ensuring vulnerable older people have well-being is an important moral value which should be maintained. In addition, we may be appealing to a principle of social justice or fairness, by implying that older people deserve to benefit from a share of society's wealth in view of the contribution they have made to society over many years.

Other terms used to express moral approval or disapproval are *acceptable* and *unacceptable*. For example, we might say, 'It is morally unacceptable to live in a society in which some people are left homeless.' Here we are appealing to the view that everyone in society should have a comfortable and secure place to live for well-being as a human right. When they do not have one, a basic norm is breached. *Appropriate* and *inappropriate* are terms also used to express moral approval or disapproval. Like acceptable and unacceptable, they can be used as synonyms (words that have the same or similar meaning) for morally right and wrong, or morally good and bad. Depending on the context in which they are used, acceptable and appropriate, and their opposites, can convey different shades of meaning. For example, instead of unacceptable or inappropriate conveying that we think there is something essentially wrong about a particular behaviour or practice, we may be conveying that something in particular does not accord with our views, or with the kind of society we would like to live in, or with our estimation of the general view on the matter which people have in society.

Distinction between Values and Principles

A distinction is made between values and principles. Parekh describes values as 'things we consider worth cherishing and realising in our lives'. They are 'things we have good reason to cherish, which in our well-considered view deserve our allegiance and ought to form part of the good life' (Parekh 2000: 127). Values include human well-being in all its aspects – physical, material, social, and mental and emotional health.

Moral principles are general statements of basic ideas which are considered to indicate the right way to behave; respect for each other is an example. Principles are similar to values in that they are considered worth living up to. However, even if we do not value principles, they imply that we should try to abide by them. There is a general expectancy that we should try to follow them for the good of others and ourselves. General principles give rise to more specific ones, for example, the principle of respecting others gives rise to the principle of seeking a client's or service user's consent for his/her care plan or care support measure.

The main values and principles relevant to social care work are in this book as chapter headings.

Ethics and Morality

Ethics and *morality* are terms used interchangeably. At the same time, ethics tends to be used more for the study or understanding of moral values and principles, whereas morality tends to be used more for the practice of values and principles. In this book, ethics as the study and understanding of values and principles is related to the ways in which they are applied in practice. We will see how values and principles are expressed through social care, and at how care standards can be improved by putting values and principles into practice to greater effect.

Philosophical ethics is called *normative*, i.e. it is the study of how people ought to behave towards each other. *Descriptive* ethics, on the other hand, is an account of social norms and standards and people's moral values, without questioning their justification and trying to establish why there should be values and principles for everybody.

APPLIED PHILOSOPHY

Rational Justification

From our upbringing, we learn about particular values and principles. We learn, for example, to be honest and kind and to treat people with respect. They are part of the means by which we are socialised into society. Philosophers go further than simply appealing to values and principles as social norms and standards. As a subject, ethics is also called 'moral philosophy', and philosophers provide reasons or rational arguments to explain why certain ideas should be considered values and principles: ones which we should use as guides for behaving in certain ways and for avoiding behaving in other ways.

Philosophical justification of values and principles provides evidence of their worth over and above the fact that they are simply there as part of culture. This is important because it gives values and principles a stronger foundation than if simply taken for granted. Also, in Ireland, and in other countries, certain practices were morally accepted as social norms but in time came to be understood as contrary to values and principles. For example, women were once legally paid less than men for the same work, and people with disabilities did not have their lives and their potential recognised to the same extent as people without a disability. By establishing rational evidence for values and principles, such as equality and respect, philosophical understanding provides a basis from which to assess whether certain practices that come to be the norm are justified or not.

Another reason why philosophical justification is important is that it strengthens the foundation of our ethical views. It adds to and can clarify more immediate sources we may have for our views, such as feelings or opinions, or beliefs we have been taught and accept. Also, where there is a shortfall in care services to meet needs, justification strengthens the case for the necessary resources to be made available to care organisations and agencies.

However, in practice social work and social care ethics is not about directly applying philosophical arguments to issues and cases. It is more a matter of dealing with the many issues, problems and dilemmas which arise naturally in care work through discussion and assessment. But when viewpoints have been formed through philosophical understanding, it can bring more insight and confidence to care decisions based on values and principles. For example, during a case conference, a number of possible courses of action may come up in trying to provide for a client's well-being where his/her independence and safety are both an issue. So, in assessing the client's circumstances, to know the philosophical justification for the value of well-being, which relates to clients making their own decisions, as well as others providing them with practical assistance, can inform the discussion and influence the best course of action.

A further reason for exploring rational justification is that, both within philosophical ethics and among people generally, there is disagreement and debate about what certain values mean, such as social justice, and, as a result, on the kind of policies which provide for the values. By exploring the justifications that lie behind people's differing viewpoints, care practitioners can develop an informed viewpoint with which to contribute to the debate.

Reflective Practice

Reflective practice is an important part of social care work. Individually, with supervisors, or in teams, care workers reflect on how cases are being handled, or review how they were handled, in terms of both the skills and practices used, and the appropriateness of the care plans or care measures. Typical of its nature, philosophical thinking requires us to step back from immediate engagement with an issue and question it. In this way, it helps to develop the kind of thinking needed in reflective practice.

Ethics and Religion

Ethics has always been central to human living. There have always been requirements or expectancies about how to behave. Traditionally these have come from the community or culture, which in turn located the source of the requirements in a belief in the existence of an all-powerful God. Historically, ethics is associated with religious belief. This is still very much the case for billions of people who believe in a particular religion such as Christianity, Islam and Judaism. They get their ethics from belief in the teaching of their religion about the behaviour God expects from them if they are to lead good lives. A central element of religious morality is care for people in need. Before the state became involved in providing care, it was provided through voluntary, charitable work, mainly by people who saw it as one practical way of living their religious belief. Such work remains a part of care services today.

However, ethics is not confined to religion. Outside religious belief, people still need to know how they should act and what they should do. They need to know where the authority lies that holds them accountable for their actions, or if there is no such authority apart from law. Also, in a democratic society there is a separation between church and state. This means that the state cannot prescribe the moral teachings of a particular religion, or religions, on the basis that they are required because of religious belief. Nor can it prescribe views of any other moral or belief system, such as the humanist one, on the grounds that they are required because of that system. In a democracy, the state has to be guided by the values of the democratic system itself. These include individual freedoms and human rights, which form part of the basic laws of society and are included in the Irish Constitution. It also has to be guided by other provisions in the Constitution on moral questions, since they have been approved by majority vote of the people in a referendum. Nevertheless, a democracy is open to churches, humanist and other organisations, and individuals advocating their moral views in order to exert influence on government. This happens in particular when legislation or a constitutional amendment is being proposed on a moral issue, such as abortion, and these views contribute to the government's decisions and policies.

As a subject within philosophy, ethics is different from religion. It does not accept views on faith. As far as possible, it is based on rational thought. Ethics tries to establish the kind of behaviour appropriate for people through rational thinking. Faith-based and other moral systems also of course provide rational justification for their perspectives. However, it is specifically within philosophical ethics that the question of what constitutes good or right behaviour is examined in-depth and shown, in so far as possible, to have an underlying basis in rational thought. As we shall see, moral requirements from the main ethical theories also have care for others as a central element.

Ethics and Law: The Overlap

Ethical and legal requirements often overlap, particularly for behaviour that directly harms others. The law supports some ethical requirements by making non-compliance with them a punishable offence. For example, while it is morally wrong to harm another person physically, the law supports this in the case of domestic violence, by enabling the spouse who is a victim to obtain a court order barring the spouse who has been violent from access to the family home. The law reinforces many ethical requirements by imposing a penalty for non-compliance in the interests of the protection of citizens and for the good of society. One way of putting this is to see law as exerting an external force to make us comply with certain minimum acceptable moral standards for living with others in society.

Another feature of the overlap is legal provision of services, and of rights, on the basis that they are ethically required. For example, a particular issue in relation to social care is legal entitlement for people with disabilities to special needs services as a right. We will look at this issue in Chapter 6.

At the same time, it is not the law's job to make us morally good. While ethics overlaps with law, it is distinct from it.

Ways in Which Ethics Is Distinct from Law

Freedom of Choice

In the interests of providing for personal freedom in a democracy, there has to be a large sphere of activity in which it is a matter for the individual to choose how to behave without undue legal restriction. People are free, for example, to end their marriage commitment if they so choose and to seek a divorce (under divorce legislation). This point about personal freedom, morals and the law was made in the Wolfenden Committee's report in Britain as far back as 1957 in recommending that homosexuality be decriminalised. The report stated, 'There must remain a realm of private morality and immorality which is, in brief and crude terms, not the law's business' (cited in Hart 1969: 14–15).

Self-regulation

Ethical behaviour can be characterised as complying with requirements where we have a certain freedom to comply or not. This highlights self-regulation as an important feature at the heart of ethics. Ethics is about regulating our own behaviour in particular ways, either because we want to or feel we have to even if we don't want to, rather than from fear of having to pay some penalty if we don't and are found out. For example, we don't have to be compassionate, speak out against injustice or always tell the truth. These are matters for us.

However, usually people behave in ethical ways because they believe they are *the right ways* to behave; they don't do so simply because they feel they have to conform or because the law requires them. Whether a law existed or not, they would still try to behave ethically. They see it as important to do the right thing for its own sake.

Ethical Basis of Law

If law is to command respect and obedience, it has to be based on what citizens in general consider ethical. For example, until the early 1990s in South Africa, successive governments of ruling white people enforced apartheid laws on black people, laws under which black people suffered from separate and unequal living conditions. Because these laws were judged morally wrong on the basis of the value of equality in particular, people felt justified in disobeying them and campaigning for their abolition. That a particular law might be considered unethical serves to highlight how law needs to be based on the understanding of what is ethical if it is to be acceptable. It highlights how ethics can be considered a deeper court of appeal than law.

Ethics and Politics

Ethical Basis for Politics: Theory and Practice

In a democracy, the purpose of politics is to provide for *the good* of all citizens. This makes ethics a natural precursor to political activity. Aristotle, whose ideas we will be looking at, was a philosopher who followed up a work on ethics with a work on politics. Since he believed he had established how we should live for our own good, both personally and socially, he saw that politics should be about facilitating us to live a good life. However, this is not to suggest that the state should enforce a strict code of ethics for our good. The idea of personal freedom is present in his ethics and, as we have seen in the previous sections on religion and on law, personal freedom in a democracy is a key value that the state is obliged to ensure. Partly under the influence of philosophers, such as Hobbes and Rousseau, whose ideas we will look at in Chapter 10, personal freedom came to be accepted as the cornerstone human right which justifies and makes legitimate democratic politics. Since we live in a pluralist society in which people hold different views on moral questions, one of the difficulties in developing a common ethics for everyone is that people ask 'whose ethics should it be?' At the same time, the general idea of providing for the common good remains part of democratic societies. It gives purpose and direction to political rule. The Irish Constitution, for example, refers to 'seeking to promote the common good, with due observance of prudence, justice and charity so that the dignity and freedom of the individual may be assured'.

While individual politicians and their parties are motivated to a greater or lesser extent by the idealism of achieving the common good, as they see it the business of practical politics in which demands are made on government from all sections of society makes it difficult for politicians to give priority to ideas about the common good. One cause of the difficulty is that political parties need to win and retain power in order to implement their policies. This has led to an emphasis in politics on providing for the demands of particular groups whose support politicians seek in order to get voted into office. There is also the view that, in the absence of agreement among the public on what constitutes the common good, politics in practice is only, and should be, a process of catering for needs and wants of particular groups. In effect, groups compete with each other to be heard by government and to have their requests granted. This is the pragmatic or managerial view of politics. As Millar puts it, 'The normal political process for government is . . . one of conciliation and accommodation of competing interests, not the automatic registration of an existing general interest (1965: 57–8).'

However, appeals to fairness in particular, which are frequent, imply in practice the notion of a common good in which all people can receive a deserved share of the benefits available from society. Also, politicians will sometimes admit that certain groups, which already do well from society, have too much influence over public policy and decisions. Such groups are often referred to as 'vested interests' because of the keen interest they take in how decisions are made in order to gain from them. There are many such groups. The main groups are the employer associations, professional associations and trade unions as well as particular industries, such as pharmaceutics, and services, such as banking. A consequence of the influence of vested interests on political decisions is that the public good of those who have social care needs may not be catered for as well as it deserves to be. At the same time, there are a number of organisations and groups who represent the interests of those in need of care, such as the Children's Rights Alliance, Age Action Ireland and Social Justice Ireland, as well as agencies set up by the government, such as the National Disability Authority.

Politics and Social Policy

Social policy in its different areas such as early childhood, custodial care, disability, and care of the elderly are developed in consultation with interested groups and decided upon by government. Politicians make the laws, and legal provision and regulation of care policies and services make them enforceable. This adds to and strengthens the moral requirement for improved services. For example, in 2013 the work of the state's Health Information and Quality Authority (HIQA) was extended to cover setting standards and providing inspections in residential centres for children and adults with disabilities. This was essential in view of the unethical conduct, poor practices and inadequate standards which HIQA inspections had found in some nursing homes for the elderly.

Social welfare (or 'social protection', as it is sometimes called) is a policy area of particular importance for many people who are likely to come in need of care services. The idea that the state should provide people with welfare arose from acceptance of the ethical argument that it was wrong to leave people who were unable to provide for their own needs to rely on charity. As a result, state provision of measures such as old age pensions and disability benefit were introduced. Utilitarian ethics, known by the *greatest happiness principle*, which was developed in the late nineteenth century, is said to have had a significant influence on Britain becoming known as a welfare state in the twentieth century. We will look at this theory in Chapter 7. Each year in Ireland the Finance Act gives legal force to the measures in the budget. From a care perspective the main measure in the budget is the amount of money by which benefits are increased or decreased. Conditions for eligibility for benefit may also be improved or made more restrictive. Also, the net overall effect of budgets on people's living standards can be judged in terms of social justice, i.e. in terms of the people who benefit the most from the measures introduced, whether they are the middle- and high-income earners or low earners and those on social welfare. We will look at ideas about social justice in Chapter 11.

Ethics and Professional Codes of Conduct

Most professions have a code of conduct which their members are required to follow in practising their profession. Codes vary and can have a number of different purposes. One purpose is to provide a service ideal of values and aspirations for professionals to try to fulfil. Another is to set down the requirement for professionals to be trustworthy in their relations with service users. Respect for the client's liberty and independence is central. This is to help ensure that all service providers are clear that any exploitation of the client is professional misconduct. Abiding by a code is particularly important for those who work in social care because many clients are vulnerable.

Professional ethics can be regarded as 'an intensification of ordinary ethics', with particular reference to 'interpersonal trust' (Kohen cited in Banks 2004: 61). Both ordinary ethics and professional ethics can be seen ultimately to derive their requirements from ethical ideas about values and principles. Banks points out that while many of the ethical issues belong specifically within the nature of the profession and the professional's role, they nevertheless draw from moral philosophy. As she puts it, 'it is important to be able to locate professional ethics in the broader field of philosophical ethics and to use the insights and arguments of philosophy to illuminate and develop our thinking' (Banks 2004: 74).

The values and principles explored in the book have particular relevance to a code of conduct for those who work in social care, notably the principle of having respect for service users. In Ireland CORU is the umbrella body responsible for regulating health and social care professions. Among the professions it regulates are social workers and social care workers. It has developed a Code of Professional Conduct and Ethics for Social Workers, which can be viewed on its website at www.coru.ie. See also 'Ethical Guidelines' on the website for the Irish Association of Social Care Workers, www.iascw.ie.

APPLICATION OF VALUES AND PRINCIPLES TO CASES

A background in understanding ethical values and principles is not just informative for guiding social care provision, but also helpful for ethical reasoning in particular care cases. Ethical reasoning is often necessary due to the complexity of cases. For example, in the particular case of an older person who is unable to cope on his/her own, there can be a clash between supporting the values of both independent living, where s/he insists on it, and ensuring his/her health and safety. Also, difficult issues can arise in some cases where, for example, the rights of parents to rear their children can be in conflict with their children's right to safety and protection. In such cases, a decision may have to be made about whether to leave the children in the care of their parents or relatives or to obtain a court order to take them into the care of the state. Such issues can take the form of an ethical dilemma, which make them particularly challenging. A dilemma in social care involves having to make a hard choice between two aspects of a client's welfare, such as his/her safety and continuing to live in the family home, when both cannot be provided for at the same time. Both aspects cannot be provided for at the same time, at least not in full, though it may be possible to decide on a compromise solution as the best outcome in the circumstances. Dilemmas may involve a care team making a risk assessment before taking a decision whether to trust people whose behaviour is a cause of legitimate concern.

Dilemmas highlight the fact that, apart from distinguishing right from wrong, ethics relates to the more challenging questions of deciding that one course of action is morally better than another, and in the client's best interest. Making ethical decisions often requires the ability to make distinctions between competing choices and to justify one choice over another. (In the next chapter, Case Study 2.2 in particular presents a dilemma to consider in applying understanding of the value of well-being.)

In social care casework there is a growing accumulation of knowledge and experience, and there are established procedures for best practice in particular types of cases. However, each client's circumstances will be unique and this can make a case complex. Also, apart from new variations of familiar factors, complexity can arise from the emergence of new and unexpected ones. This means that in assessing a client's circumstances, there has to be a certain openness to according weight to particular factors and, as a result, to the balance between them in making the best decision. Central to this process is concern for the client's good – understood as his/her best interest. Factors to do with the good of others related to the client and the good of society can also come into consideration. In short, making good decisions involves being able to reason morally on the basis of knowledge and understanding of values and principles.

Ethics requires us to think carefully with an open and questioning mind. As Banks points out, it is not possible or desirable to produce an ethics rulebook. Instead, critical thinking and reflection are required (2006: 9). Philosophy provides the tools for this thinking and reflection.

ADVOCACY

Advocacy as a particular aspect of social care is underpinned by the moral case for improvements in care. It is based on the value of the advocate helping others to have their identified needs met by speaking on their behalf to the relevant service providers, or by the advocate empowering the service user to advocate on his/

her own behalf. The service providers are usually the staff in state or voluntary agencies that make the decisions on service provision.

At a broader level in society, groups that represent the interests of people in need of care, such as Social Justice Ireland and the Children's Rights Alliance, advocate and lobby politicians and government to make improvements in care services.

The need for advocacy is based on the recognition that different sections and groups in a democratic society have varying degrees of influence over public policy in having their interests satisfied. Some lose out because they have little or no influence on public policy. Advocacy is the means for them to have a voice in achieving their needs. It is seen as particularly necessary for members of certain groups, such as older people, those with a disability or the homeless, who may have limited ability or opportunity to speak on their own behalf and are therefore vulnerable to having their needs neglected. At the heart of social care advocacy lies values such as human rights and respect. Social fairness or justice are other broader ethical ideas that arise within advocacy in social care.

Advocates try to bridge the gap between what should happen to meet care needs and what happens in practice. It is the gap between the level and quality of care provided through public policy and the needs of service users. This attempt to bring about change or improvement in practice is the moral thrust that runs through their work. In effect, the advocate draws from values when s/he argues on behalf of a client whose needs are not being provided for that those needs *should be* provided for.

AIMS OF THE BOOK

From studying this book it is hoped that you will:

- Develop a deeper and more informed understanding of the ethical purpose and practice of social care through understanding the values and principles that guide it.
- Have a means of contributing to ethical decision-making, especially in cases for best social care practice.
- Be able to evaluate social care conditions and issues in the light of knowledge and understanding of values and principles.

GUIDE TO CHAPTER MATERIAL

Each chapter explores the reasons that establish a particular value or principle. It also gives examples of practical issues and problems which care workers encounter. Then it explains why the value or principle is relevant, whether to maintain best practice relations with service users or as a guide to decision-making in casework or to advocate for improvements in care services. In each chapter there are also questions for consideration and discussion or there is an exercise or case study to provide a means of relating the value or principle to practice.

At the end of each chapter there is a section on critical evaluation of the value for those interested in exploring the philosophical aspects in more depth. One of the reasons for including this section is to show that there are limitations (as well as strengths) to our understanding of values. In general, this is one reason which can help care workers to understand why they work in an environment where values are not rationally compelling for everyone, where people differ in their moral views and where there can be moral uncertainty.

You will find that values and principles are connected and often arise together as different ways of looking at the same ethical requirement. As you go through the book you can then begin to look at a particular issue from the perspective of different values to see how informative they are for guiding the appropriate ethical response.

You could look on your exploration of the values in a similar way to how Wittgenstein is said to have looked upon philosophy, i.e. as taking you on different journeys in order to find your way about a strange town. On many of these journeys you pass the same place or close to it. No one journey is necessarily more important than another. Eventually you get to know your own way about (Drury, 'Wittgenstein': 5).

Exercise 1.1

From your knowledge and experience of social care, describe a case in which ethical issues arose in the provision of services to meet needs that had been identified for a client, and relate your response to your understanding so far of ethics and social care. Explain why you think the issues in the case are specifically ethical. (Note: If you draw from a case known to you rather than a hypothetical case, ensure you refer to the issues only and not to identifiable people. Confidentiality is an important ethical principle looked at in Chapter 4.)

REVIEW

Ethics is a distinct subject which tries to establish values and principles to guide behaviour. In practice for social care it is closely connected with law and politics. Political decisions and law-making are the main processes through which services (and their funding) come to be provided for those who are in need of care. Ethical requirements are used as justification for the need for improvements in the provision of services. Ethical requirements are also central in formulating a code of practice for those working in social care.

FURTHER READING

Social Care Ethics

Banks, S. (2004) *Ethics, Accountability and the Social Professions*, Palgrave Macmillan.

Banks, S. (2006) *Ethics and Values in Social Work*, 3rd ed., Palgrave Macmillan ('Preface', 'Introduction', Chapter 1 'Ethical Issues in Social Work', Chapter 4 'Professionalism and Codes of Ethics' and Chapter 7 'Ethical Problems and Dilemmas in Practice').

Banks, S. and Nohr, K. (eds.) (2003) *Teaching Practical Ethics for the Social Professions*, FESET (European Social Educator Training/Formation d'Educateurs Sociaux Européens). (See www.feset.org)

Bateman, N. (2000) *Advocacy Skills for Health and Social Care Professionals*, Jessica Kingsley (Chapter 3 'Ethical Principles for Effective Advocacy').

Slote, M. (2007) *The Ethics of Care and Empathy*, Routledge.

Ethics in General

Benn, P. (1998) *Ethics*, UCL Press ('Preface').

Blackburn, S. (2001) *Being Good: A Short Introduction to Ethics*, Oxford University Press.

Honderich, T. (ed.)(2005) *Oxford Companion to Philosophy*, 2nd ed., Oxford University Press (contains useful entries on ethics).

Norman, R. (1998) *The Moral Philosophers: An Introduction to Ethics*, 2nd ed., Oxford University Press ('Introduction: Ethics and its History').

Roth, J. (ed.) (1995) *International Encyclopaedia of Ethics*, Fitzroy Dearborn (a very useful synopsis of many aspects of ethics).

Thompson, M. (2003) *Teach Yourself Ethics*, Hodder Headline ('Introduction').

JOURNALS

Journal of Social Work Values and Ethics
Ethics and Social Welfare

SOME INTERNET SOURCES

Ethics

Ethics in Practice
www.stpt.usf.edu/hhl/eip

Ethics Updates (useful introductory site for students, particularly on the theoretical
   aspect of ethics)
   http://ethics.acusd.edu/

General

Comhairle
(National Agency for information, advice and advocacy on social services)
   www.comhairle.ie
FESET (European Social Educator Training/Formation d'Educateurs Sociaux Européens)
   www.feset.org
Irish Association of Social Care Workers
   www.iascw.ie
Irish Association of Social Workers
   www.iasw.ie (see especially for their code of ethics)
Manus Charleton's site
   www.manuscharleton.ie
Social Studies
   www.socialstudies.ie

REFERENCES

Banks, S. (2004) *Ethics, Accountability and the Social Professions*, Palgrave Macmillan.
Banks, S. (2006) *Ethics and Values in Social Work*, 3rd ed., Palgrave Macmillan.
Drury, M. 'Wittgenstein', *Context*, No. 3, UCD Philosophy Society.
Hart, H. (1969) *Law, Liberty and Morality*, Oxford University Press.
Millar, J. D. B. (1965) *The Nature of Politics*, Pelican Books.
Parekh, B. (2000) *Rethinking Multiculturalism, Cultural Diversity and Political Theory*,
   Palgrave Macmillan.

2

Well-being

OVERALL AIM

To explore Aristotle's virtue theory for the understanding it offers in meeting people's needs for well-being.

LEARNING OBJECTIVES

At the end of this chapter you should be able to:

- Give Aristotle's account of the relationship between satisfying desires and achieving overall well-being, understood as flourishing.
- Explain what he means by virtue and why he thinks the practice of virtues provides for well-being.
- Explain why he thinks our own well-being is bound up with the well-being of others.
- Understand that poverty and bad luck can restrict a person's chances of doing well.
- Describe the relationship between Aristotle's ethics and care practices in meeting needs for basic support, social inclusion and client self-empowerment.
- Explain why behaving according to particular virtues is beneficial for clients and for guiding care providers in complying with best practice.

INTRODUCTION

There are a number of aspects to well-being. They include physical health and fitness, mental and emotional health (feeling good about oneself and having the capacity to cope with challenges and adversity), and having the material means for living, such as money and housing. For Aristotle, as we shall see, a central aspect of well-being is making our own choices in directing our life for the good. The following are some examples of common needs which services users may require for their well-being.

- A family may have a need for support services where parents have difficulty coping because of poverty or lack of parenting skill.
- Elderly people in care and people with disabilities have needs for fulfilling activities.
- Residents in care homes have a need to exercise choice in their lives as much as possible, e.g. over the food they want and leisure activities.
- People who are homeless have needs for long-term secure accommodation.
- People with learning or other challenges who are capable of independent living have a need for support services.

VIRTUE

Aristotle's theory is known for being the prime example of ethics based on virtues. It is the practice of virtues, he claims, that will lead to well-being. So what are virtues? Virtues are qualities or character traits that a person has and puts into practice. By behaving in accordance with virtues we become a person with a certain type of character. Aristotle calls virtues dispositions to behave in particular ways. There are many virtues – they include honesty, loyalty, courage, compassion, and so on. It is important to realise that, for Aristotle, being virtuous is not about becoming 'a goody two-shoes', i.e. someone who is virtuous in a smug or sentimental manner. The original meaning of virtue comes from the Greek word *areté*, which means excellence or power. We will look at virtues more closely later on in the chapter, but it will help to see what Aristotle is getting at to keep them in mind from the start.

DESIRE TO FLOURISH

Desire to Satisfy Basic Needs

For Aristotle, everybody desires to flourish. (For an image of flourishing, think of a plant doing really well and transpose that image onto a person!) The desire to flourish is a central desire of human beings. Even though some people are not flourishing, maybe because of restrictive living conditions or because of behaving in misguided ways harmful to themselves and others, they still have a desire to flourish. It is what we all desire most.

The desire to flourish is evident first of all from the fact that we have natural desires to satisfy our physical and social needs. Much of our behaviour is directed toward achieving these desires. For example, we desire food, education, a job, friends, etc. Such things that we naturally desire are good, and they are the first step on the way to understanding moral goodness as the desire to flourish. In Aristotle's terms, in seeking to achieve our desires, we are seeking to achieve *our ends*. This makes behaviour *teleological*, i.e. always directed toward achieving some end or goal.

Aristotle points out that when we examine our desires, we see that we usually desire something for the sake of something else. We desire food for the sake of satisfying hunger or for the pleasure of taste; we desire education for the sake of knowledge and qualifications (or, of course, for the love of learning!); we desire a job for the sake of money and the satisfaction of exercising our abilities; we desire money for the sake of all the things we can buy with it; and we desire friends for the sake of the enjoyment and fulfilment that comes from close relations with others. Desire, therefore, consists of wanting various means for various ends (Aristotle 1998: 1–2).

One Overall Desire: To Flourish

Aristotle maintains that human desire amounts to more than the satisfaction of particular desires which we find are for our good. He argues that it makes sense to conclude that in satisfying our particular desires, we are at the same time seeking some overall good. Otherwise, our lives would amount to no more that a continual process of trying to satisfy our desires for one thing after another, a process that for as long as we lived 'would go on to infinity, so that our desire would be empty and vain' (1998: 2). Apart from maintaining that it makes sense to conclude that there is some overall good being sought, he also maintains that implicit in satisfying our particular desires we feel ourselves to be seeking or looking for some overall good. The overall or 'chief good' is 'that which is in itself worthy of pursuit . . . [and] always desirable in itself and never for the sake of something else' (1998: 11–12). But what is it? For Aristotle, it is to have an overall feeling that we are flourishing in our lives. If we attend closely to our experience of seeking to satisfy our desire, we can notice that we are being drawn towards wanting to flourish. For, even if we could satisfy all our particular desires, he claims we would still feel something more desirable is missing. The person who 'has everything' is still left unsatisfied. S/he would still not be happy, and to be happy is what everyone wants the most. He uses the Greek word *eudemonia*, which translates as flourishing and is sometimes translated as happiness, though flourishing is thought to be the more accurate translation.

In our ordinary use of the word, happiness of course means different things to different people. For example, some will say they experience happiness in travelling to new places, others in playing their favourite music, and others again in socialising. We generally associate happiness with the good feeling received from certain experiences, such as having success in exams, or on the birth of a child, or being in the company of friends or someone we love. If we won the lotto, we might imagine we would he happy. But these are all examples of satisfying passing, particular desires, rather than happiness or flourishing itself as a 'self-sufficient' good (1998: 12). If we are flourishing we are leading 'the good life'. Aristotle can be credited as the originator of this now much-used phrase, though somehow I do not think people see it as having the same meaning that Aristotle gives it!

So, what exactly is happiness or flourishing? It is not contentment, which suggests being in a pleasant, passive state of mind. Instead, it has the active meaning which applies to a person who feels he or she is thriving or 'living well or faring well' in relation to all aspects of life (1998: 5). But what should a person do in order to flourish? Aristotle's answer is that we should use reason to manage or regulate feelings and desires. Depending on how well we use our reason to regulate our desires, we will be flourishing. Not only that, but we will be behaving in an ethical way. Flourishing behaviour is ethical behaviour.

DEFINING FUNCTION OF REASON

Desires give rise to how we behave. We desire something and, as a result, our behaviour is directed toward achieving it. Feelings also give rise to our behaviour. For example, when we feel upset or frustrated, we will behave in some way as a reaction to such feelings. Perhaps more noticeable for us than our desires or feelings in giving rise to how we behave are the courses of action open to us from the situation we are in. But how we respond in practice to these courses of action, i.e. which one we opt for or otherwise comes to be the one we take, depends on the kind and degree of desire or feeling we have toward them. Desires and feelings are, then, the basic influences on our behaviour.

However, we are not solely under the influence of our desires and feelings. This is because we also have reason to guide our choice. We can reason about our desires and feelings in order to make the best choice of how to respond to them. For Aristotle, reason is central. Why is reason so important? It is because reasoning is something only humans can do. It distinguishes us from plant and animal life. It is our defining function. For Aristotle, man is a rational animal. We all have a function by virtue of our nature as human beings and that function is to reason well about how we should behave (1998: 13–14). He argues that if we fulfil our defining function, we are behaving as we ought to behave and will flourish. No more can be expected of us. We are living the life fit for a human being whose nature is made up of both desire and reason.

In identifying our human function with reasoning, Aristotle distinguishes it from a job function, or social function, or the function of exercising a particular talent. These functions are good. It is good that we perform these functions as well as we can. They contribute to human flourishing. For example, it is good that a builder builds a house as well as he can; it is good that a case worker uses his/her skills to the best effect; it is good that a parent performs the role of being a parent well in bringing up children; and it is good that a musician plays well. For the individuals concerned, these are examples of their human potential being realised. These are good things, and we can admire the results.

However, Aristotle's key point is that exercising neither a particular job function, nor social function nor talent on *its own* fulfils our human desire for flourishing. Human flourishing comes about essentially through reasoning about our desires and feelings in the context of the particular circumstances that have aroused them – and then making a good decision as to our response. For example, what is important is how the builder handles being let down by workers who don't turn up; it is how the parent handles the moody assertiveness of their adolescent son or daughter as they undergo the transition from childhood to adulthood; it is how a care worker handles being verbally abused or lied to by a service user; it is how the musician handles an inattentive audience or bad review; it is a whole host of other feelings and desires that they or any person experiences in the course of any day.

Ethics, for Aristotle, is particularly about the nitty-gritty, day-to-day challenges to our response. For example, on any ordinary evening you may feel tired after a long day and want to relax and watch TV. Yet you may also feel like obliging a friend who phones and wants you to go out to a disco. In addition, you may have a niggling feeling that you should start writing an essay which is due shortly. Then there's your mother, whom you promised to phone, but you have been putting off phoning her because you are afraid she will have something to say to you about your behaviour that you don't want to hear. What Aristotle is saying is that you should become as clear as you can in your mind about your feelings in response to this situation, *with a view to making the rational decision which will enable you to flourish best in the circumstances*. The right rational decision here is difficult since you are pulled in different directions, which is often the case with moral decision-making. And Aristotle is not going to tell you what your right rational decision should be. He does offer general guidelines, as we shall see, but essentially what you decide will depend on your own judgment about what will best enable you to flourish in the particular circumstances.

In this way, ethics is about making good judgments around our desires and feelings in the context of practical matters that arouse them. We need to deliberate well about what is the best thing to do in the light of how we feel.

DOCTRINE OF THE MEAN

How do we reason well about our desires and feelings to make the right decisions? Aristotle's answer is contained in his famous doctrine of the mean. This doctrine provides guidelines for making a decision. But what is the *mean*? The mean is the midpoint between the two extremes of excess and deficiency of the particular desire or feeling. Excess is over-reacting; deficiency is under-responding. He uses the role of food and drink in relation to health as an example. Health is adversely affected by eating and drinking either too much or too little. It is adversely affected by excess or deficiency. But it is produced, maintained and improved by choosing to take the right quantity (1998: 30–1).

He calls the mean between excess and deficiency a virtue. Here we meet again the word *virtue*, which we said at the beginning is central to Aristotle's understanding of ethics. But how do we find a virtue as the midpoint between an excess and deficiency? Aristotle's answer is that we find it through making a rational choice for the midpoint, which avoids both excess and deficiency. As he puts it, 'virtues are modes of choice or involve choice' (1998: 36); they are a choice of a midpoint or intermediate which we make or determine through our rational thinking (1998: 39). In choosing the mean as the midpoint between the excess and deficiency of a particular desire or feeling, we are choosing then the virtuous response. We will look next at some examples.

With regard to desire for food and drink, the midpoint, or mean, as the virtuous response is moderation. It is precisely through eating and drinking moderately in relation to our desires for food and drink that we can act best toward having good health. Moderation is also a virtue in responding to the desire for any physical pleasure. Aristotle is sometimes misrepresented as having the view that we should repress our physical desires for pleasure because they conflict with the rational side of our nature. For him it is a matter of *managing* our desires in our best interest. He claims moderation contributes toward enabling a person to flourish by keeping an edge to his appetite and preventing it from becoming dulled from either disinterest or overindulging (1998: 40). Moreover, it is up to each person to decide on and implement *moderation* for themselves in their circumstances; it is not a question of having to accept someone else's view of what moderation should mean. Though, of course, there are often recommended guidelines and measures from professionals and public bodies, for example for food and alcohol intake. Aristotle vests authority and responsibility with each individual person for deciding on where virtue as the mean lies in relation to their particular needs. One way of describing moderation as a virtue is to say that it lies between extremes of avoiding being 'a slave to our passion' on the one hand and being 'a cold fish', or passionless, on the other. So for Aristotle, a capacity to enjoy physical pleasure comes best from practising the virtue of moderation. (If true, it's not a bad incentive for being virtuous!)

Further examples of virtue as the mean between extremes of excess and deficiency include the following.

Patience

When we feel it hard to maintain hope or expectancy, then patience is the midpoint between the excess of annoyance and the deficiency of being disheartened.

Courage

When we feel challenged, courage is the rational way to respond as the midpoint between the excess of recklessness and the deficiency of fear or timidity.

Assertiveness

When we feel unsure of our self-worth or self-esteem, then Aristotle would no doubt identify with the modern-day quality known as assertiveness as the rational response. Assertiveness is the midpoint between the excess of aggression and the deficiency of submissiveness. It is emphasised today as a communication skill.

Honesty (Truthfulness)

When we feel fear or concern about the consequences for ourselves or others if certain information is known, then the deficiency is in saying or doing nothing about it and the excess is in denying the truth and perhaps telling further lies to try to protect ourselves from the consequences. Honesty also avoids the excess of desiring to succeed by misrepresenting the reality. The challenge we usually face in being honest is where the truth is inconvenient, awkward or hurts.

Self-restraint

When we feel frustrated, then restraint is the midpoint between lashing out and being indifferent to the cause of our frustration, which can linger and affect us emotionally in a negative way. Restraint is a much-needed social virtue. Many bad actions result from failure to control frustration through restraint, e.g. domestic violence, drunkenness, greed, road rage, verbal abuse or making hurtful comments.

Compassion

Compassion is feeling for others in the suffering that they are experiencing. It can be understood as the midpoint between the deficiency of being indifferent to their suffering and the excess of being self-indulgent by wallowing in pity for them. Excess could also lead to overpowering a client with care, which would not be good for the client. An example of compassion being exercised in public policy is where the Minister of Justice grants permission for an asylum seeker who has been judged not to meet the legal requirements to remain in the country on humanitarian grounds.

Due Anger

When we feel angry about some injustice done to us or to others, then, for Aristotle, due anger is the right response. It is the midpoint between losing our temper (excess) and feeling indifferent or not bothered (deficiency). Due anger is a powerful motive for social justice, especially where the lack of justice is causing suffering, as when people experience famine or abuse of their human rights.

Justice

Justice can be understood as the midpoint between the deficiency where people do not get what they are entitled to have and the excess of receiving more than they deserve. For Aristotle, a socially unjust society is one in which there is excessive wealth alongside the deficiency of poverty.

ACTION AS WELL AS THOUGHT

Of course, it is not enough to reason well and make rational decisions as to the virtuous response without doing anything. Ethics expresses itself in actions based on good decisions. Aristotle likens the good person to one who competes well in the Olympics (1998: 16). He calls the virtues, such as those listed above, the 'practical virtues'. This is because they show themselves in actions; they constitute what he calls 'practical wisdom' (1998: 39). He draws a distinction between practical or moral virtues and 'intellectual' virtues (1998: 27). Intellectual virtues enable a person to arrive at the truth and include understanding and deliberation.

BAD FEELINGS

Not every desire or feeling allows us to choose the mean as the virtuous response. Some desires or feelings are bad in themselves; it is not possible to relate to them by choosing their mean in order to respond to them in a good way. Instead we simply have to try to avoid having such feelings at all. They include feelings of hatred, malice and envy. Aristotle admits he cannot prove why they are wrong. He simply says they are self-evidently wrong (1998: 39).

However, it is easy to agree with him. We learn from experience that living a life in which we have these feelings will not lead to our own flourishing. For example, hatred eats us up emotionally, making it impossible to feel good. Envy takes our attention and energy away from making ourselves happy through its focus on the person we envy.

VIRTUE AS RATIONAL MANAGEMENT OF FEELING AND DESIRE

It is not so much a matter of applying reason to desire or feeling where they are two distinct aspects of our response. In practice, both are interfused. We respond emotionally in a way that can be rational or irrational. It is a matter of trying to ensure our feelings are appropriate to the situation whereby we don't overreact to something minor and underreact to something serious (Norman 1998: 38).

At the same time, we sometimes do need to exercise rational control in a distinctive way. We need to step back from strong emotions that have been aroused in us to gain rational control of them. We need to rein in our emotions in order to respond appropriately. The phrase 'blinded by emotion' is one Aristotle would well understand; indeed, our recognition of this state derives from his ethics. Being 'blinded by emotion' is to behave without the influence of rational control. Following the mean avoids the negative effects of acting on strong feelings without thought of the consequences for us or for others. One saying that captures Aristotle's ethics is when we say of ourselves that 'I let my feelings get the better of me.' Aristotle's doctrine of the mean has given rise to a number of sayings still much used today to point out appropriate behaviour. These include:

- 'The happy medium.'
- 'The golden mean.'
- 'The right proportion.'
- 'The well-balanced decision.'

VIRTUE AS POWER

As the mean, a virtue is not a safe middle course of action between responding too strongly or too weakly. It is not a compromise in which something is lost. As mentioned earlier, the original meaning of *virtue* is *power* or *excellence*, and that is how Aristotle understood it. The present-day term *self-empowerment* is perhaps close to the benefit Aristotle saw in practising the virtues. This term highlights the fact that it is up to each individual to achieve well-being by making good or virtuous decisions about how to relate to his/her feelings and desires in any circumstances.

In order not to misunderstand Aristotle it is important to point out that while the mean *is* the virtue, there is no mean *of* virtue (1998: 39–40). In other words, it is admirable to have an excess of virtue. People who have virtue to a high degree are described as having *heroic virtues*. Nelson Mandela, for example, would be said to have practised the virtues of courage and justice to a heroic level.

Also, being virtuous does not mean missing out on a good life for the sake of some more worthy moral ideal. It is precisely the way to behave that increases a person's power of flourishing. Aristotle also makes clear that a virtuous life is meant to be pleasurable (1998: 42). Practising virtues enables us to feel pleasure or satisfaction from the fact that we are living a fulfilling life in accordance with our human nature: 'Pleasure in doing virtuous acts is a sign that the virtuous disposition has been acquired' (1998: 31).

DIFFICULTY FINDING THE MEAN

Finding the right or virtuous response in all circumstances is not easy. Aristotle accepts 'it is no easy task to be good' (1998: 45). As he puts it, 'to miss the mark [is] easy; to hit it difficult' (1998: 38). As the mean between extremes, virtue is a particular point on a scale. This makes it likely we will miss that mark. There are many ways in which the mean can be missed, but there is only one way in which it is found. Finding the mean is like hitting the bull's eye on a target. We should try to come as close to it as we can.

He accepts also that there is no exact way of choosing the mean. In particular, it cannot be the same prescribed choice for everyone (1998: 37). We can understand why when we consider that feelings and desires are subjective states that belong to individuals. No two people are exactly the same, either in their emotional states or in experiencing circumstances in exactly the same way. Therefore, the choice of the mean that expresses the virtue for one person is not necessarily the same choice for another person in the same situation. On a daily basis, each person finds themselves in many different situations unique to them requiring a specific appropriate response. It is, then, very much up to each person to work out how to behave in order to flourish.

HELPFUL ROLE OF HABIT

The desires and feelings we have are often the same ones that have arisen from being in similar situations before. This enables us to develop virtue as habit. Habits are a way of making it easy to behave in accordance with the mean for recurring feelings that arise from similar situations we encounter. They save us from having to think what our virtuous response should be on each occasion. Good habits help to confirm a person in virtue as a settled disposition (1998: 28–9).

Habits enable a relatively smooth continuity of flourishing behaviour. The common understanding of ethics as related to developing good habits comes from Aristotle.

DEVELOPING CHARACTER

By acting in accordance with virtues as a matter of habit, a person develops a good character as distinct from personality. Virtues are the marks of good character

1998: 35–6). In the end, it is from having a good character that a person gets a sense of flourishing.

OUR OWN WELL-BEING INCLUDES WELL-BEING OF OTHERS

So far we have been looking at Aristotle's understanding of how an individual person should flourish. However, the fact that, as we have seen, flourishing is a self-sufficient good does not mean that we seek our own flourishing in isolation from others. There is a close relationship between a person's own flourishing and that of other people. The reason for this is that people have an essential need for each other's company. Our social nature is evident to Aristotle from the natural existence of family, friendships and the state as a community: 'Now by self-sufficient we do not mean that which is sufficient for a man by himself, for one who lives a solitary life, but also for parents, children, wife, and in general for his friends and fellow citizens, since man is born for citizenship' (1998: 12). Our nature is 'to be with others' and to organise our affairs by engaging in political activity (1998: 233). This basic and natural connection we have with others is a philosophically important point because it explains why we should try to act in the interests of others as well as in our own interests. Acting in the interests of others is often a challenge when our own needs and desires get in the way. It also explains why much self-interested behaviour is wrong where it results in avoidable harm being caused to others. At the same time, it is important to emphasise that, for Aristotle, behaving in our own interest is part of behaving in a morally good way, in particular when we try to achieve our potential through realising our abilities and talents. A distinction is made between self-interested behaviour and selfish behaviour. This distinction is considered further when looking at Hutcheson's ethics in Chapter 5 on empathy.

From our social nature comes natural feelings and desires for others to do well. Thus, for society as a whole to have well-being, its members need to practise virtues that provide for the well-being of others, such as for people with disabilities, who have desires which they cannot realise for themselves without help.

In practice, having a social nature means that in making good decisions about our own flourishing in how we respond to our desires and feelings, we have to include the effects of our decisions on the flourishing of others. There is always a social context to be taken into account. Otherwise a person's own flourishing will in some way be diminished. At the same time, Aristotle does not suggest that relations with others should have to restrict our own flourishing. Both aspects come into consideration for the individual in judging behaviour appropriate to flourishing in any set of particular circumstances. Here again it is a matter of getting the balance right.

Friendship

In Aristotle's time and culture, friendship was rated highly as a value and he emphasises its role in providing social well-being. He says it is 'most necessary for living' and that no one would choose to be without friends, even if they are rich and have everything else which they want (1998: 192). He writes about friendship in detail, highlighting the good things that come from it, as he does about many of the virtues. Friendship provides for well-being in a number of ways. It provides a spontaneous and informal means of expressing our social nature. Friends enjoy being in each other's company. They connect with each other's personality and are likely to share many of the same interests and experiences. Also, the close attachment friends have enables them to support each other emotionally when, for example, one or the other may be going through a difficult time. Another benefit of friendship is that it enables us to learn more about ourselves and our options from engaging with the views of others who have had different experiences to us and whose understanding can vary from ours. Alternatively, their understanding may support ours when we have doubts. Friendship broadens our horizon, particularly in relation to intimate matters of concern to us. From friends we can get a different perspective on a problem which can release us from entrapment in our view (if it is holding us back) and contribute to providing us with a more balanced outlook to enable us to flourish. Friends can help us see and judge better our good in particular situations. 'Trusting the guidance of a friend and allowing one's feelings to be engaged with that other person's life and choices, one learns to see aspects of the world that one had previously missed' (Nussbaum 1990: 44).

Because of incapacity, or other reasons, some people who require care may not have opportunities to develop friends. Thus, it is a particularly good thing for care workers to provide opportunities for clients to develop friends where they desire them. Many of the benefits of friendship also come from the love that family members have for each other. This is one reason why family support services are important.

PRACTICAL IMPEDIMENTS

Aristotle recognises that for people to flourish they need 'the external goods' (1998: 17). They need an adequate level of material prosperity, which we can easily understand. Without adequate means of living, a person will struggle and suffer. In particular, time and attention, including worry and anxiety over lack of money, for example, goes into trying to cope, especially among parents who have the responsibility of children, so it is hard for them to feel that they are happy or flourishing.

Aristotle also recognises that great misfortune or bad luck can have a devastating effect on people's prospects of flourishing, as they 'both bring pain and hinder many activities' (1998: 21). Again, it is easy for us to understand the effects of, for example, job loss, or a serious illness or accident on individuals and their families.

However, Aristotle holds that, no matter how difficult it may be, people who experience poverty and misfortune can still practise the virtues and flourish in the particular way he believes it is in our nature to flourish. If a person is truly good, then 'always, or by preference to everything else, he will do and contemplate what is excellent', a person who is truly good 'always makes the best of circumstances' (1998: 21).

WELL-BEING AND SOCIAL CARE

Client Self-empowerment

Looking back at the elements of Aristotle's ethics, the central element relating to social care is that it is in the nature of human beings to have a desire to flourish. In order to flourish, each person is required to think about what is appropriate for his/her own good within the general guidelines of the doctrine of the mean. Responsibility and challenge are given to each person to make decisions in his/her own best interest to flourish. Aristotle's ethics can be seen, therefore, to underpin the values of individual empowerment and self-determination. So the reason self-determination is important for service users is because it enables them to make their own decisions about how best to relate to their *own* feelings and desires. Put another way, while we should behave with virtue toward people in need of care, we cannot *make* them (or anybody else) virtuous. They can only do this for themselves, and the reason we should help empower them to do it for themselves is because it is the way for them to experience well-being, as it is for all of us.

Clients in need of care have their capacity to exercise their power limited by their circumstances, such as disability, age, living conditions and addictions. Aristotle's ethics, then, can be taken to support clients exercising their own power in so far as possible.

In practice, providing for client self-empowerment and independence can sometimes be difficult. The following are three types of circumstances that give rise to difficulty:

1. Where there is a shortfall between the desires of the client and the care measures which the agency can supply in needed support.
2. Where clients have varying degrees of learning challenge, difficult decisions can arise with regard to both supporting their choices and ensuring their protection.
3. Where there is disagreement between the strong view a teenager from a broken home has about her well-being needs and the views of the social care team.

Practical Assistance

At a basic level, providing for the well-being of service users involves protecting them against harm and neglect. Aristotle also makes clear that certain material conditions are necessary for people to flourish. Lack of material requirements and bad luck can seriously restrict a person's capacity to flourish. This underlies the view that it is morally good to assist clients through providing them with practical support to enable them to flourish as well as possible. This may have to do with some material or social need, such as housing or a specialised service for a particular disability.

Social Inclusion

Central to Aristotle's ethics is the recognition that an individual's capacity to flourish is intimately bound up with the flourishing of everybody else in society, arising from the social nature of being human. Thus, the well-being of the community as a whole is diminished to the extent that some of its members experience obstacles to their full participation. This underlies the care role of providing for the social inclusion of individuals and groups who are excluded or marginalised from family, friendship or the wider community, such as the homeless, refugees or migrant workers. In particular, the major good that comes from friendship highlights the value of helping service users cope with isolation and loneliness. Older people living alone and people with significant disabilities are particularly vulnerable to being deprived of the good that comes from having close ties to others.

Provides for a Full Life

Related to empowerment, practical assistance and social inclusion is the value of leading a full life in which people can realise their potential to flourish. We have mentioned this value already in the Introduction. For Aristotle, leading a full life includes being able to exercise our particular talents and abilities as far as possible – this particularly supports care practices for those who have a disability.

Gives Importance to Feeling for Others

As we have seen, deciding on a virtue as a midpoint between extremes involves responding in an emotionally intelligent or rational way. However, in another sense our emotions are involved in having a good or right response. The way in which we first respond to another person or situation is partly emotional, and Aristotle sees this as a vital element in having a fully human response. We respond with shades of such emotions as affection or concern, and they inform the appropriate good response. Along with reason, they contribute to giving us moral knowledge. In her book, aptly titled *Love's Knowledge*, Martha Nussbaum sees Aristotle as saying that if we do not cultivate our emotional responses, and go by reason too much, we can lack moral perception (1990: 78). This point about the role of emotion in giving us appropriate moral knowledge is particularly important for the traditional core values of care and empathy. We will look at it in more detail in Chapter 4.

Has Understanding for Circumstances

A significant feature of Aristotle's ethics of relevance to social care is that it is not dogmatic. Ethics arises for people in their capacity to deal with circumstances and situations as well as they can in accordance with their nature – made up of both reason and emotion. How we should respond depends on the particular circumstances of the situation that calls for our response. While the doctrine of the mean provides a general guideline, it is always under the influence of the particular circumstances. This absence of a prescriptive element, i.e. laying down the law for how everyone should behave, is characteristic of virtue ethics. A prescriptive element is, however, central to duty ethics associated with Kant, which we will examine in Chapter 3. In particular, in making a moral decision on appropriate care for a client, virtue ethics enables care workers both to recognise and to take account of such factors as a service user's:

- Physical, emotional and relationship circumstances.
- Personal pressures, which s/he may be under.
- State of well-being, e.g. how vulnerable or resilient a person may be.

Virtues and Social Care Work

Finally, the understanding Aristotle gives of virtues, in particular the virtues of compassion, due anger and justice, can be seen to inform the work not just of those who care directly for individual service users but also of policy-makers, directors of care agencies and care managers. Service users, too, can contribute to their own well-being by practising the virtues. Part of social care work is assisting clients to recognise how they may need to behave with, for example, courage or patience in the interests of their own well-being.

Aristotle's Psychological Insight

A notable feature of Aristotle's ethics is his recognition of the importance of human psychology to behaviour long before *psychology* emerged as a specific human science. He did so by pointing out the powerful role played by human desire in causing behaviour. In addition, he recognised that management of desire is essential for the benefit of both the individual and society. He also pointed out that regulation of desire is something we all have to learn, for example, through self-restraint and deferred gratification of desire. This remains an essential part of the moral guidance parents give their children and, where necessary, can feature in the care guidance given to service users.

NOTE ON ARISTOTLE'S INFLUENCE IN ETHICS

Aristotle's ethics has had a huge influence. This is partly because his ideas became incorporated into Christian ethics. They also influenced ethics in the Islamic tradition. This has meant that his theory has influenced many billions over two millennia. In particular, he provided a basis for the understanding and teaching of traditional moral values such as honesty, compassion, moderation and justice, which are as important today as in his time. In Chapter 11 we will look at his understanding of social justice, which has also proved relevant to the present day.

Exercise 2.1

For some of the particular virtues mentioned, e.g. courage and patience, describe how they can contribute to well-being if practised by:

1. The social care worker in seeking to accomplish his/her aims in a particular example of casework.
2. The service user in relating to his/her care needs.

CASE STUDY 2.1

Case Study: Issue in Residential Care

You work in a residential centre for adults with learning challenges. The parents of Paul, who has a learning challenge, are unable to care for him at home any longer on account of their age. They wish to ensure Paul gets the care he needs as a permanent resident in the centre. However, they are concerned about the upset they will cause Paul if they tell him his stay in the centre is permanent and that he will not be coming home again except, perhaps, for an occasional visit. To avoid upsetting Paul, they have already explained to him that his stay in the centre is temporary and that he will be returning home when renovations to their home are complete, even though the house is not being renovated.

They ask you to go along with the explanation they have given Paul. They add that because of his learning challenges it is unlikely it will register with him over time that there must be another reason why he is not going home. They advise you that if he knows he will not be coming home, then he is likely to become emotionally volatile. He may inflict harm on himself or strike out at staff or the other residents. They also fear he may withdraw into himself and never experience joy again.

Apply Aristotle's value of well-being to the response you would make to Paul's parents. Describe, in particular, the relevance that particular aspects of Aristotle's ethics have for the care of Paul if he is to achieve well-being.

CASE STUDY 2.2

Case Study: Home Support, Independence and Care

Mary is a 75-year-old woman who lives alone. She suffers from arthritis and is beginning to show signs of short-term memory loss and neglect of personal hygiene. Mary has been cared for by her daughter, who visits her three times a week. However, her daughter has made it known that she needs to scale back her visits to one day a week in the interests of looking after her own family. She also believes her mother would be best cared for in a public nursing home. However, Mary is adamant that she will not move into a nursing home. Mary is also on painkillers for her arthritis, but was advised to reduce their intake after a fall, as the sedation was felt to be a factor. Mary has informed her social worker that she intends to take an overdose of sedatives if she believes she will have to move. An assessment of Mary's care needs three months ago showed that she should be provided with daily home help for a significant number of hours. However, given the resources available to them, the HSE have said that they cannot provide the service for the amount of hours required. They said that even if they were to make an exception, it could lead to a reduction in services for others.

Identify the nature of the dilemma facing the care team. Apply Aristotle's understanding of well-being to decide on how the dilemma should best be resolved.

CRITICAL EVALUATION

The Problem of Identifying Human Nature

Under Aristotle's ethics all human beings have the same function, i.e. to reason, and the same overall desire, i.e. to flourish as individual and social beings. We fulfil our function by making good decisions about managing our desires and feelings in order to flourish in accordance with the doctrine of the mean. This is the core of our human nature. Good conduct is in accordance with this understanding of our nature, while bad conduct is in conflict with it. People's conduct can be judged to be good or bad, right or wrong, in the light of how well or badly they behave in relation to their human nature. If this view is true, it would provide a general, objective standard of ethical behaviour for all to follow.

However, this view has been faulted. The main fault disputes the idea that there is such a thing as human nature which can be identified with reason. Central to Aristotle's argument is the idea that human beings have their own distinct nature from animals, and that the distinction is identifiable with having a capacity to reason. But is reason unique to humans?

Studies of animal behaviour in higher primates such as chimpanzees have shown that they display a capacity to reason. Also, under the theory of evolution, the understanding of a gradual development of human life from less complex animal forms indicates a continuation of a potential for a capacity to reason rather than a distinctive break occurring with the emergence of humans. Scientists have also found evidence that some higher primates display signs of behaving in accordance with a moral capacity. Frans de Waal, who has carried out extensive studies of the behaviour of higher primates, is quoted as saying: 'We have evidence for empathy, we have evidence for reciprocity, we have evidence for pro-social tendencies and we have evidence for fairness principles' (Alsthrom 2009; see also de Waal 2006). In Chapter 5 we will look in some more detail at the scientific understanding of morality.

Benn (1998: 163) points out that human beings are distinct from animal life in other ways besides being able to reason. For example, he cites playing sports or making art as activities unique to human beings. Enjoyment of music could be considered a particular example because many people find it an essential part of their nature. In the light of the theory of evolution and study of animal behaviour in higher species, such as apes, it is not clear that having rational capacity is the distinctive feature of being human.

Also, Benn points out that while reasoning is clearly important, and is arguably the main element characteristic of the human species, that does not mean we necessarily have to base our ethics on it in terms of using it to choose the virtuous response as a means to flourish. Fulfilling our plans and activities might just as easily enable us to flourish without regard for making rational choices to behave in accordance with virtue. In practice, many people identify their flourishing with the extent to which they realise their plans and activities.

The Existentialist View

In stark contrast to Aristotle, some modern philosophers hold that there is no such thing as a specifically human nature. This view is associated with some existentialist philosophers who came to prominence in France and Germany after the Second World War. They accept, of course, that human beings can and do use their reason. However, influenced by Nietzsche's ideas (1844–1900), they regard reason as under the sway of irrational desires, such as the desire for power.

The Holocaust of the Jews and other people by the Nazis during the Second World War is said to have influenced the existentialist view that we have no human nature. If people are supposed to be rational of their nature, how could some people deliberately set out to exterminate others? It makes no sense for people to exterminate their fellow human beings if they have a nature identified with rational behaviour which links them with everyone else.

Sartre (1905–80) takes the view that a person is to be understood precisely as lacking any nature. Instead of reason, Sartre speaks of our consciousness, but this consciousness is not anything. It is simply an emptiness or nothingness which we are compelled to try and fill by whatever takes our attention or by whatever desires we have. For Sartre, this is also what makes people free, as they are not bound by any particular nature (1995: 441). In the discussion in Chapter 5 about the value of empathy, we will go a bit more into the challenge people face in managing their freedom as one of the reasons for having understanding for them in the difficulties they experience.

A feature of life that came to prominence in the Western world, particularly during the twentieth century, and which is often described in modern literature, has been a sense of meaninglessness which people experience. Symptoms of a sense of the meaninglessness of individual and social life include behaving to excess as well as anxiety, depression and despair. In other words, people can feel alienated from themselves and their world. They do not feel at home in a psychological sense, but instead feel homeless. The absence of a human nature can be seen as lying behind this feeling since, if there was a human nature that was clear to people, it would give them a sense of having a personal core in relation to which they could find meaning and value in their lives.

The 'Open Question' Argument

Norman (1998: 33–4) makes a further criticism of Aristotle when he points out that even if we accept that reasoning is the defining function, or at least the *distinctive* or *characteristic* activity of being human, this does not necessarily imply that it is the kind of activity that is best for us. In other words, there is a philosophical problem of being able to prove that just because something *is the case*, i.e. that reasoning is our defining function, we therefore *ought* to behave in accordance with it. If we accept that everybody desires to flourish, we can still ask why they *ought* to do so. This is known as *the open question* argument. This is because when we say that something is the case, it remains an open question whether we should still behave in accordance with it. (See also Norman, 1998: 102; 160.) The distinction that is said to exist between something being the case and it having value raises a core problem in ethics. It is known as the *is/ought* or *fact/value* distinction. We will look at this problem again in Chapter 3.

However, against Norman's argument, we can argue that since we have a reasoning capacity, which is at least characteristic of being human, it makes practical sense to use our reason to decide on how we should behave. We would at least be trying to act in conformity with ourselves rather than going against ourselves.

REVIEW

For Aristotle, we achieve well-being through making rational decisions about our desires and feelings, while taking into account the effect our decisions have on other people, because we are social by nature. The rational decision is the midpoint of the desire between excess and deficiency. Decisions made in this way result in behaviour according to virtues such as courage. This view supports care practices, in particular empowering clients to make their own choices for well-being.

FURTHER READING

Banks, S. (2006) *Ethics and Values in Social Work*, 3rd ed., Palgrave Macmillan (Chapter 3).

Benn, P. (1998) *Ethics*, UCL Press (Chapter 7).

Goleman, D. (1996) *Emotional Intelligence: Why it Matters More than IQ*, Bloomsbury. (This is an interesting popular application of Aristotle's insight to everyday life.)

Norman, R. (1998) *The Moral Philosophers: An Introduction to Ethics*, 2nd ed., Oxford University Press (Chapter 3).

Waal, F. de (2006) *Primates and Philosophers: How Morality Evolved*, Princeton University Press.

REFERENCES

Ahlstrom, D. (2009) 'Morality "a Result of" Natural Selection', *The Irish Times*, 12 February 2009.

Aristotle (1998) *The Nicomachean Ethics*, Oxford World's Classics.

Benn, P. (1998) *Ethics*, UCL Press.

Norman, R. (1998) *The Moral Philosophers: An Introduction to Ethics*, 2nd ed., Oxford University Press.

Nussbaum, Martha C. (1992) *Love's Knowledge: Essays on Philosophy and Literature*, Oxford University Press.

Sartre, J. (1995) *Being and Nothingness*, Routledge.

3
Equality and Respect

OVERALL AIM

To show how the values of treating everybody as equal and deserving of respect are basic moral principles which we are obliged to practise.

LEARNING OUTCOMES

At the end of this chapter you should be able to:

- Explain Kant's duty theory as a source for understanding why we should regard people as equal and deserving of respect.
- Discuss examples of what it means in practice to treat people equally and with respect, and its importance in caring for vulnerable people in particular.
- Justify a duty of care from Kant's argument for the existence of universal moral principles.
- Distinguish between duties of equality and respect and a duty of care.
- Explain what is meant by paternalism in social care, and discuss cases in which it arises as an issue.

INTRODUCTION

First, a note on the meaning of the word *equality* as used in this chapter. People are clearly not equal in lots of ways. For example, we differ in our interests, talents and abilities, family backgrounds, material circumstances and standards of living. The principle of equality does not mean that we should try to make everyone alike. Treating people equally means that we treat everyone the same in virtue as our worth as human beings; that we do not see some people as less or more deserving of consideration and appreciation because they are rich or poor, male or female, white or coloured, gay or straight, have a disability, or are asylum seekers or identify with a different culture to our own. Another way of putting this is to say that there is a basic or foundational equality of moral status among all people. This is not to say that we are all equal in how moral we are; it is to say that when considered as individuals, no one is better than or inferior to anyone else by virtue of their status as a human being.

How ever much people may recognise and accept that they should respect and treat others as equal to themselves, this is often not borne out in practice, at the cost of much suffering. Throughout history, people have been enslaved and discriminated against. People in care have also suffered at the hands of those who had responsibility and authority for looking after them. In Ireland, in the twentieth century, for example, this has included children who suffered severe and excessive physical and emotional abuse, as well as sexual abuse, from some members of religious congregations who ran care institutions on behalf of the state (see Report of the Commission to Inquire into Child Abuse 2009). In Ireland today examples of treating people unequally and disrespectfully still occur, including racial abuse, trafficking young women from poorer countries to work as prostitutes, and paying some people less than others for doing the same work. There is also concern about an acceptance of a culture of disrespect developing among some younger people through cyber bullying and the use of social media to make hurtful, personal comments, as well as making material public about people's private lives.

People who have understandable difficulty standing up for themselves are vulnerable to being taken advantage of and treated unequally and with disrespect. In Ireland there have been examples of elderly people and children suffering unequal treatment and disrespect, including while receiving care services. In 2013 the Health Service Executive released to *The Irish Times* complaints it had received from elderly people who were receiving care in their homes. Examples included an elderly person who was not able to leave her bed over a weekend because staff failed to make a visit; and a threat a support staff worker made to a person who had been disabled by a stroke not to give him more than two showers a week because of the problems he was causing (Duncan 2013). The Senior Helpline also received many complaints from elderly people of different forms of abuse, including emotional, physical, psychological and financial. Abusers are rarely strangers; in most cases, they are the adult children of the elderly person (Dempsey 2013). RTÉ's current affairs programme *Prime Time* showed in 2011, using a hidden camera, examples of an elderly person being verbally abused and another being forced to eat while receiving the home help service. An RTÉ *Prime Time* documentary, *Breach of Trust*, revealed in 2013 that treatment of children in some crèches included threats of punishment, being shouted at, roughly handled, and strapped into chairs for longer than necessary.

Respecting others means treating them as individual human beings. Care workers can come across situations where clients are not being treated with the respect to which they are entitled and this becomes an issue that needs to be addressed. Some examples of disrespect and bad care are obvious and the need for the practice to cease is clear. For example, it may be a case of an elderly person left to spend the night in a wheelchair because the staff cannot be bothered to help him/her to bed.

Other examples include not listening actively to service users, and not consulting them and obtaining their agreement for matters that affect them, such as moving a resident in a home to another room or installing another bed for a second person in his/her room. Lack of respect can also include practices of doing basic personal tasks for clients out of convenience where they are capable of doing them for themselves given time, tasks such as tying the shoelaces of a person with a disability. Respect also includes respect for the emotional integrity of clients. This means they should not be treated in a patronising, condescending, ridiculing or embarrassing manner. Respect also means ensuring that rules in residential homes are not unnecessarily restrictive of residents' freedom.

If we can convincingly establish *why* we should treat people equally and with respect, this will provide a basis for helping to ensure that treating people unequally and with disrespect is not acceptable. The main philosopher who tried to establish why we should always respect others is Immanuel Kant (1724–1804). He claimed to prove that respect and care are moral principles everyone is obliged to follow. Before looking at his argument, which can be difficult, it will be helpful to look at the problem he was trying to solve. This was the problem pointed out by David Hume, which is that we cannot prove that there are obligatory principles for everyone.

ETHICS BASED ON FEELINGS: HUME'S VIEW

A philosopher whose insight into the basis for our moral views and who convincingly shattered the wishful thinking of many people was David Hume (1711–76). Kant's ethics can be seen as an attempt to refute Hume's view. In trying to prove Hume's view wrong, Kant came up with one of the most important and influential ethical theories, a theory which has at its heart the principles of respecting other people along with caring for them. For this reason it will be helpful to look briefly at Hume's view.

From a young age we are taught that actions such as theft and murder are wrong. This teaching is reinforced throughout our lives because it is the common and deeply held view that such actions are wrong. As a result, understanding that they are wrong comes to be inseparable in our minds from them as particular actions. It can seem strange then to have to consider that there may be little or no evidence to support the view that such actions are wrong. Hume is asking us to set aside what we have been taught and look for *evidence* that such actions are wrong. When we do so, he claims, we will see that there is no evidence apart from how we feel about the action. This would make our ethical judgments *subjective*, i.e. a matter for ourselves, and not *objective*, i.e. a matter based on independent evidence which applies to everyone. The only evidence why they are wrong is our *feeling* of disapproval for them. In thinking that the evidence for right and wrong resided in the nature of actions, unbeknown to ourselves, we were only referring to our own feelings about certain actions.

Hume invites us to examine any action to see where *right* or *wrong* lies. He says that no matter how hard we look, we will never find right or wrong in the action itself. Imagine you are walking down the street and see a man in front of you snatch a lady's purse and run off. You saw what he did (fact). You heard her shout, 'Stop, thief!' (fact). You see that she is hurt because she is crying (fact). But where do you see *wrong*? The *wrongness* of the action is not there as a fact in the same way as the other things you saw and heard are there as facts. So where is it? Hume argues that the wrongness of the action lies in your emotive reaction of disapproval for what the man did. Yes, your emotive reaction is a fact, but there is nothing about the action itself that makes it wrong as a fact or wrong as a result of any other evidence besides your emotive reaction. You may say, 'Hang on a minute, what about the harmful consequences of being robbed had for the lady, her loss of money and her distress, surely these consequences make the action wrong? And what about the law? There is a law against stealing, surely that makes it wrong.' Not so, Hume would say. He would still argue that causing harmful consequences is wrong only because in the first place we *feel* disapproval for it, and it is our feeling of disapproval that leads us to make laws to try to prevent people causing harmful consequences. In this way, for Hume, our moral judgments come from our feelings and not from our understanding of the actions themselves. He sums this up by saying 'morality is more properly felt than judged' (Hume 1969: 522). Hume's view has been summed up for the way it points to a distinction between a fact and a value. It is known as *the fact/value distinction*. Facts and values are not the same thing. The only way they are connected is from the way our feelings about certain facts lead us to make value judgments about them.

However, in Hume's ethics there is a role for using reason. It can inform our understanding of an issue or condition that arouses our moral feeling, such as famine, and it can enable us to work out the best means to take action in accordance with our feeling. However, it is feeling that lies at the basis of our judgments.

Implications of Hume's View

If Hume is right, then he can be considered to have dealt a serious blow to the idea that there is a common morality that everyone has to follow, in particular that we should always respect others and care for them. This is because it follows from his understanding that morals can vary from person to person depending on how they happen to feel about particular actions. As he puts it, there is no way of showing that there are 'immutable measures of right and wrong that impose an obligation' (1969: 508). In effect, this means that there is no requirement for anyone to respect others and care for them unless they feel they want to. It is not that Hume is against principles of respect and care, it is just that he believes we can't show why they have to be moral requirements for everyone.

If Hume is right, then this leaves a big problem for how we can ever expect people to behave according to certain standards. For example, if a person feels there is nothing wrong with allowing a person with a disability to go without a service he requires, we have to accept that his view is morally valid. This is because all that matters morally is how he happens to feel about it. We may, of course, disagree with him and give reasons for our disagreements, such as providing for equality, but at the end of the day, morally speaking, it is only our feeling against his.

KANT'S RESPONSE TO HUME

Agrees that Right and Wrong Do Not Come from the Nature of Actions

Kant felt challenged to respond to Hume's view. His challenge was how to prove that morality is not some free-for-all based on personal feeling. It was how to prove that we can still understand certain actions as right or wrong for everybody.

Initially, Kant agrees with Hume on one point. He says if we look for our principles in particular actions, it invariably results in those principles getting mixed up with our own self-interest. For example, the manager of a home for the elderly or a crèche, while holding principles of respect and care, may see the practice of employing unqualified staff as acceptable because he can pay them less than qualified staff and therefore make more profit. Also, the manager of a residential centre for people with disabilities may see having minimal practices available to residents for their stimulation and development acceptable because it is administratively convenient. In such ways, Kant would see the danger in taking our cue for right and wrong from actions and practices. We may be inclined to look on those actions from the point of view of what suits us.

As a result, Kant says that the moral source must lie not in actions, but within ourselves as the agents of the actions. It is the only other available place to look. However, against Hume, Kant says that the source within ourselves does not lie in our feelings toward the actions. Our own feelings as a source would be even more likely to result in principles that serve our self-interest. Nor, for Kant, does the source lie within our inclinations and desires, for they, too, can be self-serving. It's not that our feelings or inclinations or desires are necessarily bad, it's just that they are not reliable guides and we need to eliminate them from having a role in determining the source of our values if we are to achieve certainty (Kant 1969: 55–6).

Where, then, does the source of our morals lie? Kant says the source of our morals lies in our *will*. (To help with clarity, I have put the word *will* in italics when using it to refer to our human capacity of having a *will* or to the mental activity of *willing*.)

Will

The reason Kant picks our *will* as the source for our morality is that he sees our *will* as the enabling capacity we have to act in certain ways. We exercise our *will* whenever we want to do something, in particular when it is difficult, for example, when trying to give up smoking or sticking to a diet. Our *will*, if you like, is a mental power which can direct our actions. But Kant also has a deeper reason for choosing *will*. He says our *will* when considered as a pure capacity to do something is the only thing in the world that is good in itself. Anything else that is considered good is good only with conditions or qualifications attached. For example, even if we *will* something with the best *will* in the world, it could still turn out badly because of unforeseen circumstances. Also, we might think that the virtues which Aristotle has explained are good things in themselves, but this is not necessarily so, as it depends on the purpose for which they are used. Kant points out that a person can develop good qualities such as courage and self-discipline, but use them for a bad purpose (1969: 60). Benn gives the example of people who develop qualities such as loyalty, dedication and self-sacrifice to be more effective terrorists (1998: 102).

What is so special about our *will* that it can be the source of our morals? Kant's answer is that our *will* is the only thing that is always and absolutely good. 'It is impossible to conceive anything at all in the world, or even out of it, which can be taken as good without qualification, except a good *will*' (1969: 59). Hence it must lie at the foundation of morality. This is our *will*, considered first in itself as a human capacity. Kant considers it first independently of anything in particular that we *will* (1969: 60).

Another reason Kant gives for picking the *will* as the only thing good in itself is that we do not have control over the consequences of our actions. So, when we *will* some action, even with the best *will* in the world, we can still cause bad consequences for others. For example, as a social care advocate, you may *will* that a client with a disability be set up in independent living because it will be good for him/her. However, in a particular case it may not turn out that independent living proves beneficial for the client – it could turn out badly. To take another example, you may intend the best for an older person by helping him/her as much as possible, but you might be undermining the client's own ability and hence hastening the day when s/he will become even more dependant.

It is for these reasons, then, that good *will itself*, considered separately from anything in particular that it *wills*, is the first element that lies at the source of morality (1969: 59–60). The second element that lies at the source of morality is our human reason.

Reason

The human *will* is good when considered something in itself. However, the things that human beings *will* are not always good, as the extent and nature of crime in society makes evident, for example. Therefore, we need reason to know what we should and should not *will*. Kant accepts that there is a distinct human faculty of reason and that it has a role in controlling how we act. Nature has endowed us with reason as well as *will*, and reason is attached to *will* 'as its governor' (1969: 60). Reason's role is to be of service in producing, in practice, the one thing that is good in itself – the good *will*.

Will and Reason Together

So far, Kant's theory remains highly abstract. There are just two elements – good *will* itself and reason itself. It is what he calls purely *formal*. That is to say, it is empty of any specific content. But, so far, this is how he intends it to be. It is his method. Kant claims this abstract approach is necessary if we are ever to understand why there are moral principles that apply to everyone. In other words, he sees that we have to step right back from the particulars of our experience, or go to some place well above them, if we are ever to get an overall view of the source of moral behaviour for everyone. Of course, he does accept that in practice our *will* and reason aim to produce good actions. This is the whole purpose of morality. As we shall see, he claims to show us the supreme principle of morality (1969: 57). We can then apply the supreme principle to decide what actions are right and wrong. Furthermore, he will give us examples of particular actions that are right or wrong in accordance with the supreme principle. But to get there, he first goes back to what he sees as the source of morality, which is independent of particular actions, and it lies in good *will* under the governance of reason.

The question then is, 'How does reason provide for a good *will* in practice?' Kant says it does so by enabling us to *will* actions that are *rational* as opposed to those based on feeling or inclination (1969: 62). But what is a rational action? Kant's answer is that a rational action is one which will not involve us in contradiction. Kant's key point is that it would be contradictory to *will* the action as okay for ourselves but not for others. It is in this way that Kant arrives at the supreme moral principle. He calls it 'the categorical imperative'. In the next section we will take a closer look at it.

The Supreme Principle: The Categorical Imperative

Categorical means *absolute* and imperative means *a demand*. Thus a categorical imperative is an absolute demand we have to follow in relation to how to behave morally. There is only one categorical imperative. It is so binding on us, Kant believes, that it has the force of law – not civil law, but moral law. He calls it 'a practical law' or 'the moral law' (1969: 83). It is not a law that society imposes on us for our own good, but a law we can recognise as valid from our own reasoning and therefore one that we should follow. Kant provides four different versions of the categorical imperative, each bringing out a different aspect of its meaning. We will focus on two versions. The first is the main one, and the second is concerned specifically with explaining why we are required to respect others. The main version is as follows:

> Act only on the maxim through which you can at the same time will that it should be a universal law.
>
> Kant 1969: 84

A maxim is a particular principle upon which we act. It comes from our motive or intention to do something expressed as a principle. For example, if I intend to steal something, then I have to ask myself if I can rationally *will* my intention as a universal principle. That is, can I rationally *will* that it is okay for me, and for everyone, to steal? Or can I will that it is okay for me to tell a lie, and for everyone else? 'No,' says Kant, 'I can't logically *will* this because I would be acting in a contradictory way.' Kant explains the nature of the contradiction in detail. He says that if we did *will* a universal law that it is okay to tell a lie, then 'there could be no promises at all' since no one would trust that anyone is telling the truth. This means we could not lie successfully because no one would believe us. We would not succeed because people would naturally suspect we were lying to them since we have introduced a law permitting lying. We can only tell a lie and get away with it if there is an expectancy that others will believe we are telling the truth. This makes *willing* a universal law that it is okay to lie contradictory; it makes it *futile* or self-defeating. (In practice, as distinct from logic, we still might, of course, succeed in getting away with telling a lie by deceiving a person, but this is not Kant's point.)

Kant also explains the nature of the contradiction by pointing out that if we *will* a law to allow for telling lies, then we are *willing* a law from which we ourselves could become the victim. This is because if someone did happen to believe our lie, once s/he found out that we had told him/her a lie, and that there was a law permitting lying, then s/he would be entitled to lie back to us. In Kant's phrase, s/he would be entitled to 'pay me back in like coin'. In other words, any law that I might *will* to tell lies would rebound on me. I would be putting myself into a position of being a victim. But who would logically want to *will* himself/herself to be a victim? To do so would be contradictory or irrational. Here is what Kant says:

> . . . I can indeed *will* to lie, but I can by no means *will* a universal law of lying; for by such a law there could properly be no promises at all, since it would be futile to profess a *will* for future action to others who would not believe my profession or who, if they do so over-hastily, would pay me back in like coin; and consequently my maxim, as soon as it was made a universal law, would be bound to annul itself.
>
> Kant 1969: 68

Kant, then, is asking us to exercise our reason to see what we could *will*, not just for ourselves, but for everyone. We are being asked to think through what would happen, or what we would be signing up for, if we *will* that everyone could do the same as we are intending to do. In effect, the categorical imperative means that if you wish to do something, your action will be morally right if at the same time you can *will* that everybody else should do the same as you. On the other hand, your action will be morally wrong if you find you could not *will* that it should apply to everyone. It is always wrong to act in one way while *willing* that no one else should do the same.

Rationality, Not Consequences

Kant is sometimes misunderstood as arguing that the *consequences* of permitting everyone to tell lies would lead to social breakdown and that this is the reason why it is irrational. But Kant is not saying that to *will* to tell a lie is wrong because of its negative consequences on others or on society, and so we have to have a rule against lying in everyone's interest. This is the social convenience or social contract argument. But this is not Kant's argument. He would not consider this argument strong enough. No doubt he would acknowledge that negative social consequences are a good reason why we should not tell lies, but they do not *prove* why we should not. A person can still validly say, 'In my opinion I don't see anything wrong with telling a lie to suit myself when I want to, even if it has negative social consequences.' Kant wants to prove to such a person that his view is untenable. This is why he argues that in telling a lie a person is going against reason – reason that is common to every human being. Nor is he saying we would necessarily want to tell a lie and get away with it. He is merely pointing out the irrationality of wanting to do so.

'Do to Others as You Would Have Them Do to You'

People sometimes remark on the similarity between Kant's imperative and the

Christian principle of behaving toward others as you would like them to behave toward you. A similar principle is also found in other religions. For example, we don't steal from others because we wouldn't want them to steal from us. There is a similarity, but Kant's imperative is based on a logical reason why we should behave in this way regardless of whether we accept the religious moral teaching. He claims to provide a basis in a *law of reason* why we should treat others as we would like to be treated. In ethics the principle of treating others as you would like them to treat you is known more generally as 'the golden rule'.

The Imperative as an Objective Criterion for Right and Wrong

With the categorical imperative, or supreme principle of morality, Kant is claiming that there is an objective criterion for deciding between right and wrong. Yes, a person can still ignore this criterion and behave in ways that go against it. However, in doing so he is behaving in a way that goes against his rational nature as a human being, which is common to everyone. Kant is pointing out to wrongdoers that they are in denial of what it is to be a rational human being. This, he claims, makes the reason why their behaviour is wrong *objectively* true, i.e. true for everyone no matter what their feelings or opinions are on the matter. In other words, what Kant is trying to show is that there are actions which are *wrong in themselves* and that people are going against *human* reason by doing them. This, Kant argues, gives morals their *objective* force.

EQUALITY

So far we have seen how Kant claims to prove that there is a rational basis for understanding common moral views, such as it is wrong to steal and tell lies. These are examples of behaviours we should avoid, but what about behaviour we should do, such as to treat all people as equal in their worth as persons? If Kant's supreme principle is applied, we can see that it would make no sense to *will* a universal law that we should regard people as unequal in their humanity because then we would be leaving it open to others to treat us as inferior and not having the same worth as they have.

Also, since the moral laws that Kant is arguing for have to be universal ones, this means they have to apply to everyone equally. It would make no sense to *will* universal laws and then start to make distinctions about who the laws should apply to on the basis of gender, colour, ethnic origin or disability.

However, under Kant's theory there is a more fundamental reason why everyone should be treated as having the same basic equality. The reason comes from the two cornerstones of his theory: that we are endowed with a capacity to exercise our *will* and our reason.

Individual Freedom or Autonomy

From each of us having our own *will* and reasoning ability, Kant identifies an essential freedom or autonomy at the heart of being a person. This autonomy can be seen in the way we make our own decisions in formulating moral laws and in the freedom we have to obey or disobey what those laws require.

Everyone Decides

Morality is not imposed on us from without by some higher authority or institution. Each person is in the same position of addressing his/her own rationality to determine the actions which s/he can rationally *will* all others to do and those actions which s/he cannot rationally *will* others to do. Each is an authority in his/ her own right to determine what is right and wrong in accordance with what can or cannot be rationally *willed*. There is an essential freedom which is the mark of the equality of everyone at the heart of the very process of determining moral principles. Kant calls this freedom the 'autonomy' of the individual.

Freedom to Obey or Disobey

Also, people are free in another sense. This is the sense in which they can choose to recognise, and try to live by, the moral principles that come from the categorical imperative or they can decide to not bother with them and suit themselves. Either way, their capacity to choose indicates their freedom. If they decide to ignore the principles that come from the imperative, they will then, as we saw, be acting against reason and in a morally wrong way (and perhaps breaking the state laws as well), but they will be indicating their human freedom. It's not that we should respect people's freedom as the mark of their equality when they break the law! It's people's autonomy that deserves respect, for which breaking the law is an impermissible example. In particular, the autonomy at the heart of everyone points to the care requirement to treat with respect people who have broken the law and are detained in prison.

RESPECT

Kant's argument for the requirement to respect others has the same basis as the requirement to treat them as having equal worth. As to treat others with respect is to ask ourselves if we could *will* a universal law that everyone should be treated with respect. Our answer would have to be 'Yes'. Otherwise we would be *willing* a world in which it was okay for others to treat us with disrespect and this would make no sense. Also, since people are equal, they deserve to be treated on the basis of their equality.

There is also a deeper reason for respecting others, which arises from the autonomy we have as individuals through our will and reason.

Treating People as 'Ends'

Kant describes the requirement to treat others with respect as a result of their autonomy by saying that we should always treat another person as an *end* in himself/ herself. By *end* he means that we should see a person as free and autonomous in his own right. In practice we can say that to treat each person as an *end* is to treat them in a way that recognises their entitlement to make their own choices and decisions in pursuing their plans and activities. This essential freedom or autonomy is something we value in ourselves and it is necessarily how we have to understand the way others are for themselves. It requires that we avoid manipulating others for our own ends. For example, in slavery, people are not treated as ends in themselves. Common expressions reflect Kant's understanding of the respect we should have for other people's *will*. We say, for example, that 'it is wrong to impose your *will* on someone else' and that 'we shouldn't do something to someone against their *will*'. Abusers fail to treat their victims as ends in themselves. This requirement to treat people as ends in themselves is particularly relevant in caring for those with disabilities, where there can be a tendency to restrict unnecessarily opportunities for them to live according to their own plans.

Of course, we also treat people as *means* to some end that we want. This is an inevitable part of human interaction. For example, we treat a taxi driver as a means to our end of taking us to our destination. In this sense, a care worker can be said to treat clients as a means to his/her end of accomplishing his/her work. However – and this is the crucial point – Kant says that we should never treat people 'simply as a means, but always *at the same time* as an end.' What Kant is saying, in effect, is that while using other people as a means, we should also have the greatest of respect for them as individuals. Here is the second version of the categorical imperative in full. It is called 'The Formula of the End in Itself'. In ordinary language it is known as the 'Respect for Persons' version of the imperative.

> Act in such a way that you always treat humanity, whether in your own person or in the person of any other, never simply as a means, but always at the same time as an end.
>
> Kant 1969: 91

This formula particularly brings out why it is morally wrong to ill-treat or abuse others. In doing so, a person is treating another as a thing or a tool for his/her own ends and not as an autonomous person who is an end in himself/herself as of right. This formula also highlights why all are deserving of equality of respect and treatment in society and in laws. It makes clear why many particular forms of behaviour that go against this basic equality are morally wrong. For example, people have rights under the law, so if their rights are being denied or withheld, this is to treat them with disrespect.

Kant's formula also requires that we treat *ourselves* as ends and have self-respect. For the same reasons as we have to respect others, we have to respect ourselves. It would make no sense to have to respect others while treating ourselves with disrespect. This duty includes developing our potential as best we can (1969: 92). This benefits not only ourselves but others also, since it puts us in a better position to be able to support and promote others in their needs.

CARE FOR OTHERS

Rationality, Not Self-interest

In addition to principles of equality and respect, Kant also explains why there is a principle to care for others. He argues that we should *will* a universal law of care for others because we will require help some day. It is important not to misunderstand Kant when he says this. It is not that we should *will* care for others for a selfish or self-interested motive or, more generally, from a motive of common or collective self-interest. It is not a case of 'I'll help you provided you help me'. Nor is it even a case of 'one good turn deserves another'. The point is that, as for the example of lying, it would be self-defeating or contradictory or irrational to *will* into existence a law that no care should be given to others because then we would be *willing* that no care should be given to us when we need it. If we have *willed* that there is no obligation to help others, we are *willing* that no help should be given to us. Here is how Kant puts it: 'It is impossible to *will*' that we should do nothing for 'others who have to struggle with great hardships (and whom we could easily help)'. This is the reason:

> For a *will* which decided in this way would be in conflict with itself, since many a situation might arise in which the man needed love and sympathy from others, and in which, by such a law of nature sprung from his own *will*, he would rob himself of all hope of the help he wants for himself.
>
> Kant 1969: 86

One way of expressing Kant's argument here is to say that the *effect* of the principle of acting to care for others is that others will (hopefully) care for us when we need it, but this is not the *reason* for the principle – the reason is that to disregard the principle is to act irrationally. We would be acting in a way that is inconsistent with our own *will*.

How Much Care?

Perfect Duties

Kant distinguishes between two types of obligations or duties under the imperative. The first type provides for a 'narrow (rigorous) duty'. This includes duties to refrain from lying and physically harming others, and duties to treat people with respect and having equal worth. There are simply no two ways about having to observe them. They are called perfect duties from the fact that the requirement to abide by them is perfect or absolute. (Harming others in necessary self-defence could be considered an exception, as we have a duty to preserve and develop our own life.)

Imperfect Duties

The second type refers to 'wider (meritorious) duty' (1969: 86–7). This type of duty includes the duty to care for others. There are clearly many ways in which we can care for others, and we can do so to varying degrees. Kant calls caring 'an imperfect duty' because we can never fulfil it completely. Imperfect duties include a duty to develop our own potential. For Kant, this is also an imperfect duty because we can never fulfil it completely or in all ways. As O'Neill (1993: 178) puts it, 'We cannot help all others in all needed ways, nor can we develop all possible talents in ourselves. Hence these obligations are necessarily selective as well as indeterminate.' In other words, both how much care and in what way we give care are matters for us to decide and we have discretion in doing so. No one can specify for us either the nature of the care we are required to give or the amount.

Becoming Good by Providing Care

The fact that we have discretion does not mean we are required to do only the minimum. Kant points out that the extent to which we discharge our imperfect duties is the extent to which we become good people. The more we seek to implement them to the best of our ability, the more we are doing the right thing and behaving as well as we can, as a human being ought to behave. This is what makes us a good or virtuous person. We saw with Aristotle that there is no excess of virtue. For Kant also, there is no excess of becoming virtuous through discharging our imperfect duties. In addition, we are only deserving of moral praise to the extent that we do more than the minimum (1969: 86–7). Schneewind makes the point that, if I want to, 'I may only do what is permissible within the limits of my legal duties', but 'I can become entitled to moral praise through my efforts for others. My merit increases as I make their goals my own' (1999: 324).

The Obligation to Provide Care

Example of Home Help Services

In a specific case of need, how are we to decide whether or not we have an obligation to provide care? For example, are we obliged to meet all the needs that older people have to continue to live independently and have the highest quality of life possible in their circumstances?

Kant's answer would seem to be both 'No' (strictly speaking) and 'Yes'. 'No' because neither we nor the state can provide for the care needs of everyone in every respect. All we are obliged to do is provide some care, and this does not necessarily have to include providing elderly people with all the home help they may need. However, we (and the state on our behalf) are required to provide *some* care, and it is reasonable to conclude that this should include at the very least people's basic needs, of which you can argue independent living is one. In this way we can see how his answer could also be 'Yes'. In addition, by providing help, the state is acting in a way that is morally good and praiseworthy.

This line of argument can be applied to many other examples of basic care needs, including providing long-term accommodation for the homeless and helping them overcome the causes of their homelessness. Also, following Kant's line of thinking, it would be rational to *will* a universal law that those who need to be provided with independent living or a home should be provided with it, since we may need a similar provision for ourselves some day. Since we can see we would want it for ourselves if we had the need, it is inconsistent of us to deny it for others.

DUTY ABOVE ALL

Duty is central to Kant's ethics. He argues that it follows from the existence of universal moral principles that we have a duty to obey them. It is probably true to say that many people today don't much like the idea of duty. It is seen to run counter to the sense they have of their own freedom. Yet for Kant, morality is based on freedom. Each person, as we have seen, is a free or autonomous agent – but for Kant, freedom is not fulfilled through doing as we please. He understands freedom as the capacity to be motivated to act according to reason. Moreover, as Patton points out, Kant is saying that it is only when we act according to reason that we actually achieve real freedom (Patton 1969: 33). Then we are freed from being under the sway of inclinations and desires that are not reliable guides for moral behaviour. Freedom is fulfilled through doing our rationally recognised duties.

For this reason, for Kant, duty is more important than a natural, human inclination we may have to care for others. People now tend to be more at home with the idea that they behave well toward others, not because of duty, but because they feel for them and, in doing so, experience this as an uplifting expression of being human. But for Kant this is not a good enough reason. He goes so far as to say that good actions done *solely* out of inclination or feeling have 'no genuinely moral worth' (1969: 64). In order to have moral worth, they have to be done for the sake of duty. This is because duty comes directly from the source of morality in the *will* and reason, which gives us the categorical imperative. In addition, as we will see in the next section, for Kant it is dangerous to allow feeling or inclination to dictate what is right or wrong.

Remember, too, that people often lack the inclination to do the right thing. For this reason there is much moral weakness and moral failure in society. Kant's position on duty allows us to say that just because you don't feel like doing the right thing, this does not let you off the hook. Whether you like it or not, you have a duty to do the right thing.

This point goes to the nub of our experience of feeling morally challenged. When we experience moral challenge, we experience ourselves simultaneously pulled in the opposing ways of doing something we want to do and not doing it because we recognise it as wrong.

Role of Inclinations

One practical reason why we must put aside what is 'to the advantage of our inclinations' is because once we allow anyone to have such an advantage, then everyone will feel entitled to justify their actions by special motives they feel they have (1969: 87). Kant warns against this. He says we can all find ways of special pleading. The result would be morality ending up 'looking like anything you please' (1969: 89). So we must *will* a universal law impersonally 'without basing it on any impulsion or interest' (1969: 105).

Let's look at the hard case of a poor woman who steals food from a supermarket to provide for her children. She still has to put aside her (understandable) inclination to steal, unless she and her children have no other way of surviving. She has to ask herself if she can *will* the principle arising from her intended action, which is that taking something that does not belong to her should be allowed as a moral law. Her answer has to be 'No'. Imagine if at the same time as she is taking the food from the shelf, her daughter, who had been at home, rushes up to tell her that a robber is in their house stealing their rent money. Logically, the woman would have to acknowledge that it is okay for the robber to take her rent. So, for Kant, we always have to put aside our inclination arising from our particular circumstances and base our judgment on the principle implied by the action we are intending.

Kant is pointing out that, if we want to, we can all try to find ways of arguing that our particular circumstances justify doing something we know is wrong. We see our circumstances as providing a justifiable exception to the rule. However, the reality is that we are only making excuses.

At the same time, we can argue, in the case of the poor woman (or other cases of a similar nature), that this logical answer does not adequately take account of the subjective reality of her plight given her particular circumstances. We can empathise with fact that she has felt driven to steal to provide for her children. Some critics say Kant's view is too rigid. It makes morality a matter of black and white with no shades of grey allowed. In practice, inclinations which arise from our circumstances often provide understandable human reasons why we behave as we do. After all, what if the woman finds her pride and dignity suffer unbearably if she has to seek charity or beg? It seems unreasonable of Kant not to accept circumstances in at least some hard cases as valid reasons which do not make an action wrong. We would say that, at the very least, circumstances can greatly reduce how wrong we consider the action to be, but a scale of wrongness is not something Kant includes. At the same time, his point is that to allow exceptions is to place ourselves on a slippery slope where we will have difficulty knowing how to stop allowing for exceptions.

Also, we should remember that where we have the means to relieve hardship, we have a duty to do so, admittedly an imperfect but meritorious one. So, under Kant's theory, other people (or society at large through the state's welfare system) can be considered lacking in morality through not having provided the woman with the help she obviously needs.

It is important to emphasise that Kant is not against moral feeling and inclination having *any* role in morality. The main role he sees them having is as a feel-good factor which backs up or supports us when we have done the right thing, but it is not how we know we have acted in accordance with the moral law (1969: 120).

Secondly, Kant recognises that inclination has a role as a *motive* for doing the right thing as distinct from the reason for doing the right thing. He recognises that moral feelings clearly help people to do right and avoid wrong. As such, they are invaluable in practice. Patton makes this point:

> Furthermore he [Kant] never wavers in the belief that generous inclinations are a help in doing good actions, that for this reason it is a duty to cultivate them, and that without them a great moral adornment would be absent from the world.
>
> Patton 1969: 20

KANT'S ETHICS AND SOCIAL CARE

Respect for Others

Complete respect for others underlies the following five aspects of care work.

Equality of Treatment

This includes supporting the interests and rights claims of clients who have grounds for their case that they are not being treated equally or fairly under public policy. This may be for a number of general reasons, such as that there is no administrative provision under existing policy, that policy is not being interpreted correctly or that lack of resources is preventing the policy from being implemented. In practice, equality of treatment does not always have to be followed rigidly. In cases where there are relevant and justifiable differences, making exceptions can be warranted. For example, in a waiting list for medical treatment, urgent cases will be treated before others who have been waiting for longer; in a residential care home there may be particular justifiable reasons why one person should receive more favourable conditions or allowances than others on the basis of their care needs. Equality underlines many practical issues which can arise for people with care needs.

Related to a basic equality of worth is the idea that equality in practice means that it is morally good for the state to provide equality of opportunity for all people in society. A morally justifiable equality policy is one in which people, for example, can avail of educational opportunities up as far as third level, and are not prevented from doing so for financial reasons. It would also, for example, ensure that children who come from backgrounds in which there is poverty and crime have opportunities and support to help them resist any adult or peer pressure they may come under to get involved in criminal activity. Underlying contributory reasons as to why some people come in need of care services, in particular custodial care, can relate to difficulties in their background which inhibited them from availing of opportunities.

Self-determination

One immediate principle that follows from having complete respect is the client's right to make choices. Respecting a person means respecting their right to determine their own life as far as possible. This is an important guideline for care of people with disabilities and older people in particular. In relation to advocacy, self-determination includes empowering clients to become advocates for their own needs.

Informed Choice

Related to facilitating self-determination is the need to ensure that people in care can make their own informed choices. This includes ensuring that they have, and can understand, accurate and relevant information, and where they have options that they can assess the advantages and disadvantages of each. Paternalism is the practice of making choices for others on the grounds that we believe we know what is best for them. A paternalistic approach to care is not supported by Kant's ethics of individual autonomy. However, in certain cases where, for example, a person has a significant learning challenge, Alzheimer's disease or diminished capacity in old age, it may be necessary to curtail a person acting on their preferred choice to ensure their safety and protection. Particular care may need to be taken to ensure that a person is not being unnecessarily restricted in their choice, for example, for reasons of staff convenience or the organisation's convenience. Kant's ethics of individual autonomy is reflected in Article 3 (a) of the UN Convention on the Rights of Persons with Disabilities, which provides 'Respect for inherent dignity, individual autonomy including the freedom to make one's own choices, and independence of persons'. Article 12.2 provides for 'legal capacity on an equal basis with others on all aspects of life' and Article 12.3 provides for 'support' to exercise this capacity.

Of particular note are the guiding principles and detailed provisions of the Assisted Decision-Making (Capacity) Bill 2013. They represent a substantial move away from paternalistic notions of care in supporting personal autonomy. The Bill provides legal entitlement for people of diminished capacity to exercise their own choice in so far as possible and, where necessary, to be supported by a person appointed as assistant or co-decision maker to look out for their best interests and take account of their beliefs and values. (See Bill for details.)

Kant's ethics also supports best child care practice of enabling children to exercise their own *will* and reasoning ability to understand and engage with issues and information and make choices appropriate for their age.

Informed Consent

This includes ensuring, as far as possible, a person's informed agreement for the care measures intended for him/her or for the nature and type of representation being proposed on their behalf. Where a person may not be in a position to give this consent as a result of disability, for example, it should be obtained from his/her next of kin.

Qualified Confidentiality

Respect for clients also includes ensuring that personal information about them is kept confidential. In practice, this means that information about a client and his/her circumstances should not be shared with anyone else, other than on a need-to-know basis. *Need-to-know* means where others will need to know the information in order to provide care for the client. Passing on concerns relating to poor practice is particularly important as a first step to prevent it from continuing. Confidentiality is never absolute, it is always qualified. It is important that clients know that while information they give will be treated in confidence, it will only be on this qualified basis. This is to ensure that there will be no misunderstanding. A problem can arise when a client assumes confidentiality is absolute and s/he learns that information s/he shared has been passed on. S/he may see this as a breach of trust, withdraw from taking part in care and find it difficult to trust again.

Related to confidentiality is respect for a person's right to privacy. Ensuring that people have their needs for privacy met arises in particular in residential care. (For more on confidentiality and on informed consent see the Code of Professional Conduct and Ethics for Social Workers on the CORU website, www.coru.ie.)

Duty of Care

The idea of a duty of care informs and guides social care practice. A duty of care is central to the mission statement of care agencies and is much referred to by care practitioners. Most ethical theories provide reasons why we (or the state) should provide care. However, it is Kant's theory which provides a justification for a specific *duty of care*. Also, as we have seen, Kant explains why doing more than the minimum duty is morally good. O'Neill explains the implications of a duty to care by saying, 'A commitment of this nature, taken seriously, will demand much. If we honour it, we have on Kant's account shown respect for persons and specifically for human dignity' (1993: 179).

Duty of Care for Prisoners

A duty of care for prisoners includes, in particular, a duty to treat them with respect. The fact that they have not respected the victims of their offence is not a reason for disrespecting them, and it is not a justification for the perception that they are less deserving or worthy of respect because of what they have done. A study of prisons in the UK, which was based on consultation with prisoners and prison staff, found respect to be one of the top requirements in the prison officer–prisoner relationship. Other requirements included trust, humanity and support. (See Liebling 2005, Chapter 5 for a detailed account of the meaning of these values and the part that they play in custodial care.)

Duty of Care and Advocacy

A duty of care helps us to understand the moral context of the work of social care advocates. This is because it is a matter of making the principle of caring for others apply to a particular need for care, for example, where an agency may not be willing (for lack of resources or other reasons) to grant a particular service. However, if a strong enough case is made, the agency may find a way of obtaining the required resources or of making a justifiable exception in the particular case. A society that has the resources to provide for at least basic care needs for those requiring them would seem morally obliged to do so as a universal law, and this provides justification for the advocate's efforts. By using the facts of the client's circumstances, the advocate tries to convince agency staff of the need for the service. In effect, the advocate is acting out of conviction that it should be a moral requirement.

Reporting Malpractice (Whistle-blowing)

Incidences of malpractice occur in all professions. This places an obligation on staff who become aware of any malpractice (or who have concerns that it might be occurring) to report it to the appropriate person in authority. It is important, also, that there is an official whistle-blower's charter in place for staff, so that staff can feel supported and protected by following its procedure for reporting concerns. The government published a Protected Disclosures Bill in 2013 which, when enacted, is designed to provide legal protection for people who raise concerns in good faith about potential wrongdoing in the workplace which comes to their attention.

Exercise 3.1

Questions to Consider and Discuss

From your knowledge and/or experience of examples of (i) lack of equality; (ii) lack of respect; and (iii) lack of care, consider and discuss:

1. Why the practice in each example can be considered wrong according to Kant's ethics.
2. What providing for equality, respect and care would mean in your examples.

Exercise 3. 2

Consider and discuss whether it is always wrong to tell a lie. If you think there are cases when it is okay to tell a lie, identify and explain a moral principle or value that you think supports and justifies it.

In the following example, consider and discuss whether the care staff are justified in telling the service user a lie. Deirdre is 70 years old and has Alzheimer's disease. Each morning she asks a staff member in the home where she is being cared for if her husband will be coming to visit her today. The staff used to tell her the truth, which is that her husband passed away some years ago and cannot come to visit her. On hearing the staff say this, Deirdre had become very upset, which also upset other residents. Before she got Alzheimer's she had been able to acknowledge and understand that her husband had died and to mourn his loss. However, since the onset of her disease she has forgotten this. After discussing the matter, the staff decide to tell Deirdre that her husband will be along later to visit her. This has the effect of pleasing Deirdre and she carries on her day without getting upset. Yet, each morning she continues to ask staff if her husband will be visiting her and they continue to tell her that he will be along later.

CASE STUDY 3.1

Case Studies: Self-determination and Safety

Drawing on Kant's principles of equality, respect and care, consider the appropriate response of a care team to the following situations. Include details relating to the client's level of challenge and other circumstances. If certain conditions are proposed which support attendance, consider whether they adequately respect the client's freedom.

1. An eighteen-year-old boy with a learning challenge in a residential centre who insists on going into pubs in the town at night.
2. A seventeen-year-old girl with a learning challenge who wishes to attend a disco.

CASE STUDY 3.2

Case Studies: Privacy and Safety when Monitoring Residents

Drawing from Kant's principles of equality, respect and care, consider and discuss the case below. Also consider and discuss the general issue of respect for privacy in a society where the use of technology has made it increasingly possible to access personal information about other people.

In his report for 2012 the Data Commissioner found that a private nursing home was using CCTV cameras to monitor residents and accessing live film from the cameras using smartphones. This was reported 'as a substitute for on-the-ground staff'. The management company for the home said the cameras were for the safety, protection and quality of care for its residents and staff. However, the Data Commissioner said that under the Data Protection Act,

CCTV images are personal data and that their use has to be 'proportionate and transparent'. The company voluntarily removed the cameras. The Commissioner also made the point that in workplaces workers were concerned that their work performance is being monitored on a live basis.

(*Source*: E. Edwards, 'Nursing Home Used CCTV "as Substitute for Supervisory Staff" in *The Irish Times*, 21 May 2013)

CRITICAL EVALUATION

Abstract and Rigid: Overlooks Circumstances

A problem with Kant's principles is that he arrives at them through an exercise of pure reason without consideration of circumstances. In arriving at valid principles, we have to go only by our intention to do some act formulated as a universal principle, and not by particular circumstances. In the example of the woman who steals to feed her children, it is the principle that counts, not her circumstances. Kant doesn't allow for circumstances to influence how principles are to be understood in particular cases. However, in practice it is only within our understanding of particular circumstances that moral questions and issues arise for us. It is these circumstances which influence our application of the principles to particular cases. This is particularly so in social care decision-making. For example, the morally appropriate response of whether it is right or justified for the state to take into care the child of a young mother with an addiction will depend greatly on the particular circumstances. Kant's principles don't help us to understand the influence we should allow circumstances to have in guiding our decision. At the same time, his principles do provide guiding benchmarks. It is only because we know we should have respect and care for both mother and child that the appropriate response is an issue in the particular circumstances.

Also, we find that in complex cases different principles can contend with each other in their claim on us to give them the most weight. We need to consider the circumstances of the cases to decide on which principle (or combination of principles) should have priority. For example, in the case of a client with a disability who desires assistance to live independently, there are at least three principles that will lead to a morally appropriate decision to do so, when providing the assistance with safeguards or not. On the side of a decision to provide the assistance are principles of respect for the client's autonomy to make his/her own choices and determine his/her own life, and a duty of care. However, on the side of turning down the client's request (or perhaps meeting it in a partial way which s/he considers inadequate) are principles of protecting the client from harm and perhaps also the principle of equality of treatment (if there is a question of providing preference to one client over others in the allocation of limited resources). Thus all these principles can be in the mix and contend with each other for our support, but the only way we can decide on which principle (or combination of principles) should guide the actual decision is by considering the particular circumstances of the case. In this case, circumstances could include the client's level of ability to cope in his/her own judgment and the judgment of the care team, the level of support, or opposition, from the client's parents and the availability of required services, etc.

So, the problem is that Kant develops his principles using abstract reasoning, but morality only arises for us embedded in a set of circumstances. It therefore becomes a question of whether or not we can *will* principles as universal laws in their attachment to particular circumstances and not in the abstract. For more on this difficulty with Kant's theory, see Norman (1998: 79–81).

So, while Kant's principles can guide decision-making, his approach overlooks a crucial element: the details of the case. It's not that we could expect Kant (or anybody) to provide a detailed account of all the various types of circumstances that can arise which are relevant to moral decision-making in relation to his abstract principles, and then to tell us how much weight we are to give to them. It is that the factor itself – of allowing the moral weight of circumstances to guide the application of principles – is not included in his theory. Other theories do allow for circumstances. In Aristotle's ethics, as we have seen, a good or virtuous decision depends on a person relating to his/her feelings and desires in the context of the particular circumstance that have aroused them, and in the context of the courses of action open to him/her.

The problem is also that, in practice, human situations can be complicated, so it is hard to have a rule that fits every case that will arise. We may find that circumstances require us to make justifiable exceptions to principles. Mill, whose Utilitarian Theory is examined in Chapter 7, makes this point:

> It is not the fault of any creed, but of the complicated nature of human affairs, that rules of conduct cannot be so framed as to require no exceptions, and that hardly any kind of action can safely be laid down as either always obligatory or always condemnable. There is no ethical creed which does not temper the rigidity of its laws, by giving a certain latitude, under the moral responsibility of the agent, for accommodation to peculiarities of circumstances.
>
> Mill 2008: 157

In other words, life can be more complex than principles allow for. However, in fairness to Kant's position, it needs to be emphasised that, as Patton points out, his main aim is to establish the principles according to which we should act. His aim is not the application of those principles to particular cases (1969: 15). It is therefore a matter of speculation regarding what he might or might not have thought about how his principles should be applied in the circumstances of specific cases. The few examples he gives are intended only as general illustrations. At the same time, as we have said, he does not make taking account of circumstances an integral part of deciding between right and wrong.

Distinction between an Action being Contradictory and Wrong

This criticism requires making a fine distinction, which may be hard to see. The distinction was pointed out first by another famous philosopher, Hegel (Norman 1998: 81–2). If our behaviour is contradictory, does this also make it wrong? Hegel pointed out that it is not the same thing to say an action is contradictory and to say it is wrong. To see the distinction, we need to look a bit more closely at Kant's argument. Kant argues we could not rationally *will* a universal law that permitted telling lies because then no one would trust that anyone else was telling the truth, so it would be logically impossible to succeed in telling a lie as others would be wise to the fact. If you like, such a law would collapse from being contradictory. Also, we would, in effect, be *willing* as acceptable a practice by which we ourselves could become a victim of someone lying to us, which would be an irrational thing to do. In this way, Kant's argument claims to prove that telling lies is wrong. But does this argument prove it wrong? We can understand that it would be contradictory for us to *will* a law that lying is okay without this necessarily meaning that we have to regard telling lies as wrong. You can argue that Kant *assumes* that because lying is contradictory that this *makes* it wrong, but an action being contradictory can be regarded as different to it being wrong. When Kant points out that it is contradictory to tell a lie, he is still assuming that lying is wrong, that there is something bad about it, but he is not *proving* lying to be wrong. While Kant certainly offers a good reason why we should not lie, it is not a reason that shows lying to be wrong as such. This criticism can also be applied to show that Kant does not prove to us why respect and care are moral principles we have to follow, even though he gives us good reasons for doing so.

Assumes We Have Free Will

Freedom of the *will* means that we have the capacity to choose between two courses of action without our choice being the result of factors acting on us, such as our inclinations and desires. We always exercise our *will* in the context of factors acting on it, so does this mean it is the factors that give rise to our choice, or can we make a decision by being able to discount the factors? For example, imagine you are faced with a choice to have a night out or to stay in. Can you make a completely free decision? Will your choice not be the result of how you feel in one way or another, such as a feeling of boredom or restlessness giving rise to your decision to go out, or a feeling of tiredness or a need to save money for another occasion giving rise to your decision to stay in? Even if you try to prove you have free will by going against your desires and saying, 'I really want to go out, but I'll stay in just to prove I have free *will*', is this desire to prove you have free *will* not now the factor that gives rise to your choice? Clearly, we can know our intention to act in a particular way, and we can decide whether to act in accordance with our intention or not. In this sense we have free *will*. At the same time, there is always something that inclines us to act in one way or in another, and the question arises then as to the extent to which we can say that we have free *will*.

Kant is one of a number of philosophers who have grappled with the question of the *will*'s freedom, and his account is difficult. The freedom of the *will* is a particularly important question in ethics, and his account can help bring into focus the key point in the question, even though, as we will see, fault has been found with it. The question of the *will*'s freedom is important for social care ethics because if we lack freedom of the *will*, or if it is at least always restricted by factors affecting us, then this is one reason why we should have empathy for people who develop a habit or practice such as an addiction, which can become a problem for them and for others. (We will look at empathy in Chapter 5.)

For Kant, as we saw, the *will* is central. It is only those principles that we can *will* to become universal laws which establish how we should behave. But, for Kant, it is crucial that we regard the will as free in its *willing* of principles as universal laws (1969: 109). This is because if our *will* is not completely free but influenced by forces external to it, then it is these forces that will cause us to will universal laws (or at least contribute to willing universal laws) and not the will on its own. In other words, our *will* in attempting to establish universal law will, if you like, be discredited by some influence personal to us, which will make it impossible for anyone to consider that the laws could therefore be ones which have the standing of being universal for everyone. Influences or forces acting on our *will* typically include our inclinations and desires. For example, we *will* ourselves to get fit out of a desire to lose weight or to feel healthier. So, in *willing* himself to develop a theory to establish the existence of universal moral principles, Kant could have been influenced by his desire for moral security, or to become a great philosopher!

On the face of it, some inclination or desire always affects how we behave, and Kant accepts this. He goes further and claims that our behaviour is always caused by some inclination or desire. This means he is faced with a contradiction. On the one hand, he is saying our behaviour is always caused, and on the other hand he is saying we have to regard our *will* as free in how it wills moral principles. So the question is, how can the apparent contradiction be resolved? How can our *will* be free while at the same time our actions are always caused or determined for us?

Free Will as a Presupposition

Kant's answer is detailed and can be difficult to understand. At the outset he accepts that 'the idea of freedom' of the *will* is merely 'a presupposition' (1969: 109). He accepts that he has not proved it exists, and he does not think the existence of free *will* can be proved. To find a proof for it would mean having to go beyond the bounds of knowledge. However, he does try to explain how the freedom of the *will* can be understood in relation to *willing* principles as universal laws.

The Two Standpoints

By way of explaining how we have free *will*, he says we can look on ourselves from 'two standpoints'. From one standpoint our actions are caused – from the other we have free *will*. From one standpoint we live in the world of sense experience, of sight, hearing, etc. This is the world as we experience it through our five senses. He calls it 'the sensible world'. This world is the world as it appears to us, the world of appearances. It is the world as we can only know it in its relation to us. In belonging to this world, our behaviour is caused by our inclinations and desires.

In the sensible world, considered on its own, we do not have free *will*. If we ask ourselves why we have behaved in such a way, some inclination or desire will appear to our 'inner sense' as the reason. So, for example, if I go for a walk, it is because it appears to my inner sense I did so because I wanted to take exercise. (Kant was so well known for always taking a daily walk at the same time each day that the story goes that the townspeople used to know what time it was by seeing him leave his house!) We are always able to find some reason why we behave, and so in this world of the senses we are not free. Our behaviour is always caused by something or other; it is not the outcome of free *will* or free choice.

This is the first standpoint from which we can look on ourselves, the standpoint of living in a sensible world where our actions are governed by our inclinations and desires.

But, for Kant, we can also look on ourselves from a second standpoint. This standpoint is one in which we must assume another world existing behind all appearances of things in the sensible world. This is a world of things, not in their relation to us but simply in relation to themselves, a world of 'things in themselves'. We cannot know this world as it is in itself, but only in the way in which it affects us through appearances. We must assume that this 'intelligible world' exists if we are to make sense of our experience of having freedom of the *will* (1969: 111–112).

How does this solve the apparent contradiction of finding that our behaviour is both free and caused at the same time? Kant explains this by simply saying we belong to both worlds. When we act to *will* a principle as a universal law, we are solely in the intellectual world where there is freedom. But when we want to know what we should do in some situation that arises, we belong both to the sensible world – the world governed by desire and inclination – and to the intellectual world. This means we can respond with free *will* either through abiding by the requirements of the principles or by going against them, while still finding that our behaviour is caused by a particular desire. Through having a foot in both worlds at the same time, we are placed precisely in the experience of moral concern or challenge in that we can either do as we ought and act in conformity to universal law or we can allow ourselves to be governed by a desire or inclination that is contrary to it (1969: 113).

Difficulties with Kant's Account of Free Will

As we have seen, Kant's theory depends on accepting that our *will* is free in being able to *will* rationally principles as universal laws without being influenced by anything else. The *will* has to be pure, detached from any motive or desires we may have. Otherwise, their influence will enter into *willing* universal laws, making them personal and subjective to us rather than objective for all. But he has great difficulty showing that we have free will. This account of the problem of free *will* is generally acknowledged to be both difficult and obscure, and critics have found fault with it. One problem Kant leaves us with is that we have no idea how our deliberations in the intelligible world can act upon the sensible world (Benn 1998: 100). There is no obvious bridge between them, since Kant sees them as quite separate.

From a social care point of view, the difficulties Kant encounters in trying to explain free *will* show just how difficult it is for people to know for certain that they have free *will* and are responsible for their actions. Even if Kant is right, it is still a major challenge for people to use their free *will* in practice and to appropriately address the pressures they feel acting upon them as causes of their actions. As he says, in our ordinary everyday experience our actions are not merely influenced by our inclinations and desires, but actually caused by them. Thus it is a task for the intellectual side of our nature, where our freedom resides, to combat these causes where the need arises, assuming it is possible, through exercising free *will*.

Especially from a social care point of view, Kant's difficulty with the problem helps bring out how people are likely to have difficulty relating clearly to free *will* in themselves as a means to avoid behaving in ways that are not good for them, or to behave in a different way to improve their independence.

We will look at free *will* again in Chapter 5, where people's lack of free *will* is considered as one reason why having empathy for them is understandable as a value.

Provides Understanding for Common Moral Standards

Kant is said to have made one of the best attempts to demonstrate the commonly held view that the essence of morality lies in everyone abiding by the same principles. This is something that accords with people's general understanding and expectancy. As Patton points out, this is at the heart of Kant's ethics: 'He [Kant] holds that a man is morally good, not so far as he acts from passion or self-interest, but so far as he acts from an impersonal principle valid for others as well as himself. This is the essence of morality' (1969: 30).

Provides Rational Understanding of Guilt

Some people may feel Kant's moral laws are unduly restrictive, and that the primary good is to fulfil ourselves in achieving our plans even if it requires us to do things we could not agree that others should be allowed to do. However, Kant's point is that if we do so, we are not really fulfilling ourselves because we are going against our rational nature as human beings. So, if we are feeling justifiably guilty for something we have done (or not done when we feel we should have done it), it can be understood as a sign that we recognise we have behaved in a way that no one should. One of the merits of Kant's theory is that it can be considered to provide a rational explanation for the psychological experience of moral guilt.

REVIEW

That people are of equal worth; that they should always be respected; and that we should care for each other, at least to an extent, are common basic moral principles and central to social care ethics. Often these principles are not lived up to in practice. Kant enables us to understand that they are not just 'nice ideas'. He shows that from the fact that everyone has his/her own will and reason, there are rational grounds for why we should try to live in accordance with the principles.

FURTHER READING

Banks, S. (2006) *Ethics and Values in Social Work*, 3rd ed., Palgrave Macmillan (Chapter 2).

Benn, P. (1998) *Ethics*, UCL Press (Chapter 4).

Commission to Inquire into Child Abuse/Department of Health and Children (2009) 'Report of the Commission to Inquire into Child Abuse 2009', available at www.dcya.gov.ie.

Glover, J. (1999) *Humanity: A Moral History of the Twentieth Century*, Jonathan Cape ('A Study of Ethics and Inhumanity').

Government of Ireland, Assisted Decision-Making (Capacity) Bill 2013, available at www.oireachtas.ie.

Norman, R. (1998) *The Moral Philosophers: An Introduction to Ethics*, 2nd ed., Oxford University Press (Chapter 6 'Kant' and Chapter 10 'Facts and Values').

REFERENCES

Dempsey, A. (2013) 'Scandal of Elder Abuse Must Be Tackled Now', *The Irish Times*, 13 June 2013.

Duncan, P. (2013) 'Absence of Homecare Inspection Puts Elderly at Risk' and 'Home is Anything but a Safe Haven for Some Vulnerable Elderly Citizens', *The Irish Times*, 4 June 2013.

Edwards, E. (2013) 'Nursing Home Used CCTV "as Substitute for Supervisory Staff"', *The Irish Times*, 21 May 2013.

Hume, D. (1969) *A Treatise of Human Nature*, Penguin Classics.

Kant, I. (1969) *The Moral Law: Kant's Groundwork of the Metaphysic of Morals*, translated and analysed by H. Patton, Hutcheson University Library, London.

Liebling, A. (2005) *Prisons and their Moral Performance, a Study of Values, Quality and Prison Life*, Oxford University Press.

O'Neill, O. (2004) 'Kantian Ethics' in *A Companion to Ethics*, P. Singer (ed.), Blackwell.

Patton, H. (1969) 'Analysis of the Argument' in *The Moral Law: Kant's Groundwork of the Metaphysic of Morals*, Hutcheson University Library, London.

Schneewind, J. (1999) 'Autonomy, Obligation and Virtue' in *The Cambridge Companion to Kant*, Cambridge University Press.

4

Care

To show how feelings of care for others are natural in human relations and are an important part of the basis for understanding ethics.

LEARNING OBJECTIVES

At the end of this chapter you should be able to:

- Explain caring as a basic value.
- Explain why Hutcheson considers benevolence or kindness an essential emotional human response which provides a basis for ethics.
- Explain the feminist moral philosophy of care.
- Identify and describe the elements of a caring ethical approach, such as attachment, interpersonal relations, attention to the individual and empathy.
- Contrast and connect the two 'organising frameworks' of an ethics based on caring and an ethics based on rational considerations of equality and justice.

INTRODUCTION

Historical Note

In the history of ethics as a subject, a specific ethics of care came to prominence through the writings of mainly women philosophers in the second half of the twentieth century. In the 1980s they began to write about an ethics based on the caring experience which people have naturally in their relationships, such as that which parents have for their children. In 1982 Carol Gilligan published an article called 'In a Different Voice: Women's Conception of Self and Morality', which launched what came to be known as 'the feminist ethics of care'. From a study of male and female responses to ethical problems, Gilligan found that females tended to think differently to males and to reach different conclusions. While men tended to interpret moral issues in terms of what is rationally justifiable based on equality between people and a concept of fairness, women tended to interpret the same issues based on feeling empathy for people who have needs and problems (Held 1995: 1).

Subsequent studies have found that there is not a distinct gender-specific way of relating to morality, with males taking a detached, independent, rational approach and females an attached, interdependent, caring approach. Both tendencies are found in males and females (see Tronto 1993: 82–5; Friedman 1987: 63; Jagger 1995: 182). Regardless of whether we are male or female, there is now a recognition of two distinct, though related, ways of looking on ethics. There are what Gilligan calls two 'different organising frameworks' for understanding and assessing moral issues (1987: 34), which are encapsulated by the terms 'care' and 'justice'.

Gilligan and others highlighted that caring had largely been ignored as a basis for ethics within moral philosophy. A caring response had become sidelined or subordinated to an understanding of principles, such as we saw with Kant, or to an understanding of the virtues, such as we saw with Aristotle, rather than being itself the basis for morally good behaviour. They argue that a caring relationship is at the heart of ethical concerns and responses. Appropriate moral responses and judgments emerge from empathising with other people in their problems or needs. As Tronto puts it, 'In Gilligan's different voice, morality is not grounded in universal abstract principles, but in the daily experiences and moral problems of real people in their everyday lives' (1993: 79).

While a distinct ethics of care dates from recent decades, there have been philosophers in the past who argued for an ethics based on natural feeling for others, which is similar to the current basis for care ethics. We have seen, for example, the role that feelings of concern or distress play in Hume's ethics when we witness a robbery and see the victim's suffering. We feel joy or pleasure or a warm glow when we witness an act of kindness. For Hume these feelings form the basis for our moral judgments of disapproval and approval. Francis Hutcheson (1694–1746) is a philosopher who emphasised that ethics is based specifically on feeling for the good of others, which he called benevolence or the love of others. From the Scottish immigrant community in Ulster, he was born in County Down where his father was a Presbyterian minister. He lived in Dublin for ten years where he taught in an academy and wrote his works on ethics. In this chapter we will look at his arguments for an ethical basis in benevolence before looking at the more recent emphasis on an ethics of care.

CARE AS FUNDAMENTAL TO HUMAN LIFE

At a deep level, care lies at the heart of human existence. No other response that we have is more basic than care. It is not merely ethical but also goes to the core of being human. Care has what is called *ontological* reality, i.e. the deepest possible reality. Heidegger, a philosopher who wrote about what it means to be a person at the deepest level, describes care as lying behind everything we do: 'When we ascertain something present-at-hand by merely beholding it, this activity has the character of care just as much as does a "political action" or taking a rest and enjoying oneself' (Heidegger 1967: 238; see also Furrow 2005: 133). Caring is something people do immediately and naturally; it describes our very being in the world. People who do not care will usually have mental health problems, perhaps chronic depression or despair. They are seen as in need of care so that they can begin to care again about their lives. Moreover, it is because we care about our life, health, family and friends, and material prosperity that these things and relationships come to have meaning and value for us.

From the earliest times, care has been a theme in the recorded stories of the peoples of the world. The stories revolve around the kind of things and relationships that people see as having meaning and value for them, such as deeds of heroes and heroines who accomplish great feats and protect their clan or social group from harm. There is one story that features care itself as a person who accomplishes the most basic feat of all, i.e. the creation of a human being. In this fable (see below) we can see that care, in having created a person, is given the reward of possessing the person, and one way of understanding this is to consider people as both imbued with care and in the hands of care.

Ancient Latin Fable: Care and Being Human

Once when Care was crossing a river, she saw some clay; she thoughtfully took up a piece and began to shape it. While she was meditating on what she had made, Jupiter came by. Care asked him to give it spirit, and this he gladly granted. But when she wanted her name to be bestowed upon it, he forbade this, and demanded that it be given his name instead. While Care and Jupiter were disputing, Earth arose and desired that her own name be conferred on the creature, since she had furnished it with part of her body. They asked Saturn to be their arbiter, and he made the following decision, which seemed a just one: 'Since you, Jupiter, have given its spirit, you shall receive that spirit at its death; and since you, Earth, have given its body, you shall receive its body. But since Care first shaped this creature, she shall possess it as long as it lives. And because there is now a dispute among you as to its name, let it be called homo, for it is made out of humus (earth).

(cited in Heidegger 1967: 242)

HUTCHESON'S ETHICS OF BENEVOLENCE

Possession of a Moral Sense

Hutcheson believed that people have an innate moral sense through which they experience goodness in being benevolent, that is, in having kind feelings toward others and in wanting to help and not harm them. The moral sense is similar to our five external senses in that it gives us our experience of the world. But it is an 'internal' sense through which we receive perceptions of approval and disapproval of certain actions. We find the actions we approve of give us pleasure or joy, which make them attractive; actions we disapprove of, on the other hand, make us uneasy, upset or angry, and we have an aversion toward them. Approval and disapproval come to us naturally, not by an act of our will or by working anything out. When we examine in our minds what is making us feel approval, we discover that 'kind affections' and 'kind intentions' are the marks of actions we approve of, and that they are the characteristics of good actions to which we are drawn (Hutcheson 2004: 90–91; 116).

The moral sense is 'some instinct' that comes before our will, reasoning or calculation, and it arouses our desire for benevolence and avoidance of harm. It 'influences us to the love of others' (2004: 112). An example is when we see images of the suffering of famine victims. These images immediately affect us with the moral disapproval that this should not be allowed to happen, without our needing to work out a judgment; we are simply moved or affected, and our desire to help is aroused.

For Hutcheson, this is how we find we are of our nature; our minds are given to receive perceptions of right and wrong actions by being moved through an internal sense. He also calls an internal sense a 'natural power' (2004: 67). It gives us a natural desire to act for the good of others. When we examine further our perception of the actions we approve, we discover also that they 'tend towards the good of the whole' or 'the public good' (2004: 109–110; 116). Also, since there is a natural unity among people by virtue of their status as human beings, this means that when we act benevolently for the good of others we are also being benevolent toward ourselves. From being part of the whole of humankind 'every moral agent justly considers himself . . . an object of his own benevolence' (2004: 122). In this way, we discover that ethics is about acting with kindness as a settled disposition of virtue in so far as our influence extends toward others, and in so far as we have prudent knowledge of their interests (2004: 132).

In Hutcheson's day, as in ours, people have argued that morals are not endowed in us by nature. Instead, they come from our culture. In arguing for an ethics based on nature, he recognises the diversity of cultural practices and the differences that exist between cultures in how people regarded the same practices morally, but points out that in all cultures children, before they are educated, identify with kindness and recoil from cruelty and hate (2004: 145–6). In this way, our individual moral sense reveals an experience of ethics that is both universal and inherently related to helping others meet their needs and interests. So in making his case for an ethics of benevolence, Hutcheson also brings in as evidence the universal feeling of concern that parents have for the happiness of their children (2004: 112–14; 147–8).

Reason and Human Nature

Hutcheson's account is at variance with much actual behaviour, and he was well aware of this. He knew that throughout history people have engaged in practices such as incest and slavery without it seeming to offend their moral sense, at least not enough for them to feel straightaway they should desist from such practices and to have done so. Hutcheson's explanation is that reason can be deficient in not enabling us to see the harmful consequences of our actions. People can be conditioned into finding practices that are offensive to the moral sense acceptable under the mistaken impression that they provide good. He also points out that we are liable to be overcome by selfish and violent passions. But when people do bad things, it is more a sign that they cannot see where their own and other people's best interests lie rather than them lacking a moral sense (2004: 135–146). As a result, he sees a need for us to think out the consequences of our actions to be able to recognise the harm they cause others, a recognition that will bring out a natural feeling of aversion toward such acts (2004: 125). Reason can enable us to see whether or not practices accord with natural human feeling. It is nature that provides the bedrock on which our ethical sense is founded, and we can experience our moral human nature more clearly, and implement it to greater effect, by using our reason to reflect on the consequences on others and ourselves of certain behaviours and practices (2004:133-4).

He is also aware of the argument that when we seem to act for the interests of others we are only disguising some self-interest, that some philosophers 'will rather twist self-love into a thousand shapes' rather than acknowledge that we can genuinely act for the interests of others without it being in some way to our own advantage (2004: 93). The view that we act only for our own interests is now known as psychological egoism, and we will come back to it when considering moral relativism in Chapter 8. But Hutcheson appeals to the genuine nature of our experience of acting for the interests of others, and he makes the point that 'If there is to be any benevolence at all, it must be disinterested; for the most useful action imaginable, loses all appearance of benevolence, as soon as we discern that it only flowed from self-love or interest' (2004: 103).

Self-Interest and Benevolence

Moreover, Hutcheson recognises that acting from self-interest is as natural to us as acting toward others with kindness, and so he does not criticise self-interest as something necessarily bad which should be avoided. Pursuing our own private good makes us capable of putting our benevolence into practice because it can give us the means to do so. A neglect of our own good can show a lack of interest in the common good (2004: 122). He accepts that desires for wealth and power are as natural to us as feeling for the good of others. In fact, the desires for wealth and power are 'the most effectual means, and the most powerful instruments' to achieve the good of everyone in practice (2002: 19–20). He recognises, too, that we often act from mixed motives, but he distinguishes between acts that are useful to others and those that are benevolent in a moral sense (2004: 103–4; 116). Much that is useful to us has come from individuals pursuing their own desires in all spheres of activity, whether it is done for our good in a moral sense or not. But for an act, or portion of an act, to be morally worthy, the motivation for it must be for the good of others, he believes. It is then that an act has 'a moral beauty' which is absent from an action that is merely useful to us (2004: 109–110).

While the moral sense is instinctive, it is often a struggle to act benevolently toward others as self-interest gets in the way. This is why he sees that 'what . . . properly constitutes a virtuous character is not some few accidental motions of compassion, natural affection, or gratitude' but 'a fixed humanity or desire of the public good of all' (2004: 132; see also p. xv, editor's footnote 16). It requires, in other words, an act of will over and above being drawn to act benevolently.

Hutcheson also describes the moral sense we have been given as a 'passive power' (2004: 67). By this he means that we find ourselves acted upon in wanting to care for others. For him the moral sense would seem to be the conduit for our conscience. As a Christian, Hutcheson believed in God as the 'Author of nature', and so the ultimate source of the human experience of moral sensibility. It is possible also to see the moral sense as having come down to us through evolution, and, as we shall see in considering a neuroscience understanding of ethics in Chapter 5, it also makes use of the idea that people have a moral sense similar to the one which Hutcheson is claiming we have.

FEMINIST ETHICS OF CARE

The Bodily Basis

By experiencing our environment primarily though our five bodily senses of sight, hearing, touch, taste and smell, we orientate ourselves toward things in the world and other people. To perceive is to leave ourselves, however momentarily, and focus on something or someone. Merleau-Ponty makes this point in his philosophy of the body. He locates our sense of having a subjective self within the way our bodies lead us out into the world. In his account of care ethics, Hamington draws from Merelau-Ponty's philosophy of the body: 'When confronted with another person, my senses focus on the other, and I become part of the background. The other is the foreground, or source of perceptual focus. This transition makes care possible' (Hamington 2004: 51). The very way we relate to the world through our bodily senses provides the basis on which we relate to other people, which includes providing the basis on which we care for them.

Care is also fundamental from its origin in the body's capacity to experience sensations of pain and pleasure. The fact that we are sensitive to pain in particular underpins our knowledge and disposition to care for others who show signs of suffering in some way. Hamington draws further from Merleau-Ponty's philosophy in pointing out that we naturally develop habits through which we care for our bodies. We move, adjust or treat our bodies to avoid and relieve pain and discomfort, and to obtain greater levels of ease and pleasure. Because we have highly sensitive bodies, we respond to stimuli in order to protect and develop bodily well-being. Our bodies are naturally given to self-care, but they are also given to the care of others. This is noticeable in the way parents have natural bodily habits in caring for their babies and children, habits such as holding, feeding, soothing, hugging and so on. (Hamington 2004: 57). For Hamington, 'the habits of the body make it appear to have been "built for care"' (2004:31).

Also, it is first and foremost through our bodily senses of sight, touch and hearing that we come to learn about the needs other people have. For example, 'we see distress in the eyes and face of others; we hear their suffering in their voice' (2004: 48). This sensitive, perceptual knowledge of other people, which comes to us through our bodies, is detailed and complex and enables us to build a picture of someone as a distinct person. A lot of the information affects us below our conscious awareness, but it still contributes to enabling us to care: 'The information my body garners when confronting others – knowledge of the expressions, mannerisms, gestures, smells, and sounds – far exceeds what is available to my consciousness and allows me to know others as perceptual wholes. Our perceptions are rich and complex, providing an enormous amount of information and making it possible for us to care' (Hamington 2004: 48).

At the same time, as well as receiving knowledge through the body, we build up a store of cognitive or intellectual knowledge from our study of, for example, psychology or ethics, which we also draw from for our knowledge about other people and their needs; there is 'an intertwining of embodied and cognitive knowledge' (2004: 58). We can notice especially the intertwining of the two sources of knowledge when we make a deliberate choice to care, or when we modify our care to make it more suited to a person's needs. So for Hamington, too, 'Care is more than the basis for an ethical theory; it is a basic aspect of human behaviour integral to our interrelationships' (2004: 13). For moral philosophers of care, the understanding of the basic role that care plays in human experience underlies and justifies care as the basis for ethics. Virginia Held observed that 'I find care the most basic moral value. Without the actual practice of care, there cannot be human life at all' (cited in Hamington 2004: 32).

Dependency

Care philosophers point to the fact that we all have basic dependency needs. From birth and throughout our childhood, we are all vulnerable and greatly dependant on care for our survival and well-being. As adults we have independence and autonomy but are also interdependent and reliant on others, and continue to need care (Tronto 1993: 62; 135). This may be as a result of, for example, difficulty coping with being unemployed, family pressures, career or other disappointments, or illness. In older age, people are likely to become more reliant on receiving care because of diminished capacity and/or medical need. The recognition of dependency as part of the human condition changes the way care is regarded. Having our dependency needs met – and met in an ethical manner which fully respects independence and supports empowerment – is a hugely important part of our lives. Care is no longer seen as something certain unfortunate people need because of their particular circumstances. It becomes something we all engage in daily as both care givers and care receivers (Sevenhuijsen cited in Held 1998: 28).

Universality

To support their claim that morality should be based on care, care philosophers also point to caring as a universal human practice. Care practices can vary between different cultures and different groups, but the caring attitude and practice itself is constant in all of them (Tronto 1993: 110). For Noddings, the universal human inclination to care provides an overall basis on which to judge whether behaviour and practices are good or bad. It provides the guiding standard for moral responses and judgments. If the responses and judgments are morally good, then they will meet criteria for good care understood as everyone's need and desire to experience well-being. To draw on this understanding of care is a way of arguing that there can be one universal basis for ethics. If a particular response adequately expresses the caring inclination by meeting standards of good care, for example, by adequately respecting the other person as having his/her own will, then it is morally justifiable; if it does not then, depending on circumstances, it may be morally lacking (Noddings 1984:14; 20).

As caring is a universal human disposition and practice, Noddings claims that it overcomes moral relativism, which is the view that there is no one overall understanding of ethics for everyone to go by in deciding between good and bad behaviour. Instead, ethical judgments are a matter of personal feeling or desire. We will look at moral relativism in more detail in Chapter 8 on diversity.

Self and Relationships

Caring is bound up with being in relationships with other people, and being in relationships is seen as part of how we define a human person. For Addleson, the human person can be defined by the fact that people engage in relationships with others and are not separate, autonomous agents who have an identity completely independent of others. It is through our 'interactive patterns of behaviour, perceptions and interpretations' that we get our sense of self (Addleson cited in Sevenhuijsen 1998: 56). As Baier puts it: 'Thus, the insight that each person needs some others in her life who recognise, cherish and respect her particularity in its richness and wholeness is the distinctive motivating vision of the care perspective' (1987: 72).

Also, our identity is bound up with the unfolding story of our life, and this story has meaning and value for us from the fact that it relates in some way to the stories of other people's lives. No matter to what degree an individual pursues an activity in a self-interested way without apparent regard for others, his/her activity has meaning and value only because there is a society that confers meaning and value on the activity in the first place. This underlying dimension serves to show how indebted we are to others in society for what we do. We will return to this point in considering the *narrative* basis for ethics in Chapter 9 on social well-being.

The Moral Challenge to Care

Noddings, too, refers to the basis for an ethics of care in 'the more fundamental and natural desire to be and remain related' (1984: 12-13). Relatedness to others gives rise to caring for them. In a fundamental way 'caring is not itself a virtue', one among others such as honesty or loyalty. It is prior to any virtue. It is 'the genuine commitment to maintain oneself as caring' which 'gives rise to the development and exercise of virtues' (1984: 23-4).

Noddings distinguishes between two levels of caring; the first of which she calls 'natural sentiment'. This is the immediate, unreflective response to help others who are in need. We care instinctively without any moral struggle (1984: 11). It is an enabling sentiment that paves the way for the second level, which she calls 'ethical caring' proper. Ethical caring is dependent upon natural caring, but it is ethical because we feel ourselves to have a choice whether to care or not. We feel we should care but do not always want to, or feel unable to for some reason, usually because it would conflict with our own desires of what we want to do. To care would mean having to go out of our way for another person. However, we have a *memory* of being cared for ourselves, whether as a child or as an adult. This memory reminds us of how good it felt to be cared for, and we feel the memory obliging us as a matter of natural human emotion to care in turn for others. But it does not oblige us on the basis of returning a favour, or out of fairness; it obliges us because the memory we have of being cared for 'speaks' to 'our best self' when we experienced something good and valuable. So we try to follow the call of 'I must' care over the resistance of 'I don't want to'. We are being ethical when we respond to the impulse to care arising from our memory of how good and valuable the experience of care has been for us. The root of the care impulse is present 'in our best picture of ourselves caring and being cared for' (1984: 10). As Noddings puts it: 'I am obliged, then, to accept the initial "I must" when it occurs and even to fetch it out of recalcitrant slumber when it fails to awake spontaneously' (1984: 13). In finding the ethical response of care in our memory, Noddings draws from an observation Nietzsche made about the word 'love'. Nietzsche refers to love as a word that 'speaks to memory and to hope' (cited in Noddings 1984: 10).

FEATURES OF A CARING RELATIONSHIP

Attending to Another

Attention to a particular other person and his/her circumstances is central to caring. One of the early women philosophers to single out attention as the primary ethical response was Iris Murdoch. Drawing from Simone Weil, she refers to attention as 'a just and loving gaze directed upon an individual reality' and as 'the characteristic and proper mark of the active moral agent' (Murdoch 2014: 34).

Genuine attention communicates interest in the other person, that it is not one-way; it is interactive. The process involves 'expression, interpretation and adjustment between persons' (Walker 1989: 140). What distinguishes care ethics from other ethical approaches is that attention to people's needs is the primary way of obtaining morally relevant knowledge. Ethical insight and understanding come out of 'a shared process of discovery' between people directly involved in a relationship. 'Morally relevant understanding' is constructed through 'communication'. The aim is 'to know how it is with others towards whom I will act' (Walker 1989: 140; 142). This may come from what a person says, or from picking up on non-verbal signals, such as tone of voice when a person says 'I'm fine' but the strain in their voice indicates otherwise.

For Gilligan, 'care represents a way of knowing and a coherent moral perspective' (1987: 41). It is not a matter of applying principles or virtues in a form that has already been prepared but of allowing whatever response we make to be intrinsically informed by the needs of the other person.

For Noddings, also, the care approach to ethical understanding is not essentially about justifying good judgments through rational thought, though this may come into it. Instead, it is primarily about 'heightening moral perception and sensitivity' (1984: 18). It is 'the commitment to remain open to that feeling [for others], to remember it, and to put one's thinking in its service' (1984: 20). Moral views are derived from a caring attitude, not from pre-given ways of understanding facts or supposed moral truths (1984: 22). Traditional moral theories are based on the sameness between people, but care ethics is based much more on recognising and allowing for particular difference. Recognition is given to a plurality of individual voices, each expressing individual care needs, and morally appropriate care measures and plans respond, in so far as possible, to the needs individuals express (Sevenhuijsen 1998: 64).

Also central to care ethics is seeing a person's problem or need in the context of his/her life as a whole and of his/her story made up of events that are ongoing. What is moral is thus individualised to a particular person's life course and so it is not necessarily repeatable for others who will be on different paths (Ruddick cited in Walker 1989: 141).

A consequence of regarding attention as a moral requirement is that inattention is seen as a moral weakness or failure (Tronto 1993: 128–9). It includes a requirement not to turn a blind eye, wilfully or otherwise. For example, a children's care worker who uses judgmental moral criticism and threats of punishment to try to cope with a child who is crying inconsolably, or throwing away food, is failing to attend to, and have an understanding of, why the child has particular needs which cause him/her to behave in this way. It is this attention that enables an appropriate caring response.

In *Love's Knowledge*, her re-interpretation of Aristotle's ethics of practical wisdom, Martha Nussbaum has also pointed to the need to be sensitively attuned to the rich particulars of life to make good judgments. She sums up this point using a phrase by the novelist Henry James about 'being finely aware and richly responsible . . .' (cited in Nussbaum 1990: 84). For Nussbaum, too, the ethical response is not about imposing a perceived moral ideal or applying it in the abstract. She argues that this is likely to lead to an imposition of a standard already felt to be understood in full. She points out how working solely from an ideal can lead to 'an extraordinary blindness . . .' (1990: 132). In her view, traditional ethical theories make the mistake of trying to extricate us in advance from 'bewilderment in the face of the present moment' through an ethics based on rules and procedures (1990: 141). Instead, she refers to 'the primacy of intuitive perception', which she finds in her reading of Aristotle's ethics (1990: 141).

Context Has Moral Weight

In care ethics, moral decisions and judgments are situated and particularised in the specific relation between the care giver and person cared for. They arise from the circumstances or context. Referring to virtues such as honesty and loyalty,

Noddings argues 'they must be assessed in the context of caring situations' (1984: 24). As we saw in Chapter 2, virtue ethics theory does allow for circumstances to have weight in making the appropriate virtuous response, but the response is still guided overall by a prior understanding of what it means to be, say, honest or loyal. With care ethics, we come to understand what honesty and loyalty mean *through* the context in which honesty and loyalty arise for us.

Relevance of Carer's Subjectivity

In care ethics the life experience of the caring person helps to form and develop the caring relationship. Care workers do not have to deny their own individuality in an effort to appear impartial. (At the same time, there are also of course professional boundaries and procedures to be observed.) As Held points out, care ethics recognises that 'there is no impartial point of view' capable of transcending and assessing all perspectives in a detached way (1993: 163). There is no 'view from nowhere'. At the same time, the care worker has to be genuinely seeking a caring response, one open, in so far as possible, to the complexity of a case and to the implications and consequences of a particular response for the person cared for and relevant others. It is the care worker's 'appropriate motivations, attitudes, sensibilities and qualities of character . . . which are indispensable to morally acute perception' (Jagger 1995: 191). This includes allowing for the care worker's affective or emotional response to the person cared for. Knowing from emotion is not something to be avoided as unreliable or too personal: 'Caring is partly emotional. It involves feelings and requires high degrees of empathy to enable us to discern what morality recommends in our caring activities' (Held 1995: 157).

Distinguishing between Needs and Desires

Since having empathy for another person is at the centre of the care relationship, there is a risk that a care worker will be persuaded by whatever the service user says s/he needs. But a care worker needs to assess a service user's real needs and distinguish them from her/his desires, and this is a challenge. As Tronto puts it: 'Genuine attentiveness would presumably allow the caretaker to see through pseudo-needs and come to appreciate what the other really needs. Such a commitment to perceiving the genuine needs of the other, though, is not easy' (Tronto 1989: 106).

Also, while the particular care a person wants for his/her needs can, of course, coincide with the appropriate measures needed, for when they differ the care worker has the challenge of explaining and justifying to the service user what their real needs are and what care measures are appropriate (see also Jagger 1995: 189). Professional know-how and experience are needed. However, a care worker can meet with strong resistance, for example, in caring for a teenage girl who has left home and is living rough, and who, as a result of understandable past experiences, no longer wants to have anything to do with her family, but where regaining contact with them is assessed as part of an appropriate care plan for her.

CARE AND JUSTICE

Justice Inherent in the Caring Relationship

There are many examples that show the shortcomings of a *solely* care perspective which point up the need for it to be corrected by justice. As Bubeck points out, care workers often face questions of justice in their care relationships, which makes justice an inherent and not separate part of care. For example, care workers of people with disability in a residential home have to care for all residents equally. The just thing to do is to act impartially. It would be wrong to give priority to those who are easiest to work with, or whose company they might enjoy over others. At the same time, what is called the 'minimizing of harm principle', or 'the principle of greatest need', justifies giving more attention to one resident who, for example, may be at risk of self-harm over another who may have attachment needs. Care workers in practice are involved in making decisions on prioritising who they give time and attention to based on their assessment that one person needs more care than another, or needs it before other people do (Bubeck 1995: 205). Principles of justice are needed to 'discern more or less urgent needs' or 'to make judgments about the worthiness of competing needs' (Tronto 1993: 140).

Also, questions of injustice and justice are paramount in certain situations, such as in caring for women (or men) who find themselves in abusive relationships (Jagger 1995: 192). There is, for example, the continuing injustice where a woman finds she has to remain within an abusive relationship because of a lack of support services which would enable her to leave.

Justice as Corrective to Power Imbalances

Tronto points out that while the justice ideas of equality and autonomy are important, especially for helping to ensure protection for vulnerable people, the reality is that many relationships are not based on equality. There is a power imbalance between parents, children and other dependants, and also between care workers and people with intellectual disability or mental illness. In the relationship the care worker has resources and expertise, both of which the person cared for lacks. There is not equality or autonomy between them in practice (Tronto 1989: 108). The fact that equality needs to be upheld, while at the same being absent in practice in many relationships 'masks what the moral relation should be' (Gilligan 1987: 55). So the care worker has to be aware of and carefully handle the power imbalance, for example, to avoid the risk of being paternalistic by assuming s/he knows what is best for a person (Tronto 1993: 146). Principles of justice are also needed as a safeguard against the care worker unjustly taking advantage of the power imbalance between him/her and the person cared for, for example, by being bossy. Held maintains that justice considerations are needed to protect service users from care workers who may be 'too capricious or domineering' (Held cited in Bubeck 1995: 253).

Justice as Corrective to Exploitation

Justice considerations arise also as a corrective to exploitation, whether the exploitation is of people cared for or of care workers. Some care workers may be unsuitable for care work and, whether intentionally or not, try to maintain the cared for person in a relationship of dependence rather than bring about the person's greater independence to which they are entitled. As we will see in the next section, there can be a risk of vulnerable people in residential homes being exploited, for example, for financial gain in privately run homes where management put making a profit for their owners and shareholders before providing for required standards of quality care. Also, within some families, vulnerable adults can find themselves exploited. The emotional, physical and financial abuse of older people by adult children or relatives is a fact of life in some families in Ireland. In 2007 the Health Service Executive set up a national, dedicated Elder Abuse Service, and there is also a Senior Helpline which is managed by older people for older people. Ruddick makes the point that within families it cannot always be taken for granted that members will look after each other, and that therefore it is not enough to rely on an ethics of care. An ethics of justice is also needed to counteract some people's selfishness and desire for power (Ruddick 1995: 207).

Bubeck also argues that to leave justice out of consideration is to leave care workers – women especially, who have traditionally been seen as having a caring role more than men – open to having their desire to work in care exploited. She points out that people who care are particularly vulnerable to having their willingness to do care work exploited, for example, through low pay which can be considered unjust given the demands and responsibilities of the job. Also, where a person experiences a clash between doing extra work out of response to the immediate needs of another person and not doing so because it is unfair (for example, because they already have their quota of work to attend to), the caring person will usually respond to the immediate needs rather than to the claims of justice (1995: 10). There is also a justice issue in that they may be restricting employment opportunities for other care workers by doing extra work beyond what they have been contracted to do.

Justice is seen as an important corrective to the shortcomings of a care ethics alone. Though in an underlying sense, care could be considered to encompass concerns for justice in that such concerns arise from caring about the circumstances of others.

CARING AND CARE MANAGEMENT

A number of writers have written about the difference between the work of frontline care workers and the work of care managers in organisations and agencies. They see the difference as presenting a challenge for managers in particular, but also for social workers, to follow in practice an ethics of care based on empathy.

Typically the work of care managers includes:

- Implementing policies and procedures.
- Deciding on the allocation of resources within budgets.
- Organising the delivery of services.
- Arranging and chairing case conferences and formulating care plans.
- Maintaining records of how care cases are dealt with and conducting reviews.

In carrying out these and other functions, managers take a rational approach in using resources such as staff and budgets efficiently. While the whole purpose of their work is caring for others, their role means that they operate at some remove from the individual people who are cared for by frontline care workers. Their main focus tends to be on achieving efficiencies and providing for fairness rather than on responding in an immediate empathetic way. It is not that managers are, or have to be, less caring in an empathetic way than frontline workers; it is that their job role requires that they focus on general issues of managing care instead of exploring with service users their individual needs. For Tronto, management has been termed as 'caring about' or 'taking care of'. Managers are judged on their competence 'to take care of' problems rather than on taking care of individual people (1993: 133–4; 139). For her this presents a problem in that it may take away from a specific ethics of care, in particular in large bureaucratic organisations: 'Often in bureaucracies those who determine how needs will be met are far away from the actual care-giving and care-receiving, and they may well not provide very good care as a result' (1993: 109).

Writing about health care organisations, Green also makes the point that there is a presumption that a manager's good management practice will result in good health care, but this does not necessarily follow. It may be good management practice according to management teaching, but it can miss out on being directly focused on the good of individual patients (2009: 120).

Also, in reporting to managers, frontline care workers are obliged to comply with work practices and procedures which can take away from maintaining an empathetic relationship with clients. Banks sees a problem in the UK where social workers are required to account officially for their compliance with polices and procedures in their handling of cases through form-filling and reports. While these activities are understandable and necessary to ensure accountability, they can be at odds with a carer worker's empathetic engagement with service users. It can also affect the quality of the caring relationship where care workers are focused more on the requirements and less on the service user's immediate needs and well-being. She sees it as making the caring relationship more impersonal. She also sees it as leading to a risk that service users will distrust their social worker if, in providing answers to meet form-filling requirements, they feel they are being monitored and checked (Banks 2004: Chapters 6 and 7; Banks 2006: Chapter 6).

In addition, there is a danger that the necessary, and increasing, professionalisation of care work is taking away from its empathetic nature and resulting in it becoming more depersonalised. President Michael D. Higgins drew attention to the use of the terms 'client' and 'service user' which carry connotations of a business relation and which may come between a care worker and her/his recognition and appreciation of the human capacities and qualities of the person s/he is caring for (see McGreevy 2012; also O'Toole 2012).

Care is also provided through private organisations as well as through state or public agencies and voluntary organisations. There are, for example, privately run nursing homes for the care of the elderly and children's homes for the care of children as well as crèches. Privately run organisations are different to state and voluntary ones in that, as well as aiming to provide quality care, they operate to make a profit for their owners or investors. A service is offered, paid for and received by agreement between the contracting parties. There are risks that, in providing care in this businesslike or market-forces way, the *care relationship itself* becomes seen as based on an exchange of the service for payment. This risk is not confined to private for-profit organisations. State-run nursing homes also require a financial contribution from residents or their families. To see care in a market framework, where it is sometimes referred to as 'a service delivery', can make it difficult for managers and care workers to retain and practise the interpersonal attentive dimension of care. In particular for organisations that have an essential need to make a profit, it raises the question whether management and care practice can be successfully combined with a specific ethics of care. For Tronto it is a serious question, the answer to which 'depends on whether market relationships and attentive care can coexist, and if so, how? (1989: 107). Phillips, too, refers to care as 'increasingly big business' and to 'trends toward the commodification of care' (2007: 156; 157).

One serious consequence is where profit is pursued at the expense of ensuring proper care standards. Coulter acknowledges that in Ireland there are many private for-profit institutions providing quality care in a caring environment. However, if profitability is made a priority over care standards, for example, through the employment of unqualified or under-qualified staff on low pay, there is increased risk of mistreatment. She links this to the mistreatment of older people in Leas Cross nursing home in 2005 and to the mistreatment of children exposed by RTÉ in some privately run crèches in 2013. She also cites the report of a UK inquiry into the abuse of residents with intellectual disabilities in a privately run home, which found that the company appeared to have made decisions about profitability above providing proper standards of care. For her, 'This report goes to the heart of the matter – there is an inherent conflict between the push for profitability and the provision of care, stimulation and support needed by vulnerable people' (Coulter 2013).

Care organisations are subject to state regulations and inspections to help ensure quality care. While this is essential, there is also a risk of regulation and compliance becoming seen as the primary factors in how care is provided rather than frontline and managerial staff, as well as company owners and boards of directors, being guided by and practising an ethics of care for its own sake.

Ultimately, the means by which care is provided in society is a matter of government policy, which in turn is influenced by the ideas and beliefs of the political party (or parties) in government, as well as by practical considerations. In Ireland there are a range of state, voluntary and private care organisations, and the relative extent to which each sector contributes is also ultimately a matter of government policy. In considering social contract ethics in Chapter 10, we will look at some of the philosophical ideas and beliefs underlying the approaches of the main types of political parties.

Need for Influence of Care Ethics in Management

Card sees a need for 'an active ethics of care' to have more influence in the way organisations are run than strictly managerial considerations of efficient allocation of resources, or measuring performance through indicators, such as achieving targets. The justification for this, she argues, comes from the fact that our personal and informal relations with each other are more basic than organisational procedures. They underlie and circumscribe what organisations do (1990: 81). For Walker, too, a care ethics needs to inform organisations so that they are not 'distancing, depersonalizing or paternalistic', but at a more human level are open and expressive in the way that people working for them communicate with those who need their services (1989: 147). In writing about health care organisations, Green draws from Aristotle's ethics in pointing out that the good is that which all things aim toward, and that the good of a health care organisation is the good of individual patients, which should therefore be the foremost consideration influencing how the organisations are run (2009: 120).

Care of Oneself

Living a Life of Value

Generally speaking, people understand ethics as having to do with the way a person relates to others, or with how a government relates to the people. In particular, it is seen to be about not causing harm, and looking after people in need who are unable to help themselves. This view of caring about, and caring for, others does identify the main dimension of ethics, but there is another dimension closely related to it. This is the dimension of caring for oneself. We have seen that Kant emphasises a respect for oneself as well as others, and that Hutcheson recognises providing for our own self-interest can enable us to be better able to provide for the interests of others. To care for ourselves means more than looking after our own needs, whether physical, mental or emotional, so far as we can. More specifically in an ethical sense, it means having self-knowledge in order to recognise certain things as having worth or value. We are then in a position to try to live our life according to what we value, by giving attention and energy to the activities and practices that express those values.

Taylor points out that even if morality is seen only in terms of how we should relate to others, this still leaves another big dimension of life in which we need to make value choices. It relates to making value choices to have 'a rich meaningful life' or 'a full life' for ourselves, one that is suited to us as an individual with particular talents and interests (1989: 14–15).

Care of the self in this sense has long been recognised as central to ethics. Before Socrates was put to death in ancient Athens (for going against the norms of his society in trying to get people to think about how they should live), his friends asked him how he would like them to care for his wife and children. He said his wish was for his friends to care for themselves. He was not advising them to be selfish, or to do nothing for his family. He was expressing the view that the best basis from which to care for others is to have a developed sense of care of oneself. 'Socrates' last wish, prompted by his concern for his family, is that his friends care for themselves; only in that way will they be able to care for his children or, for that matter, for anyone else. The care of the self, as I have argued, precedes, or perhaps constitutes, the care of others' (Nehamas 2000: 167).

Avoiding Using Care to Compensate for Unmet Needs

A particular reason for care workers to develop their own life that they can value is to avoid the risk of caring for others to compensate for their own unmet needs. Care workers need to have a highly reflective sense of self, along with an understanding of what best care practice means, if they are to avoid transforming the needs of the person cared for into some need they have for themselves, or projecting their own needs onto the person, such as a need for recognition or praise. Some parents, for example, have a tendency to care for their children in ways that are more about trying to meet their own unmet needs for success, love and affection, or friendship, rather than meeting their children's need to develop independently within a loving family (Tronto 1989: 106). Unless care workers develop as individuals through meeting their own needs and desires, they may be 'entirely lost as one caring'. The carer needs to be 'strong, courageous and capable of joy' (Noddings 1984: 26).

Avoiding 'Burn-out'

At a practical level, unless the care worker cares for himself/herself there is the risk of burn-out. Care work can be emotionally challenging and demanding, and as Tronto puts it, 'attentiveness involves a commitment of time and effort that may be made at a high price to the self' (1989: 106). Insufficient staff numbers can mean that some care workers find they have more work to do than they can reasonably cope with. For example, social workers may have sizeable case loads and be aware of having on file reported cases of child abuse without having the time or means to investigate the cases immediately or adequately. They may also have to fill in for colleagues who are absent on sick leave or for other reasons. Also, some people who the care services try to help may resent the fact they need to be cared for. They find it a restriction on their autonomy, and they can be resistant and even hostile to receiving care. Work pressures such as these can be emotionally challenging, and care workers may even find themselves having to combat feelings of rage at what they perceive as the injustice of their work circumstances in order to avoid letting their feelings impact on how they do their work (Tronto 1993: 153).

CASE STUDY 4.1

Case Study: Treatment of Billy

In the light of your understanding of Kant's justification of principles of equality, respect and care, consider and discuss the following case. Assume you are a new member of the care staff in a residential home for clients with particular physical and learning needs. Billy is a nineteen-year-old who appears generally unhappy and is easily upset. He complains about the food and says there is no choice and he frequently throws food or cutlery on the floor. When Billy becomes particularly upset, the practice has been for a staff member to insist that he go to his room and remain there until he has learned to behave himself.

Billy has noticeable speech and language difficulties, which make it difficult for him to communicate orally. In addition, he gets frustrated if asked to write points down and you have noticed that his literacy level is below that which would be expected of a nineteen-year-old. He has had speech and language therapy in the past while attending school, but since he finished school last year the treatment stopped. Another staff member has said to you that Billy's problem is that he does not try and gives up too easily, with the result that he has lost some of the progress he had made. From talking to Billy, you are aware that he would like to do a computer course and have opportunities to meet and socialise with people his own age from outside the centre.

You brought up your concerns about Billy at the next staff meeting. However, none of the other staff felt there was anything further they should do for Billy. Some staff took the view that he was 'playing up' in order to get his way, and that provided they did not give in to his 'whims' he would learn in time to co-operate when he realised he could not get his own way. They added that the more attention they gave to him, the more he wanted. One staff member said she did not think Billy morally deserved any special consideration because he has been upsetting other clients.

You have also noticed that quieter clients are left to spend a large part of the day watching TV.

Exercise 4.1

Role of Hiqa

Research the role of the Health Information and Quality Authority (Hiqa) in setting standards for the provision of care services and for monitoring the implementation of standards through inspections and reports.

Relate the role of Hiqa to care ethics, in particular to the argument that an ethics based on care also requires an ethics based on justice.

CRITICAL EVALUATION

Insufficiency of Care

A problem with an ethics based on care is that natural feelings of care cannot be relied upon to ensure that people will have their care needs met. A caring concern for others is a real and vital human response, but many examples can be cited where it has been lacking and people in need have been, and continue to be, treated with either indifference or harm. Hutcheson recognises that self-interest can easily come between a person acting for their own interest and acting for the good of others, and that moral action requires an act of will. That moral action requires an act of will shows how prone we can be to taking the easier course of doing something that suits us rather than making the effort to care for others, even though we experience care for others as a natural feeling.

Also, there is the risk that emphasising a care ethics based on natural interpersonal relations will take away from the role the state needs to have in both setting care policy and in delivering care through state agencies on the basis that all people have a human right to care. In Chapter 6 we will look at human rights ethics.

Overlooks Structural Causes of Need

Structural causes of need are certain conditions that are seen to be embedded in society, such as poverty, or crime, or barriers to educational or employment opportunity. Jagger points out that, with a focus on empathic care, there is a tendency to overlook the root causes in the way society is structured as a factor in why some people have care needs. As she puts it: 'In care thinking, social structure occupies a place comparable to the frame of a picture one is viewing; one must be aware of it in some sense but one pays it little direct attention' (1995: 195). The lack of focus on social structures which contribute to problems means that care solutions tend to be partial and incomplete, band-aid remedies rather than transformative ones (Jagger 1995: 195). A further point is that the direct caring approach is ill-equipped to deal with large scale care needs, such as world hunger or exploitation of child labour (Jagger 1995: 197). Solutions to these problems require changes in how governments and business operate nationally and internationally. So, it is a challenge for the care worker to focus also on the bigger picture in trying to bring about change, as well as maintaining a direct relation of care for individuals.

At the same time, care attentiveness can bring into focus the plight of groups and countries with particular need, along with the structural causes of that need. Furthermore, governments and public agencies can be called to task for ignoring people's needs on the basis that dependency, vulnerability, and the need for care are a feature of all our lives (Tronto 1993: 168).

Difficulty Combining a Care and Justice Approach

It is generally accepted that care and justice imply each other and that they are 'aspects of a single practice' (Jagger 1995: 185). At the same time, it is recognised that the demands of each are not easily reconciled in practice. 'Most proponents of the ethics of care now dispute the possibility of an easy synthesis of care with justice' (Jagger 1995: 187). A care response may clash with a justice principle. For example, youth workers can experience opposing pulls between, on the one hand, the best caring response to a troubled young person who commits offences and, on the other, a justice response where people have suffered as a consequence of his actions. A manager of a women's refuge can experience conflict between granting refuge to a particular woman and her children due to their pressing, immediate needs and having to turn down, for reasons of lack of accommodation, another applicant who applied first but whose need may not be quite as urgent.

Ruddick sees justice and care as quite distinctive. They cannot be assimilated into each other in some third overall approach. They:

- 'foster distinct cognitive capacities
- elicit distinctive moral emotions
- make distinctive requirements on institutions' (cited in Jagger 1995: 187).

For Gilligan the justice perspective and the care perspective are two different ways of seeing the same issue or need. She likens this to the way we can see certain ambiguous images in either of two ways. For example, there is the famous image that can be seen as either a duck or a rabbit, depending on our perspective. Her point is that justice and care are each – separately – a particular way of arranging information to provide for a perspective. They provide a different 'organising framework', with justice orientated toward achieving a balanced outcome between independent individuals and care orientated toward meeting people's needs within a web of relationships which they have (1987: 34).

In essence, as Jagger puts it, 'justice requires a commitment to general principles; care to individuals' and it is difficult to draw from both at the same time in relation to the same issue (Jagger 1995: 185). The more a person becomes caught up in considering the justice of a case at an abstract level, the more they lose touch with the individual's need; they find they are caring about a problem rather than a person (Noddings cited in Bubeck 1995: 155). But arguably the reverse is also the case, i.e. the more a person becomes caught up in caring, the more they may be inclined to lose sight of the justice aspects of the case.

Clearly there is a need for both care and justice. Which one is given priority is a matter for discussion in light of the particular circumstances.

Care's Broader Significance

The ethics of care challenges radically the social tradition and forces that have relegated the work of caring to low importance and low pay. From its importance for everyone at all stages, in particular in early childhood and old age, to its demands, challenges and skill level required in caring for people with often complex emotional needs, it deserves to be valued more highly in society (see Tronto 1993: 63–4; 111).

Care ethics also challenges a social contract understanding of ethics which is based on the ideas of Hobbes that people are individuals whose primary ethical relation with others is not of care, but a legal one of not causing them harm or interfering with their freedom. Baier adverts to this challenge to social contract ethics which a care ethics provides (1987: 52). We will look at Hobbes's social contract ethics in Chapter 10.

REVIEW

Care for others can be considered a distinct moral philosophy, with a basis in how people behave naturally for each other's good. Caring is associated in practice with a number of features, such as having a close interest in and attention to the needs of other people as individuals. It is not considered sufficient as a basis for ethics on its own, but requires also principles of fairness and justice, to account adequately both for moral questions and for best care practice.

FURTHER READING

Grimshaw, J. (2004) 'The Idea of a Female Ethic' in A *Companion to Ethics*, P. Singer (ed.), Blackwell.
Phillips, J. (2007) *Care*, Polity Press (esp. Chapter 2).

REFERENCES

Baier, A. C. (1987), 'The Need for More than Justice' in *Justice and Care, Essential Readings in Feminist Ethics*, V. Held (ed.) (1995), Westview Press.
Banks, S. (2004) *Ethics, Accountability and the Social Professions*, Palgrave Macmillan.
Banks, S. (2006) *Ethics and Values in Social Work*, 3rd ed., Palgrave Macmillan.
Bubeck, D. (1995) *Care, Gender and Justice*, Clarendon Press Oxford.
Card, C. (1990) 'Gender and Moral Luck' in *Justice and Care, Essential Readings in Feminist Ethics*, V. Held, (ed.) (1995), Westview Press.
Coulter, C. (2013) 'State Must Not Offload Care to a Profit-driven System', *The Irish Times*, 7 June 2013.
Friedman, M. (1987) 'Beyond Caring: The De-moralization of Gender' in *Justice and Care, Essential Readings in Feminist Ethics*, V. Held, (ed.) (1995), Westview Press.
Furrow, D. (2005) *Ethics*, Continuum.
Gilligan, C. (1982) 'In a Different Voice: Women's Conception of Self and of Morality', *Harvard Educational Review*.
Gilligan, C. (1987), 'Moral Orientation and Moral Development' in *Justice and Care, Essential Readings in Feminist Ethics*, V. Held, (ed.) (1995), Westview Press.
Green, J. (2009) 'The Deformation of Professional Formation: Managerial Targets and the Undermining of Professional Judgement' in *Ethics and Social Welfare*, Vol. 3, Issue 2 (Special Issue: 'Towards Professional Wisdom'), Routledge (accessed online from Taylor & Francis, 17 August 2009).
Hamington, M. (2004) *Embodied Care, Jane Addams, Maurice Merleau-Ponty and Feminist Ethics*, University of Illinois Press.

Heidegger, M. (1967) *Being and Time*, Oxford: Blackwell.

Held, V. (ed.) (1995) *Justice and Care, Essential Readings in Feminist Ethics*, Westview Press.

Held, V. (1993) 'Feminist Moral Inquiry and the Feminist Future' in *Justice and Care, Essential Readings in Feminist Ethics*, V. Held (ed.) (1995), Westview Press.

Hutcheson, F. (2002) *An Essay on the Nature and Conduct of the Passions and Affections, with Illustrations on the Moral Sense*, Garrett, A. (ed.), The Online Library of Liberty (accessed 3 July 2013).

Hutcheson, F. (2004) *An Inquiry into the Original of our Ideas of Beauty and Virtue*, Liedhold, W. (ed.), The Online Library of Liberty (accessed 3 July 2013).

Jagger, A. M. (1995) 'Caring as a Feminist Practice of Moral Reason' in *Justice and Care, Essential Readings in Feminist Ethics*, V. Held (ed.) (1995), Westview Press.

McGreevy. R. (2012) 'Mind Your Language, Higgins Tells Voluntary Sector', *The Irish Times*, 14 December 2012.

Murdoch, I. (2014) *The Sovereignty of Good*, Routledge.

Nehamas, A. (2000) *The Art of Living: Socratic Reflections from Plato to Foucault*, University of California Press.

Noddings, N. (1984) 'Caring' in *Justice and Care, Essential Readings in Feminist Ethics*, V. Held (ed.) (1995), Westview Press.

Nussbaum, M. C. (1990) *Love's Knowledge, Essays on Philosophy and Literature*, Oxford University Press.

O'Toole, F. (2012) 'No Longer Citizens, Just Customers', *The Irish Times*, 4 June 2013.

Ruddick, S. (1995) 'Injustice in Families: Assault and Domination' in *Justice and Care, Essential Readings in Feminist Ethics*, V. Held (ed.) (1995), Westview Press.

Sevenhuijsen, S. (1998) *Citizenship and the Ethics of Care*, translated by Liz Savage, Routledge, London and New York.

Slote, M. (2007) *The Ethics of Care and Empathy*, Routledge.

Taylor, C. (1989) *Sources of the Self: The Making of the Modern Identity*, Cambridge University Press.

Tronto, J. C. (1989) 'Women and Caring: What Can Feminists Learn About Morality from Caring?' in *Justice and Care, Essential Readings in Feminist Ethics*, V. Held (ed.) (1995), Westview Press.

Tronto, J. C. (1993) *Moral Boundaries: A Political Argument for an Ethics of Care*, Routledge, New York.

Walker, M. U. (1989) 'Moral Understandings: Alternative "Epistemology" for a Feminist Ethics' in *Justice and Care, Essential Readings in Feminist Ethics*, V. Held (ed.) (1995), Westview Press.

5
Empathy

OVERALL AIM

To explore why having empathy for people in their need for care is understandable in terms of the restrictions they face in coping adequately with their lives.

LEARNING OUTCOMES

At the end of this chapter you should be able to:

- Distinguish empathy from sympathy and pity.
- Describe empathy as a natural human emotion of feeling for others who have difficulties.
- Explain practical difficulties, such as coping with poverty, which provide reason for having empathy.
- Explain why people can be considered to lack free will, and relate it to a reason for having empathy.
- Explain why managing personal freedom can be a difficult challenge, which provides a reason for having empathy.

INTRODUCTION

Empathy can be described as the power of mentally identifying oneself with another person in his/her thoughts, feelings and life circumstances. It is the main response which makes possible a good, caring relationship. Drawing from the work of Blum and Vetlesen, Banks links a capacity to have empathy specifically with a capacity to have a moral perception of other people, whereby we respond to them in a caring way through recognising factors that are having an adverse effect on them. To have empathy for people means being able to see the features of their life that matter to them, in particular features that are causing them some difficulty and that draw us to respond (Banks 2004: 169–70).

Empathy can be difficult to describe accurately. For Edith Stein, empathy is a distinctive act. She calls it 'a kind of perceiving' which is '*sui generis*' (of its own kind). For her, there are three stages to the experience of empathy. First, empathy is aroused in us, as she puts it, 'all at once', for example, by the sight of someone's sad face. From seeing another person's sad face, we are confronted by empathy as an object. The second stage is when, as she describes it, the other person's sadness, 'having pulled me into it, is no longer really an object'. Instead, we have a subjective experience of the other person's sadness. Finally, the third stage is when we experience empathy again as an object; however, this time, on account of having gone through the second stage, we have a more comprehensive perception of it (Stein 1970: 10–11).

From this account, we can see that *feeling with* another person their need or difficulty is at the heart of empathy. When we empathise, the knowledge we have about the other person's need is not neutral for us; it affects us emotionally. It is affective knowledge as much as factual knowledge. As Slote puts it, empathy involves 'having the feelings of another (involuntarily) aroused in ourselves, as when we see another person in pain' (Slote 2007: 13). It involves a naturally occurring emotion of feeling with others in the experiences we perceive them to be having, especially experiences of difficulty. This brings its meaning very close to the meaning of compassion, which is also feeling *with others* in their suffering. But empathy is said to differ from sympathy in that sympathy has the meaning of feeling *for others* in their suffering without actually experiencing something of their feeling (see Slote 2007: 13–16). Pity, on the other hand, is quite different from either sympathy or empathy. Pity suggests a difference between the person who is feeling pity and the person pitied because of their suffering. It can suggest a difference to an extent that the person pitying feels they are looking down on someone for being less fortunate or capable than other people, and where they feel glad or relieved they are not in their position.

Through empathy we feel *we know* what a difficulty is like for another person; and what they are going through. We feel we know this from our own experience of something similar, or from understanding accounts of the experience we have heard or read. If we do not have personal experience of it, we can imagine it. For example, we know what it is like not to have enough money for what we want to buy, and we know what it is like to feel hungry. From this knowledge we can imagine what it is like for families who do not have enough money to buy adequate food. Also, we need imagination to appreciate the care needs of others who are distant from us geographically, culturally or through their circumstances, for example, people who seek asylum, or refugee children from a war-torn country. Cultivation of imagination is crucial to go beyond attending only to our own needs or of those closest to us (Hamington 2004: 68–9; 104–5). 'Much of the insensitivity and hardness of the world is due to the lack of imagination which prevents a realization of experiences of other people' (Addams, J. cited in Hamington 2004: 115). Hamington adds: 'When we cannot realize the experiences of others – when our imagination prevents an affective response – the result is insensitivity' (2004: 115).

It is important to realise that we cannot know another person's experience exactly as they experience it for themselves. For Stein, empathy 'is the experience of foreign consciousness'. The other person is ultimately unknowable in his/her uniqueness as a distinct consciousness which has opened on the world, no matter what they disclose to us or how perceptive we may be of them. We may *feel we know* what they are going through, but our feeling of knowledge can give us only a faint picture. Our knowledge can at best only approximate to another person's experience. We cannot literally get into another person's head and experience their thoughts and emotions as they experience them for themselves. At the same time, when we say genuinely, 'I know how you feel', it can help to convey empathy to the other person. However, to over say it, or say it with false sincerity, can make the other person feel we are belittling their experience. So, while we cannot live other people's experience of need for care, we can see that they are in need. We can see need 'displayed' in their bodily signs and we hear it in their account of how things are for them. We hear 'an echo' or catch a 'trace' of what it means for them (Merleau-Ponty cited in Hamington 2004: 55). Edith Stein goes further and believes 'a single bodily expression, such as a look or a laugh, can give me a glimpse into the kernel of the person' (1970: 11; 99).

Hamington emphasises that while empathetic knowledge is a necessary condition for care, it is not a sufficient condition. Apart from identifying with the causes of another's suffering, empathy means being moved to act on another's behalf to try to relieve their suffering (2004: 44; 48). To a greater or lesser extent we naturally have empathy for others, especially for those who are close to us, such as family members and friends who are physically ill or depressed, and we are moved to help them, but empathy is a response that can be developed or left undeveloped depending on how open we let ourselves be to the suffering of others, especially those distant from us.

EMPATHY AS A RESPONSE TO PRACTICAL RESTRICTION

There are many factors in people's lives that we can identify with and that prompt an empathic response. Poverty is an example of restriction in living conditions, while disability and old age are examples of restriction from incapacity. Nobody is free in the sense of having no practical limits on what they can do. People are always restricted to some extent by their economic and social conditions, but people who are poor are more severely restricted than those who are well-off.

At the extreme, people in developing countries who suffer from absolute poverty have almost no freedom because they are restricted to mere physical survival. For the same reason, in Ireland, consistent poverty also restricts freedom. The factor of restricted freedom to participate in activities that are considered the norm is included in the definition of poverty used in developing and implementing polices:

> People are living in poverty if their income and resources (material, cultural and social) are so inadequate as to preclude them from having a standard of living which is regarded as acceptable by Irish society generally. As a result of inadequate income and resources people may be excluded and marginalised from participating in activities which are considered the norm for other people in society.
>
> *Source*: Office of Social Inclusion, available at www.socialinclusion.ie.

For example, people who are poor may not be able to afford the same range and quality of food that most people take for granted, or take part in common leisure activities such as having a night out or a holiday. People in need of social care can have practical limitations on their freedom through, for example, lack of simple services such as respite care or home help.

EMPATHY AS A RESPONSE TO LACK OF FREE WILL

Do We Have Free Will?

Within philosophy, the question of whether or not we have free will is debated. If people are considered to lack free will, and therefore not fully responsible for their behaviour and circumstances, then this provides a reason to have empathy for them, especially when they have need of care.

For practical purposes, notably for holding people responsible for their behaviour, both morally and under the law, having some power over our actions is taken to be the reality. If we had no power, it would make no sense to blame or praise people for their actions. Without power there is no personal responsibility. There is also a danger, especially in care work, that we may show a lack of respect for the capacity people have if we relate to them on the basis that they do not have at least some power over their actions. At the same time, it is accepted that the power we have can be reduced by influences acting on us which incline us to behave in a particular way. The justice system allows for such influences as mitigating factors where they can be shown to have reduced a person's responsibility for committing an offence.

The following sections contain an account of two views which suggest that we do not have free will, at least not completely: Spinoza's theory of the emotions, and neuroscience's findings about how the brain works in responding instinctively to stimuli. It is important to understand at the outset exactly what these two views are saying: we are not the *conscious source* of our actions. The source lies in causes or influences acting on us, of which we can know only a small part; the causes or influences arouse our emotions or instincts, which we then seek to satisfy. However, neither view is saying we have *no power* to influence our choices. How we respond by engaging with our conscious thoughts and intentions to the influences acting on us still matters, and how we respond affects how we behave in practice. We are aware of our intentions to do something and are conscious of having the power to act on, ignore or alter our intentions in some way. Nevertheless, the two views discussed claim we are under an illusion if we believe ourselves to be completely in charge of our actions and not subject to deep-rooted forces acting on us.

Spinoza's View

Spinoza identified a lack of free will as central to understanding people's behaviour and to understanding what they needed to do to still lead good lives. Spinoza accepts that we think we have free will. It is just that we are mistaken in thinking we have it. The reason we think we have it is because we are aware of what we want to do, but we ignore the fact that there are causes lying behind any choice we make (Spinoza 1995: 30–31). We can see clearly two options before us, and imagine ourselves free to opt for one or the other, but this is to ignore the causes that lie behind our option. As he explains, 'Men are mistaken in thinking themselves free; and this opinion depends on this alone, that they are conscious of their actions and ignorant of the causes by which they are determined' (1995: 64).

Spinoza argues that our emotions act on us to cause how we behave. By emotion he means not just anger, frustration, anxiety, happiness and so on but also our desires, such as all our ordinary desires for food, friendship, love and sex. Lying behind the emotions are external factors which may cause an emotion to arise. For example, suppose we are frustrated because we are stuck in a traffic jam while being in a hurry to get to our destination. There is a whole chain of factors external to us causing our frustration, some of which we may be aware of but for most we may not be. For example, we are likely to be aware of the reason why we are in a hurry, say, we are doing an errand as a favour for a friend. But let's say we do not know the reasons for the traffic jam, since it is unexpected, and can only speculate. It could be because there are road works, or a protest march against cuts in government services. We may also feel under some time pressure, for example, to get home to prepare for going out that night. Further back in the chain of causal factors, there are the reasons why our friend asked us to do him/her a favour. What was going on in his/her life that she needed to ask us a favour? Further back again there are reasons why we find we easily get frustrated. Maybe it is because of our childhood when we were let do pretty much as we liked and now find we cannot always do as we like in the adult world. These are just *some* of many possible causes acting on us to make us feel frustrated, most of which act from below the surface of our conscious mind.

So, how are we going to behave in response to our frustration? Are we going to exercise our free will and make a fully rational decision? Spinoza would say we cannot do this. This is because we do not have rational control over all the causes. It is also because we always come under the sway of three primary emotions in how the causes act on us. He identifies three primary emotions which govern how we respond to emotions being caused in us by external factors. The primary emotions are desire itself, pleasure and pain. All our particular emotions are *filtered through* these three primary emotions of desire, pleasure and pain to bring about our response. Desire, pleasure and pain are meant in the broadest senses. They include, for example, a desire a person might have to succeed in some challenge, such as completing a marathon or competing in the Special Olympics, or to improve strained relations with their family or among their friends. Pleasure and pain include emotional satisfaction and dissatisfaction. Satisfaction comes not just from success in completing a challenge but also from the need, where it arises, to give up or drop out. This is because, in the circumstances, giving up or dropping out has been the best a person has been able to do. It provides the least dissatisfaction compared with a greater dissatisfaction of continuing to do something s/he feels difficult or painful. So, to go back to the example of being frustrated while stuck in a traffic jam, if we take a deep breath or turn on the radio, this is because it is the action we find that gives us the most satisfaction as a response at the time. Alternatively, if we ring our friend and give out about being stuck in traffic, this is the behaviour that gives us the most satisfaction or least dissatisfaction in the circumstances.

The primary emotions, desire, pleasure and pain are always in operation. Through their operation, we seek the least pain or the most pleasure or satisfaction within our power from any desire we have and within whatever circumstances that are affecting us. The following is a more detailed example of how the primary emotions of desire, pleasure and pain act on a person to filter the causes of what seems to be a free choice.

Example: Deciding on Legal Action for a Care Service

A father imagines himself free to take a legal action against the state, or not take it, in order to get the best professional service for his autistic child. The father thinks he is considering two images that consist only of thoughts in his mind. But this is to overlook the fact that first and foremost the father is automatically drawn emotionally on the basis of primary emotions of desire, pleasure and pain toward or away from any image he envisages as the best way of caring for his son.

Let's say the father is a careful and thoughtful man. He weighs up all the pros and cons of taking legal action and of not taking it. Ultimately his decision will not be caused by his rational consideration of the options. Instead, those considerations will have more or less weight depending on how they relate to his desire to avoid emotional pain and achieve emotional satisfaction arising from his problem of finding the best care for his son. The decision will be due to whichever emotional pull proves strongest in avoiding emotional pain and providing him with emotional satisfaction in meeting his desire. If he decides to take legal action, then this is the course that emotionally satisfies him. It will result from a mix of emotions at play in him, emotions of parental love as well as frustration and anger. These emotions in turn will be caused in him by external factors which are largely below the surface of his conscious mind. For example, he may have lacked love himself as a child and is determined to do the utmost for his own child, or his wife may constantly ask him to do something to relieve her of the pressure she feels under, or he may have got legal advice from his solicitor which bolstered his view that his son's lack of treatment is an injustice. Whatever the causes, they will be acting on him to have caused the emotions of love, frustration and anger. It is these emotions that impact on his need to reduce his emotional pain and thereby achieve some emotional satisfaction. The emotions that give him most satisfaction in relation to his desire win out, and in this case let's say they are the ones that lead to taking legal action – they win out over other emotions of, say, resignation or worry about the financial cost of going to court. In this way, the option of taking legal action proves stronger in him on the basis of his experience of the primary emotions of desire, pleasure and pain. While he has thought carefully about the advantages and disadvantages of the two options, nevertheless *the deciding movement* for one option over another is due to his rational considerations taking on an emotional colour of a particular strength or intensity. Knowledge, in short, only leads to action from being under the influence of emotion (1995: 150).

In this way, for Spinoza, our actions are always under the influence of our emotions. The only way to avoid being under the sway of one emotion is by another emotion taking over. Only an emotion can overcome an emotion: 'An emotion can neither be hindered nor removed save by a contrary emotion and one stronger than the emotion which is checked' (1995: 146).

For Spinoza, then, we think we are free to choose from our awareness of the choice presented to us, but behind this choice lie causes we are never fully aware of, which are filtered through the primary emotions of desire, pleasure and pain. Spinoza goes so far as to say we are 'in servitude' to the emotions because of our lack of power to control what is causing them in us (1995: 139).

Emotional Complexity

Spinoza gives a detailed account of the emotions, defining and describing many of them. From his account, a picture emerges of people as emotionally complex given the range of different emotions to which we are subjected. He makes much of the fact that we experience emotional pressure. He refers more than once to the human experience of 'being assailed by emotions' (1995: 159). He also refers to the common experience of emotional conflict where more than one emotion is acting on us at any one time and we experience them in opposition to each other. He speaks of people as 'harassed by contrary emotions' (1995: 87).

All this, he says, is a sign that people often do not really know what they want. He sees people as often confused about their desires, whereby 'a man is drawn in different directions and knows not whither to turn' (1995: 126). As for those who do not experience any particularly strong emotions, they are easy prey to being taken over by any one emotion that surfaces (1995: 88). They are prone to act on a whim or impulse in seeking a satisfactory outcome to the primary emotions of desire, pleasure and pain.

These kinds of emotional experiences, which he believes are common, emphasise how much we are in the grip of emotional causes and lack freedom in relation to them. Perhaps you are familiar with the feeling of having mixed emotions such as divided loyalty, or both anger at, and attachment to, a person you love. From having mixed emotions, we experience how emotions can be strong, complex and a block to feeling free.

Power of External Causes Exceeds the Mind's Power

Spinoza emphasises that the power of our mind to overcome the restrictive effect of external causes is limited. It is an unequal contest between the power of all that can affect our behaviour and the power we have to relate to it through a detached insight into it as a causal process. All we can do is survey the process and relate our experiences to it, but we can't prevent the events occurring that lead to our own frustration at (in an earlier example) being stuck in traffic. Nor can we prevent the causes of certain events occurring that greatly affect us, such as our ageing and dying. As he says, 'The force with which a man persists in existing is limited, and is far surpassed by the power of external causes' (1995: 144–5). External causes 'far surpass human power or virtue' (1995: 124).

In particular, how other people are affected by, and respond to, all that causes their behaviour is outside our control. A big source of the causes acting on us comes from how other people's behaviour impacts on us (1995: 84–5). Everyone is liable to emotions that particularly make us inconstant and variable. As a result, people are 'often drawn in different directions and are contrary one to the other, while they need each other's help' (1995: 165). If what Spinoza is saying is true, it will be difficult for anyone to have control over what affects them for their own benefit. Consequently, we can understand that it will be all the more difficult for social care clients, especially those who have deep-seated problems. It will be hard for them to have the kind of detachment required to be able to manage the emotional causes of their behaviour. This, in turn, serves to highlight an aspect of the role of the care worker in enabling clients to gain greater awareness of factors contributing to their need for care – as part of the process of helping them to develop their well-being.

If Spinoza is right about the extent to which there are causes acting on our emotions, emotions which then cause us to behave in a particular way, and which are far more powerful than our mind's capacity to be aware of them, then he is providing strong understanding why we should empathise with people in their difficulties and challenges. However, we are not totally in the grip of the causes of our emotions; we have some capacity to manage them for our good.

Historical Note

Spinoza did not use the terms *psychoanalysis* or *unconscious*, yet there is a sense in his ethics that he was aware of how forces could act on people unconsciously, in a restrictive way in particular. This is an understanding that was taken up and developed in the early twentieth century and has proved a valuable insight for therapeutic care.

Ethics as the Effort to Become Aware of Causes

For Spinoza, we are always seeking to have more emotional pleasure or satisfaction over pain in relation to our desires. The best we can do to achieve this, in so far as possible, is to become aware that our behaviour is the result of our emotions and that there is a chain of causes as to why we are feeling a particular emotion. More particularly, it is to bring to mind specific factors which are causing us to experience a particular emotion at any time, in so far as we can. The more we do this, the more we will become liberated from being blindly dictated to by causes. He expresses this by saying that when we become aware of factors acting on us, this has the effect of increasing *our active power* of mind over that which is causing our behaviour. We are then, if you like, acting less blindly or in the dark, or, as he puts it, we are less passively restricted. Also, the more we manage to have this awareness as a clear and distinct idea in coping with the experiences life throws up, the more we are behaving ethically. It is, for him, the essence of being ethical. He understands good and bad in relation to whether we strive to have clear awareness of the causes acting on us, or whether we simply allow ourselves to be driven by them unaware (1995: 147). To be virtuous is to have power over whatever is affecting us from the point of view of regarding it as caused in us. This is because our mind can then be less restricted and more active (1995: 143).

For Spinoza, the terms *good* and *bad* refer only to the means of achieving this greater active power of mind or living power for ourselves. It is the essence of ethics. 'We call that good or bad which is useful or the contrary to our preservation, that is, which increases or diminishes, helps or hinders our power of acting' (1995: 147). Here we find one of the ways of understanding the ethical roots of self-empowerment. Moreover, it is the kind of power that also directly benefits others. Once we are acting according to reason in this way and recognise the true nature of what is to the advantage of our living power, we will recognise that we desire the same for others (1995: 153). He gives three particular reasons for this.

1. Improved Human Relations

If everybody is seeking his own genuine good by increasing his living power in accordance with having awareness of the causal process at work in his responses and actions, then each person will be pulling in the same direction. As a result, we will be less likely to act restrictively toward each other by, for example, venting our restrictive or negative emotions on others. Also, we will be more inclined to act to increase other people's living power because then they will be less inclined to act restrictively toward us. While we do not have free will, we are of most benefit to others by becoming freer in ourselves, that is free, in so far as possible, from being passively restricted by our emotions. As he puts it, 'Only free men are truly useful to one another and are united by the closest bond of friendship and endeavour to benefit each other with an equal impulse of love' (1995: 185).

2. Human Nature

He also points out that helping others is in our nature. We are naturally empathetic. 'For he who is moved neither by reason nor pity to help others is rightly called inhuman, for he seems to be so unlike a man' (1995: 173).

3. Common Advantage

Like Aristotle, he points to the obvious fact that no one is self-sufficient. It stands to reason that we should unite with others for mutual benefit. 'From the common society of men far more conveniences arise than the contrary' (1995: 161).

Fortitude

The ethical task, as Spinoza sees it, is to develop in ourselves the virtue of fortitude. Fortitude normally has the meaning of having strength to withstand adversity and setback and to persist in trying to do what we believe is right. In relation to his ethics, Spinoza (1995: 124) divides fortitude into:

- Courage to persist in trying to have the one measure of freedom available to us, which is freedom of mind in being aware that our behaviour is determined by a causal process, and to do this especially by developing presence of mind when in danger of allowing emotional reaction to rule us restrictively.

- Generosity to help others by joining with them in trying to have mutual increased living power rather than be a hindrance.

A NEUROBIOLOGY VIEW

Brainwaves and Behaviour

Research studies in neurobiology indicate that our behaviour is partly caused by patterns of activity in the brain. These patterns of activity have been instilled in the brain over the course of human evolutionary development through natural selection and adaptation, which include the influences of cultural requirements and expectancies. As we go about making choices and decisions, we are not aware of the brain patterns which are stimulated when we are faced with making choices and decisions, yet it is the patterns that affect what our choices and decisions will be.

Drawing from scientific research, Harris, in his book *The Moral Landscape, How Science Can Determine Human Values*, claims that 'All of our behaviour can be traced to biological events about which we have no conscious knowledge'. In providing evidence for his claim, he points to discoveries that conscious decisions and, in general, our varying forms of conscious awareness can be detected in activity in the brain before we become aware of them in our minds. 'While we continually notice changes in our experience – in thoughts, mood, perception, behaviour etc. – we are utterly unaware of the neural events that produce these changes' (2010: 103). As with Spinoza, and so for Harris, we feel we have free will because of being able to entertain in our minds thoughts about a choice we have, for example, to go out for the evening or stay in. However, we have this feeling only because of our 'moment-to-moment ignorance of specific prior causes' (2010: 105).

The neural events or brain patterns are instinctively triggered by our organism's reaction to what it finds beneficial or adverse to its survival and well-being in its environment. Once triggered by some experience, in a fraction of a second a pattern arouses in our mind a feeling of approval or disapproval. The patterns arouse what Harris calls 'positive and negative social emotions'. The positive ones indicate that an experience is for our well-being; the negative ones indicate that it is not. Positive emotions come from 'heightened activity in the brain's reward regions'; negative ones come from patterns that indicate we are processing distress of some kind (2010: 1–2; 92).

Morality and Brain Reactions

One of the things coming from the instinctive brain reactions, which give us positive and negative social emotions, is our sense of right and wrong, which feeds into our moral judgments. Harris claims this is shown by the fact that reward-related brain activity, and consequent positive emotion, comes from being stimulated by such experiences as empathy, co-operation and fairness. The reason we regard these values as morally good is because our brains respond positively to them for giving us well-being. On the other hand, distress-related brain activity, and consequent negative emotion, comes from being stimulated by conditions of deprivation and oppression. And the reason we regard these conditions as morally wrong is because they block our well-being and threaten our survival (2010: 15–16).

On this view, the basis for genuine morality lies in instinct and not in rationality or beliefs. Reasons why we should behave in a certain way are an after-the-fact attempt to rationalise what has already been formed in us by instinctive brain reactions. This moral instinct view of morality, which holds that the source of our morals is not in our conscious minds but hidden from us in how our brains react, is shared by others, such as Jonathan Haidt, who have been developing it on the basis of providing for 'a new science of morality (see Harris et al. 2010; and Haidt 2010; 2007).

They are not suggesting, however, that we have been determined by our biology to act from moral instinct alone. Since we have become conscious of our intentions, we are able to calculate the consequences of our intentions in deciding how best to act in the interests of well-being. We can, and should, reflect on what our instincts are prompting us to do and, by using our reason, develop a more informed and considered judgment about moral questions in the light of what is genuinely in the interests of well-being. The positive and negative social emotions coming to us from neural activity show that we instinctively associate our own well-being as bound up with the well-being of others.

Neuroscience also shows that while the source of our behavioural responses are hidden from us in triggered patterns of brain activity, the patterns are not fixed. They are open to change from being influenced. Brain activity is malleable, which enables the patterns to undergo change from the influences of thinking, culture and habitual practice.

Nevertheless, a neurobiology view shows that our immediate behaviour is partly caused in us to an extent that we cannot consider ourselves to have free will (Harris 2010: 102–6). On the basis of this view, then there is also a reason to have empathy. In particular, it shows why empathy is justified as a care response to those in need, as neither they nor we have complete control over how we behave.

Freedom as an Existential Challenge

In contrast to a neurobiology-based ethics, existentialist philosophers have highlighted human freedom to choose. They point out that we experience ourselves as free to try to have the kind of life we want. But deciding on the kind of life we want can be a challenge. This is because we don't have certainty that any choice we make will necessarily be the best one. Freedom, in other words, can be experienced as an existential challenge.

Some existentialists, notably Sartre in his early works, say that people find themselves born into a world that has no absolute meaning or value. While there is a range of cultural meaning and value available, and while we may (or may not) have adequate material and emotional support for our needs, the real challenge is to cope with our life in terms of finding fulfilling meaning and value. We recognise that we have freedom to choose what will have meaning and value for us, but have no guarantee that the choices we make will be good ones.

Sartre says that we become who we are through the choices we make. As he puts it, 'For human reality, to be is to choose oneself' (1995: 440). We make ourselves by our choices, large or small, from the career we follow to the recreation we enjoy. Through my choices 'I am more and more sculpting my figure in the world' (427). Because we are free and, at the same time, have to express ourselves in some way, how we do so produces who we are. It makes us who we are essentially (438).

However, as Sartre saw it, this presents a big challenge. This is because whatever we choose, whatever we desire, whatever we give our attention to, has no intrinsic worth or purpose. Its only worth or purpose comes from the meaning and value we choose to give to it, but our choice will always be quite subjective and a matter for ourselves. There is nothing definite and objective to guide our choice. Even though our choices may relate to our needs and interests, they will still ultimately be random in that they could have been different to the actual ones we made.

At the same time, Sartre saw us facing the challenge of having to choose in the full light of the recognition of being responsible for our freedom – he describes this as a daunting challenge. He points out that the tendency is for people to hide from their responsibility. This results in people leading false lives of 'bad faith' in which, consciously or unconsciously, they hide from their freedom to make their own responsible choices. They hide it, for example, in their social roles or in subservience to some established authority. Living in denial of their essential freedom can exert on them an unconscious pressure, pressure which in some cases may lead to unhealthy submissive or authoritarian behaviour (see Charleton 2012).

If this description of the human condition is correct, then it provides a reason for having understanding for difficulties people face in coping with their lives. It provides one possible element in understanding why people may become depressed, or homeless, or develop addictions. It may also be an element in the underlying cause of some suicides, and suicides among young male adults is a particular problem in Ireland. Immediate contributory causes may be seen to lie in drinking to excess or depression. However, difficulties coping with the existential challenge may be an element lying behind such causes.

EMPATHY AND SOCIAL CARE

Trust

Empathy in particular enables care workers to have the trust of people with care needs.

Acceptance

An empathetic understanding includes accepting clients as individuals, for the person each has become in relation to her/his circumstances, no matter what s/he may have done in the past. It also provides understanding for why there is no justification for moral judgments which are critical of clients, i.e. narrow, moralistic judgments, or for authoritarian or controlling practices.

Encouragement

From the appreciation of the restrictions on behaviour that service users can experience, encouragement is an appropriate response to enable them to cope with their restrictions and to tackle and overcome them, in so far as possible. In particular, empathy highlights that demanding of clients that they do better, or pressurising them to meet the requirements of their care plan, is not appropriate.

Understanding for Offenders

The understanding that people do not have complete free will and, as a result, can be considered to have reduced responsibility for their actions is a particular reason for treating offenders with empathy within the prison service as part of custodial care.

For a discussion on the broader question of the moral justification of criminal punishment, see Murphy (2002), whose view is based on having empathy for offenders and working with them to enable them realise the harm they have done, feel remorse, and not offend again. For a contrasting view, see Rachels (2002) who argues that since offenders have voluntarily harmed their victims, they deserve to be punished according to their crime if justice is to be served.

Respect for Capability

Even though people may not have free will in the sense of being the conscious source of all their behaviour, they still have the power to act to improve their behaviour, attitude and circumstances through being aware of their intentions. People still have personal responsibility, and it would be disrespectful to clients, and people in general, to regard them as not being capable of exercising a level of personal responsibility.

CASE STUDY 5.1

Case Study: Empathy and Allowing for Exception

Consider the case of a family of asylum seekers whose children have been attending school in Ireland for over a year (or perhaps a shorter period) and who have become part of the local community. They now find that their application for asylum has been turned down because the details they gave in their application were found not to be in accordance with the facts. They have been issued with notice that they are to be deported back to the country of their origin, where welfare services are undeveloped and where they are likely to face serious poverty. Having regard to reasons for empathy, consider and discuss the response Irish society should have to the family's needs. Also include in your study of the case Kant's principles, which include a duty to tell the truth (as well as the criticism of his principles that they can be harsh in not allowing for exceptions), together with his principles to respect and care for others.

CASE STUDY 5.2

Case Study: Paula and her Problems

Analyse the case study below by addressing the following questions:

1. What are the ethical issues involved?
2. What are the factors that have contributed to the issues? (Include the consideration of further possible background factors.)
3. What care action would you recommend?
4. Drawing from a philosophical understanding of empathy in particular as an ethical value, how would you justify your care action?

Paula is a forty-five-year-old woman who is a service user of the family resource centre. She takes part in a parenting course. Her two older children, fourteen-year-old Mike and fifteen-year-old Meg, also come to the centre for a homework club in the late afternoon. During a recent parenting class, which a care worker was giving, Paula became verbally abusive of the other women when she felt she was being criticised by them. From their contribution to a discussion, she understood them to be inferring that she was a bad parent because she did not praise her children for their schoolwork and also for maintaining that it would be best for her children if they leave school at sixteen and get work to bring home money. Paula is separated from her husband who left her for another woman. She speaks openly about this and is very bitter toward him, especially since he has cut off all ties with the family, including financial support. Her only income comes from social welfare allowances.

The care worker was able to smooth over Paula's outburst, even though it had been shocking for the group, and she continued with the class. However, Paula came back to the centre later in the day, smelling of alcohol, and started shouting and roaring, which upset the service users present, especially young children. The manager had difficulty getting Paula to leave, and Paula only left in the end when the manager threatened to call the gardaí.

Some members of the parenting class complained to the manager about Paula's behaviour in class, and the manager criticised the care worker for not reporting the incident to her immediately. The manager said she was at a disadvantage in not knowing in advance about the incident when talking with the parents, and she was made to feel incompetent in front of them. She said she needed to be informed of problems as soon as possible to be able to make appropriate decisions for the safety and well-being of service users. The care worker had thought of reporting the incident but was afraid it might get Paula into trouble. Also, she hoped it was a one-off incident which would blow over. The manager said to the care worker that a number of the women in the group, who are young first-time mothers, told her they will leave the group if Paula continues in it. The manager said it would be for the best if Paula is asked to leave. She said that to spare Paula's feelings, the care worker should tell Paula that the centre has had its funding cut and that the course will no longer be running, even though it still will be.

The care worker is concerned that if Paula leaves the course it will have an impact on Mike and Meg. She is afraid that Paula will remove them from the homework club, which will be a setback for their education. The care worker is concerned because both children show signs of being withdrawn and, in the company of their mother, fearful. The care worker has plans to encourage the children to engage in other activities in the centre, such as social events and outings, which will help them develop their social skills. She is also aware that both Mike and Meg are bright, and it would be a pity if they had to leave formal education so early. She had been talking to them about the courses available in universities and institutes of technology. Mike confided to her that he loves science and would like to become a scientist, and Meg has said she would love to be a doctor. The care worker also felt that Paula had been benefiting from the parenting course as well as the informal contact with other service users until the incident occurred.

Exercise 5.1

Question to Consider and Discuss

Are psychological and social pressures (e.g. criminality in family background, lack of educational opportunity, unemployment, peer pressure) adequate reasons to relieve people of responsibility for actions considered morally wrong?

Moral Challenge and Empathy for Characters in Novels and Films

Some novels and films can be of absorbing interest from the way the characters handle moral challenges. They are frequently the kind of challenges we can imagine ourselves having in different, if less dramatic, circumstances. This is particularly the case where the challenge is not presented in black and white, but in shades of grey. By 'shades of grey' it is meant that from the circumstances portrayed there can be understandable reasons why people act as they do, even though at some level they know it is wrong and likely to get them into trouble with other people and usually also with the law. Alternatively, they know their action is right and are determined to do right even though it will get them into trouble. Such novels and films also show how people can be led by their emotions, by desire or anger or care for others which proves to be their downfall, or their heroism. Check out the films *The House of Sand and Fog*, *The Constant Gardener* and *Lincoln*.

Exercise 5.2

Describe a moral challenge experienced by a character(s) in a novel or film that has struck you, and give an account of the way the character(s) handled the challenge in the light of your understanding of empathy and responsibility for actions.

CRITICAL EVALUATION

Empathy as a Variable and Uncertain Emotion

Empathy is clearly an important natural human emotion which gives rise to people wanting to help and care for others, including political parties in the social polices that they adopt and try to implement. At the same time, whether people as individuals, or through politics, act with empathy is a matter for them, and empathy can easily be lacking, or insufficient to provide for care, especially when it will require some cost to the individual by way of his/her time and effort or, in the case of politics, in view of lack of money to fund a service. During the economic austerity which followed Ireland's economic collapse in 2008, financial cutbacks have included reductions in welfare and care services. In deciding on the various ways in which savings can be made, empathy has not been sufficient to ensure that those who experience hardship from their circumstances can be spared reductions in support.

Spinoza Overemphasises Emotions?

Spinoza is known for being the first philosopher to identify and describe the powerful and volatile role that the emotions have in causing people's behaviour. But it can be argued that in claiming they *cause* behaviour rather than saying they *influence* or *contribute* to how we behave, he may be overstating their role. Spinoza seems to assume that just because we can see that lots of things in the world are caused, for example, a foot striking a ball causes it to move, this does not have to mean that everything is caused, in particular human behaviour. Spinoza is said to have been influenced by the scientific view current in his time (in the seventeenth century) of a mechanised world in which everything has a cause. But, in having consciousness, self-awareness and a capacity to exercise reason, human beings can be considered different in being able to act more freely than he allows for.

At the same time, we don't have to agree with Spinoza's view in full to recognise that people can come under a lot pressure, often severe, from causes which result in them behaving in ways that are not good for them or for others close to them. An example is a young, single parent from a broken home in which there was unemployment, poverty and alcoholism who resorts to drugs to try to alleviate his/her problems. We can understand that in his/her case there are strong factors contributing to, if not actually causing, his/her behaviour. Spinoza's theory, while it is a bit difficult, helps us to understand how it is that our actions are influenced by such factors, over which we may have little or no control. It can also help care workers in understanding why clients may have difficulty following care plans devised for them.

Difficulties with the Neurobiology View

Through evolution, human beings are creatures of the physical universe, and the brain is a physical organ. This makes it understandable that at least some source of our behaviour lies in how the brain has been conditioned to function to bring about our survival and well-being, rather than enabling us to act with complete free will. As a result, there is an understandable reason for having empathy for others since we are not completely in charge of our lives. However, there are a number of difficulties with this account. For example, as Harris acknowledges, the essential point that brain reactions are the underlying cause of our states of mind, which includes our moral states, remains an assumption: 'The assumption that the mind is a product of the brain is integral to almost everything neuroscientists do' (2010: 180). This is an assumption that is disputed within philosophy. Also, it remains unclear exactly how, and to what extent, our behaviour is determined by patterns of activity laid down from our evolutionary history. Harris acknowledges that the study of the workings of the brain, especially in relation to our moral responses, is still in its infancy and is complex. Apart from the technical complexity of unravelling and matching up electrical impulses operating in the brain with moral responses, there is the broader, more philosophical point, of reconciling the brain's more instinctive functioning with the extent to which thinking and culture influence the formation of its patterns of activity, 'Cultural norms influence our thinking and behaviour by altering the structure and function of our brains' (2010: 9). Also, as Harris acknowledges, his scientific account of morality is not reducible to an evolutionary account of instinctive drives causing behaviour. Through language and culture, 'meaning and morality have flown the perch built by evolution' (2010: 14). This suggests that we have more freedom in how we behave than his brain reaction account allows.

REVIEW

Empathy is central to a caring relationship. It is a naturally occurring emotion through which care workers can identify with the needs and challenges of the people they are caring for. There are also understandable reasons why we should empathise with other people. For example, they may be suffering misery and restriction from poverty; their capacity to act rationally can be restricted by the power of hidden causes acting on their emotions, and their behaviour can partly be the result of neurobiological impulses of which they are unaware. A difficulty people may have in coping with their sense of personal freedom can also be a reason to have empathy for them. Among other features of best practice, empathic relations are needed to develop trust.

FURTHER READING

Benn, P. (1998) *Ethics*, UCL Press (Chapter 6).

REFERENCES

Banks, S. (2004) *Ethics, Accountability and the Social Professions*, Palgrave Macmillan.

Charleton, M. (2012) 'Abuse of Children in Institutional Care in 20th Century Ireland: An Analysis Using Fromm's Psychology' in *Journal of Social Work Practice*, Vol. 26, Number 3.

Haidt, J. (2007) 'Moral Psychology and the Misunderstanding of Religion', available at http://www.edge.org/conversation/moral-psychology-and-the-misunderstanding-of-religion (accessed 15 November 2013).

Haidt, J. (2010) 'The New Science of Morality', available at http://edge.org/conversation/a-new-science-of-morality-part1 (accessed 28 June 2013).

Hamington, M. (2004) *Embodied Care: Jane Addams, Maurice Merleau-Ponty, and Feminist Ethics*, University of Illinois Press.

Harris, S. (2010) *The Moral Landscape, How Science Can Determine Human Values*, Bantam Press.

Harris *et al.* (2010) 'The New Science of Morality', an Edge conference consensus statement, available at www.edge.org/documents/archive.edge (accessed 28 June 2013).

Murphy, J. (2002) 'Repentance and Criminal Punishment' in *Ethics in Practice, An Anthology*, 2nd ed., H. La Follette (ed.), Blackwell.

Rachels, J. (2002) 'Punishment and Desert Punishment' in *Ethics in Practice, An Anthology*, 2nd ed., H. La Follette (ed.), Blackwell.

Sartre, J. (1995) *Being and Nothingness*, Routledge.

Slote, M. (2007) *The Ethics of Care and Empathy*, Routledge.

Spinoza, B. de (1995) *Ethics*, Everyman.

Stein, E. (1970) *On the Problem of Empathy*, Martinus Nijhoff.

6

Human Rights

OVERALL AIM

To explore human rights theories as a basis for understanding how rights provide moral justification for meeting people's social care needs.

LEARNING OUTCOMES

At the end of this chapter you should be able to:

- Explain the main philosophical sources for the existence of human rights.
- Show familiarity with the main rights relating to care in international agreements and Irish law.
- Appreciate rights as a force for social and political change.
- Understand and assess the value of rights for particular care provision, such as equality of treatment for people with disabilities and provision of basic living standards.
- Explain the theoretical difficulties in proving rights exist.

INTRODUCTION

Of all ethical ideas, the idea that everybody has certain rights has come to have the most practical significance. This is because there is a general acceptance that where a right can be shown to exist, it must be met, as far as possible. In particular, governments are seen as having an obligation to provide for and uphold the rights of all citizens. Mill makes this point well:

> When we call anything a person's right, we mean that he has a valid claim on society to protect him in the possession of it, either by the force of law, or by that of education and opinion. If he has what we consider a sufficient claim, on whatever account, to have something guaranteed to him by society, we say he has a right to it. If we desire to prove that anything does not belong to him

by right, we think this done as soon as it is admitted that society ought not to take measures for securing it to him, but should leave him to chance, or to his own exertions.

Mill 2008: 189

To have a valid claim to a right implies, in other words, that a government has an *obligation* to provide for and protect you in the exercise of your rights. Rights imply responsibilities or obligations on others, and, under human rights agreements in international law, governments have obligations to uphold people's rights. Almond also points out the practical relevance of rights in the obligation they place on governments:

Appeal to rights is widely understood and accepted everywhere in the world under all types of political regime. It is no small advantage to a moral notion that it should be regarded as valid across so many nations and cultures, and that it should have at least the potential of binding governments to the observation of important moral constraints.

Almond 2004: 263–4

Where a right is claimed and accepted politically to have justification, it may receive the backing of law. This cements its practical significance in place. Under international law, for example, there is a right to asylum for a person whose circumstances meet specific requirements. In Ireland, equality rights are provided under the Employment Equality Acts of 1998 and 2004. These Acts prohibit discrimination in the workplace. The Equal Status Acts of 2000 and 2004 prohibit discrimination in the provision of goods and services, accommodation and education. This legal provision in domestic law of some rights gives them a particular practical significance.

The care worker can come across issues relating to rights in providing care. It may, for example, be a case of a family from an ethnic minority or the Travelling community experiencing discrimination in trying to get accommodation or places for their children in a crèche or school, and where reasons other than discriminatory ones are used as a pretext. Also, as we shall see, under the EU charter people have a right to the protection of social welfare where they cannot provide for themselves, and care workers can come across cases where clients may not be receiving the welfare support they are entitled to have. Also, in providing family support services in cases where parents have separated, care workers need to ensure the rights of both fathers and mothers to be involved in continued care for their children and in care plans for them.

Since rights have come to have practical importance and force as a moral claim, we will look next at the main sources that give rights their moral justification. 'At bottom, the idea of human rights is a moral one. It becomes a legal and political idea only because of its supreme moral importance' (Gewirth 1982: ix).

SOURCES FOR RIGHTS
Philosophical Sources

Natural Law

How is the idea that we all have rights justified? Rights come from the idea that there exists something called *natural law*. It is a law, or set of laws, based on how human beings are believed to be of their nature. Natural law is something we are said to be able to recognise as existing of itself from basic inclinations or desires that are natural to people. Recognition of *natural law* goes back over 2,000 years when it emerged in ancient Greece. It was prominent in both Greek, and later Roman, Stoic philosophy where there was a notion of universal brotherhood based on the recognition that people have a common human nature identified with having rationality along with other basic natural capacities, and inclinations or desires such as for continued life. In the same way that there are obvious features naturally occurring in nature, such as day and night, the seasons and the movement of the planets, the ancient philosophers concluded that there are obvious features to human behaviour that are natural and from which we can derive natural laws.

Natural is contrasted with the notion of *convention*. In other words, natural law is not something regarded as made up for human convenience, like the idea of the social contract, which we will be looking at in Chapter 10. Natural law is something we are said to be able to recognise as existing of itself and providing an absolute standard for understanding actions that are right or wrong. Over time the natural laws came to be understood as providing for what are called 'natural rights'. People are said to have these rights simply by virtue of being born as a human person. They are regarded as both fundamental and having universal validity.

But what exactly is it that people have a natural right to? Arising from the idea of a natural law, which is based on everybody having a common human nature, is the idea of *human equality*. 'Human equality is the direct consequence of natural law, its first and essential tenet' (d'Entreves 1964: 22). Also directly linked to natural law is the idea of the right of people to be accorded the same *intrinsic value* as everyone else, regardless of ability and social status.

Aquinas

For Aquinas (1225–74), natural law, properly speaking, can only be understood in the light of reason. It takes reason to recognise that something is natural. The provisions of natural law come from reason reflecting on natural human inclinations. There is one overall inclination, which is to do good and avoid evil, and we can recognise that we are drawn toward good and away from evil through rational reflection on the nature of human behaviour. In light of this overall inclination, three basic inclinations follow.

The first natural inclination a person has is to preserve his own existence (self-preservation). It is, if you like, the most basic human instinct. Through our reason reflecting on this inclination, Aquinas claims it can be seen that those actions are naturally good by which a person's life is preserved and his death avoided. From this comes the first provision of natural law, which is that life should be preserved. The second natural inclination is for men and women to form relationships and have children. Through reason reflecting on this inclination, it can be seen that those actions are good which contribute to the welfare and development of children. The third natural inclination we have is for knowledge and to live in society. Through reason reflecting on this inclination, we can see that those actions are good which seek truth and sustain a society (Baumgarth and Regan 1998: 46–8, see also Copleston 1957: 214–5; Finnis 1980: 30–36, and esp. 94).

If these are three precepts of natural law, how then do they relate to natural or human rights? For Aquinas, because all people have a capacity to reason along with the same basic inclinations, there are natural rights relating to justice on the basis of equality (1988: 138–40). Also, you can argue that from the first natural law to preserve life comes certain fundamental rights, for example, the right to life and also a right to the practical means to preserve life, means such as adequate food and shelter since they are necessary to provide basic security and protection, without which life would be at risk. Also, from the second natural law relating to procreation, you can argue it is rational to conclude that children, for example, have a right to protection and to basic education and of families to basic social services where they cannot provide for themselves, such as an income in unemployment and in old age. From the natural law relating to living in society, you can derive the right not to suffer discrimination. In this way, we can see how certain economic and social rights, which are of particular importance for people with care needs, could be derived from Aquinas's natural law theory.

However, Aquinas's system is a system of natural law, not a system that emphasises rights (d'Entreves 1964: 45–6). Aquinas's theory is based on his view of the proper way to live in accordance with his understanding of natural law which, as a Catholic theologian, philosopher and saint, he regarded as participating in divine law. That is, he was seeking to identify natural law provisions from within the religious belief that God had given human beings a particular nature, and by living in accordance with this nature people would be living the life God intends them to live. Also, Aquinas's particular understanding of what is rational in relation to right or wrong arising from natural human inclinations is one of the sources for Catholic moral teaching. For example, it is a source for the Church's teaching on sexual relationships and marriage between same sex couples. (For an account of the difficulty in being able to demonstrate that specific moral requirements of right and wrong follow from general principles of natural law, see

Finnis 1980: 34; Buckle 2004:170–73.) Aquinas's theory was not for the purpose of providing the modern, secular view of the rights, the view that fuelled revolutions and that is now the main moral appeal for social improvements. At the same time, Aquinas's understanding of natural law shares some common ground with the modern view of rights. This can be seen today in particular in the emphasis church representatives place on the dignity and worth of each individual and in their criticism of social conditions that undermine that dignity and worth.

Natural Law Versus State Law

As we will see in the critical evaluation section, some philosophers dispute that there is such a thing as natural law. Also, where it is accepted that there is a natural law based on human nature, people differ both on the legal status it should be accorded, as well as on the understanding of the particular natural rights which come from it. One view holds that since natural law comes from nature, it is prior to state law, and therefore state law has to accord with the provisions of natural law. This view arose in 1995, after the president referred to the Supreme Court the Act that permitted people access to information on abortion to test whether or not it was in accordance with the Constitution.

In the hearing, council for the unborn argued that the legislation could not be permitted because it conflicted with the natural right of the unborn to life under natural law, and that natural law is superior to state law. A law that endangered the right of the unborn to life must be wrong, even if the people voted for it in a referendum, as the Irish people had in permitting access to abortion information. However, the Court judged that the Constitution, and not natural law, is the fundamental law of the state. The judgment also quoted from an earlier judgment, in what became known as 'the McGee case', which related to a right to have access to the means of contraception: 'In a pluralist society such as ours, the Courts cannot as a matter of constitutional law be asked to choose between differing views, where they exist, of experts on the interpretation by the different religious denominations of either the nature or extent of these natural rights as they are to be found in the natural law' (see Jeffers 2003).

Grotius

Grotius (1583–1645) was a leading natural law philosopher, who is said to have been the first to have interpreted natural law provisions specifically as rights provisions. Like Aquinas, he believed that we are born with a sense of natural law, and that it has been given to us by God. From Grotius comes the idea that 'a right is a moral quality of a person'. He believed a right is a quality we have similar to the way we have physical qualities such as a brain or a heart, even though it is not something physical which we can actually see. For Grotius, the big significance in having rights is that they confer the authority of law on what we can do or on what we can have. A right provides an entitlement even where the law of the state does not, or has not yet, supported it in legislation (Buckle 2004: 168).

Locke

Grotius's understanding is said to have influenced Locke (1632–1704), and the roots of modern thinking on human rights can be found in Locke's philosophy in particular. Locke's method to establish the existence of rights was to ask the question what human life would be like in a state of nature, that is, a state of living in which there is no government or common authority to control how we behave. The state of nature is a hypothetical state, i.e. imagined or put forward for the purposes of argument, and for the real purpose of identifying the kind of laws that would accord with a realistic picture of how people need to behave from their nature.

Locke maintained that people would try to satisfy three basic requirements in a state of nature. These are to sustain their lives, maintain their liberty, and acquire property, which are all interrelated. From our nature we find we have to work to acquire property (or things in general, especially the means of living) both to sustain our lives and to increase our measure of freedom. For Locke, who was a Christian, this is how we have been created to be by God. Everyone since Adam and Eve has had to work to sustain their life and increase their freedom. Also, following the introduction of money through which goods can be sold and purchased, it is natural for us to acquire money to secure our lives and increase our freedom. In this way, Locke seeks to justify the existence of natural rights to life, liberty and property.

Locke also believed that in this state of nature, we would recognise not only that we personally have these rights, but that other people have them, too. These rights are, in other words, universal. However, it is also a feature of our 'fallen' or morally weak nature that some people will interfere with our rights by, for example, attacking us and stealing our property. It therefore becomes the role of government to protect us in our natural rights, and the only legitimate government we would accept is one we could agree to trust with the power to protect us in our rights. So, from Locke comes the idea that there is a natural morality of rights, which the laws of government further provide for and protect. 'An ongoing practical morality exists independent of government, so that legitimate government exists to protect and defend that morality' (McClelland 2002: 236; see also 233–236).

Kant

Kant's moral theory is also seen as a source for the modern understanding of human rights. As we saw in Chapter 3, Kant claims to have shown from the fact that because each person is naturally endowed with reason and will, there is a natural equality of moral status between people. As a result, it is argued that people have a natural right to be treated equally. Also, from Kant's idea that each person is a free or autonomous individual in being able to exercise his/her own reason and will, it is argued that rights belong to people as individuals. This idea can be seen in many social practices relating to social care. For example, in the emphasis placed on caring for the child's best interest as an individual within the family and in the best practice of taking a child's own views into account, having regard to the child's age. Also, for example, people have the right to personal privacy, and to how they want to live as long as they are not harming others. The right to individual freedom is also much emphasised in politics in opposition to the suppression of people's human rights in oppressive, non-democratic regimes and in support of democracy.

Essential Interests Theory

One justification of human rights, which relates more directly to the human rights claims of today, is known as 'the essential interests' theory. Finnis identified seven essential interests which he sees all human beings as having for well-being. He argues that these essential interests form the basis for understanding why human beings have rights. We can see how Finnis is more comprehensive in selecting the basic features of being human than Aquinas is with his three primary human inclinations. The essential interests Finnis sees humans as having are for:

1. Life and its capacity for development.
2. The acquisition of knowledge, as an end in itself.
3. Play, as the capacity for recreation.
4. Aesthetic expression.
5. Sociability and friendship.
6. Practical reasonableness, i.e. the capacity for intellectual and reasonable thought processes.
7. Religion or the capacity for spiritual experience. (Finnis 1980: 86–95; for an account of essential interests theory, see Fagan 2013, 'Human Rights')

Finnis regards each of the seven as equally and self-evidently a form of human good. People, then, whose living circumstances prevent or interfere with them having these essential interests are without their human rights, and there is an obligation on others, on governments especially, to ensure they have a life that enables them to engage with these interests. In relation to the fifth interest, a social care example would be a right for older people living alone in rural areas and suffering from a lack of social contact to a means of transport, where it is lacking, to bring them to centres to engage in community social activities.

Rational Agency Theory

Gewirth argues that it is the capacity human beings have to act in a rationally purposeful way which is most characteristic of their nature. To be able to act with purpose, people have two requirements: freedom and well-being. As he puts it, 'Because every agent regards his purpose as good, he must regard as necessary goods the freedom and well-being which are the necessary conditions of his acting for any purpose' (Gerwirth 1982: 4). Human rights, then, relate to the kind of things that enable us to be a rationally purposeful agent. This would include well-being from having the basic means of living, such as food and education. It would also include freedom from economic or political oppression. Also, because everyone has requirements of freedom and well-being, these rights are universal. They are universal in a way which implies that people can demand that their rights are not interfered with, and that other people, in effect governments, should provide them with their rights when they do not have them:

> For a person to have human rights, then, is for him to be in a position to make morally justified, stringent, effective demands on other persons that they not interfere with his having the necessary goods of action and they also help him to attain these goods when he cannot do so by his own efforts.
>
> Gewirth 1982: 11

Political Sources

The idea that everyone has natural rights, especially in relation to an equality of moral status and to freedom, has been a powerful force in history. It has provided justification for people to strive to give practical expression to the idea of equality by taking action against conditions of inequality and oppression where they existed socially and politically. In other words, people have sought to change conditions under which they felt some people were not valued equally. Natural law has provided this justification because it has been seen as more basic than state law and having the authority to direct state law. The fact that, arising from natural law, rights were believed to have been created in people by God gave them additional moral authority and force. The idea of natural rights lay behind both the American Revolution of 1776 and the French Revolution of 1789, both of which highlighted the natural law basis of human rights in their declarations (d'Entreves 1964: 60). For d'Entreves, the revolutions in particular turned the idea of natural law into a theory of natural or human rights, and for practical purposes natural law theory since then has been a theory of rights (1964: 59).

The American Declaration of Independence claims that rights are self-evidently true. It famously states, 'We hold these truths to be self-evident, that all men are created equal, that they are endowed by their Creator with certain unalienable Rights, that among these are Life, Liberty and the pursuit of Happiness'. In a similar vein the French Declaration of the Rights of Man and of the Citizen refers to 'natural, inalienable and sacred Rights of Man' (cited in d'Entreves 1964: 48). Appeals to rights have also been instrumental in abolishing slavery and apartheid laws and in the many struggles, up to and including our own day, to overthrow undemocratic governments. In particular, freedom to vote in free and fair elections for a government of choice remains a basic right underpinning democracy, along with freedom from being exploited. Human trafficking of people from poorer countries into richer ones, including into Ireland, for sexual or labour exploitation is a particular violation of an individual's human right which occurs today. People who are trafficked have need of care as well as legal services.

LEGAL RIGHTS RELEVANT TO SOCIAL CARE: SOME EXAMPLES

Apart from the philosophical and political sources for human rights, practical legal status was achieved in 1948 through the United Nations which declared them to be universal and fundamental. The UN Declaration divided rights into civil and political rights, for example, rights to vote and to freedom of expression, and economic, social and cultural rights, for example, the right to the basic means of living, such as food. In addition, there are a number of articles in the Irish Constitution, domestic laws and other international agreements which provide legal acceptance that people have rights, including 'social' and 'economic' rights which are the ones of most relevance to social care.

Basic Rights

There are basic, general rights that have social care relevance. For example, a key phrase in the UN Declaration of Human Rights states that people have a right to 'an existence worthy of human dignity' (Art. 23.2). This is a general phrase and open to interpretation, but suffering and death from preventable disease and food shortage, which is the plight of many in the world, is clearly not an existence worthy of human dignity and so people in such circumstances have a right to assistance.

The UN Covenant on Economic, Social and Cultural Rights recognises 'the fundamental right of everyone to be free of hunger' (Art. 11.2). Article 11.1 'recognises the right of everyone to an adequate standard of living for himself and his family, including adequate food, clothing and housing, and the continued improvement in living conditions'. Article 6.1 recognises 'the right to work, which includes the right of everyone to the opportunity to gain his living by work which is freely chosen or accepted'. Other articles recognise rights to health, physical and mental (Art. 12.1), and education (Art. 13). These provisions include the recognition of a right everyone has to a level of income and social care services needed to have an adequate standard of living where they cannot provide for themselves.

Children's Rights

The Irish Constitution 'recognises and affirms the natural and imprescriptible rights of all children'. It also commits the State 'as far as practicable, by its laws' to 'protect and vindicate those rights' (Art. 42A 1). The Constitution also makes explicit the duty of the State to 'supply the place of the parents in exceptional cases, where parents, regardless of marital status, fail in their duty towards their children to such an extent that the safety or welfare of any of their children is likely to be prejudicially affected' (Art. 42A 2).

Article 24 of the Charter of Fundamental Rights of the European Union lays down the rights of children as follows:

(1)   Children shall have the right to such protection and care as is necessary for their well-being. They may express their views freely. Such views shall be taken into consideration on matters which concern them in accordance with their age and maturity.

(2)   In all actions relating to children, whether taken by public authorities or private institutions, the child's best interests must be a primary consideration.

Children's rights are also provided for under the UN Convention on the Rights of the Child. This is a particularly important document for the worldwide protection of children. One example is Article 37 (C). It provides for the right of children (those under eighteen) who are detained by the state under the law to be held separately from adults, unless it is in their best interests. In his annual report for 2012, the Inspector of Prisons referred to the detention of 17 year olds along with those in the 18 to 20 age group in St Patrick's Institution for young offenders. He also found in a visit to St Patrick's in March of 2013 'very disturbing incidences of non-compliance with best practice and breaches of fundamental rights of prisoners' (Annual Report of the Office of the Inspector of Prisons 2012: 19; see further for details). The Inspector made a number of recommendations, including the closure of the Institution, which the Minister for Justice accepted (see also Lally 2013).

Rights of Older People

Article 25 of the EU Charter states, 'The Union recognises and respects the rights of the elderly to lead a life of dignity and independence and to participate in social and cultural life.'

Rights of People with Disabilities

Article 26 of the EU Charter states, 'The Union recognises and respects the right of persons with disabilities to benefit from measures designed to ensure their independence, social and occupational integration and participation in the life of the community.'

Article 19 of the UN Convention on the Rights of Persons with Disabilities also identifies a right to live independently and be included in the community. Article 23.1 relates specifically to rights to enter freely into relationships, marriage and parenthood on an equal basis with others. This is an important right because sexuality is central to a sense of self, and a healthy relationship to sexuality is necessary for well-being. There has been a perception that denied or discouraged sexuality for disabled people for the mistaken reason that it is somehow inappropriate, or due to over-protection. In practice, disabled people's right to express their sexuality means they have a right to support. This includes relationship and sexuality education to enable them to make informed choices as far as is possible, as well as providing them with opportunities to socialise. It also includes practical support for couples who wish to marry and live independently. In the case of those who have learning challenges, there are understandable protective concerns relating to emotional vulnerability and willing consent, and there are risks of exploitation and abuse. However, with proper safeguards and supports it should be possible for many people with disabilities who want to enjoy their right to a fulfilling sexual life to do so safely.

EFFECTIVENESS OF INTERNATIONAL RIGHTS AGREEMENTS

In view of human rights agreements, you may be wondering why it is that the rights of some people are not provided for in practice. For example, why are there still people homeless if the UN covenant says people have a right to adequate housing? Also, having to sleep rough is not an 'existence worthy of human dignity', and people have a right to such an 'existence' under the UN Declaration. You would think, too, that having to sleep rough is 'inhuman and degrading treatment' and so goes against a person's rights under the European Convention. Also, why are people with disabilities left without access to services to integrate them with the community when both the UN Covenant and the EU Charter provide for their right to services, including means of education appropriate to their needs.

The central question here is this: 'When a person has a human right to something, does this mean the state has to provide him with it?' The answer is 'Yes' if the right in question has been turned into a legal right by the laws of the state. Basic civil and political rights are also legal rights in the Irish justice system. For example, a right to vote, to freedom of speech and to equality before the law is provided for under the Constitution, which lays down the state's basic laws. Also, there are a number of specific laws prohibiting discrimination, so under the provisions of such laws a person has a legal entitlement, enforceable through the courts, to these rights.

However, the answer is not a straightforward 'Yes' in relation to what are called 'economic and social rights'. The reason for this is because the agreements oblige governments to *progressively realise* people's rights and not to have to provide for them immediately and in full as a matter of law. Under Article 2 of the the UN Covenant on Economic, Social and Cultural Rights, for example, legal obligation on governments is 'to take steps . . . with a view to achieving the full realization' of rights. This was the observation in 2004 of the Irish Human Rights Commission on the then Irish Disability Bill (see the Commission's website for observations, www.ihre.ie). In effect, this means that governments have leeway in providing people with their social and economic rights provided by international agreements.

Another point to note is the meaning of the precise wording in legal provisions. For example, in the EU Charter people have a right to housing *assistance*, which is not the same as having a right to be provided with a house. Also in the EU Charter, people with disabilities have a right *to benefit from measures* designed to ensure their independence and integration, which is not the same as having a right to those measures in the sense that a government has to provide them.

For people who have a valid, but as yet unmet, claim to a right, the problem with 'progressive achievement' is that it allows governments leeway in making sure the measures needed to give people their rights are provided. From the government's perspective, however, progressive achievement recognises the reality of the cost implications of providing the services, particularly in the light of other demands on government spending. At the same time, both the letter and the spirit of the agreements is for governments to do as much as they can to ensure that people's economic and social rights are met in practice.

Governments could, of course, further their obligation under international law to progressively achieve implementation of economic and social rights by introducing laws that specifically provide people with required measures as a right just as they have laws that provide a right not to suffer discrimination. This would then mean people would have a legal as well as moral automatic entitlement to the measure. It would mean that if a government was not providing the service, then people would have clear legal grounds on which to force the government through the courts to provide the service.

This is why the European Convention on Human Rights is a particularly important international agreement in Ireland, because in 2003 the government introduced an Act which gave legal effect to the provisions of the Convention in Irish law. Social care cases have rarely been taken on the basis of the Convention, but one that was successful is given below.

Rights of Traveller Family to Respect for Private and Family Life, and their Home

In 2007 a Court found that South Dublin County Council's failure to provide a Traveller family, which included three members who were severely disabled, with a second mobile home was in breach of the family's rights under Article 8.1 of the European Convention on Human Rights, which states that 'Everyone has the right to respect for his private and family life, his home and his correspondence'. The Court ordered the Council to remedy the family's living circumstances. The judge said that the case was 'very unusual and unique'. The three who were severely disabled lived with seven other family members, including their parents, in one specially-adapted mobile home. She said, 'It is difficult to comprehend the level of hardship and deprivation' which the three disabled members 'endure between them'. One is confined to a wheelchair and the other two have Hurler syndrome.

Source: Irish Human Rights Commission available at www.ihrc.ie; see also Carolan M. 2007.

Can you think of other examples of living conditions experienced by people living in Ireland which might be considered a breach of their human rights?

EQUALITY RIGHTS FOR PEOPLE WITH DISABILITIES

The Right to Equality

Equality rights are basic rights. They include the right to equal employment for men and women, and for both to be treated equally in pay for doing similar work. These rights are legally established in full, i.e. they do not have to be provided for over time, or progressively realised. A question which then arises is whether people with disabilities should have the same legally provided right for the services they need in order to have the same (or as close as possible) level of equality of opportunity that able-bodied people have. It can be argued that, as things stand, they do not have the same equality rights as everyone else. This is because society does not provide service for their particular needs in a way that would put them on an equal footing with everyone else. When the government was drafting the

Disability Act of 2005, groups representing people with disabilities sought to have an automatic provision of adequate services to meet identified special needs incorporated as a right.

The main point in the argument is the right of disabled people to equal treatment, which for them means having their particular needs provided for so that they can be in the same position as everybody else as far as possible. We live in a society that is organised primarily for the benefit of people who don't have a disability. Health and education services and access to transport and buildings are provided for the majority. However, for people with a disability, society is not organised to meet their needs in a similar way to the way it is organised to meet the needs of the rest of its citizens. You can argue that a child with speaking difficulties has an automatic legal right to the services of a speech and language therapist in order to benefit from their right to a primary education in a way comparable to children without language difficulties. You can argue that a deaf child has an automatic right to have all classes in school provided in sign language and a blind child to have all reading material provided in Braille. As has often been pointed out, if the majority had speech and language difficulties or autism, there would be little question that state services to help overcome these difficulties would be in place, and that people would be seen as having a moral right to get such services automatically on the basis of equality copper-fastened as a right in law. So, through shortcomings in getting adequate services for identified special needs, you can argue that the minority with special needs are not being placed on an equal footing with everyone else, as far as it is possible. The extent to which they lack the provision of services is the extent to which they suffer unequal treatment in society. They are equal members of society who, through no fault of their own, need special services to be able to benefit from society as near as possible to the way everyone else benefits. The extent to which they do not receive needed services is the extent to which they are at an unfair disadvantage and are not being treated equally. There are, of course, special needs services, and there are measures in place to provide for the access to transport and buildings. There is recognition that people with special needs have a right to such services and there is legal provision for services in the Disability Act. However, entitlement to have all services that have been identified to meet special needs *provided in practice* automatically and in full is not seen as a legal right. Much remains to be done to ensure that people do, in fact, get the services they need.

Government's Argument

The main point in the argument against people with disabilities having a legally enforceable right draws from the notion of what Mill calls 'social expediency', and this, in effect, was the government's argument. This is the argument that if providing services for everyone's disability needs is not feasible given the practical implications of doing so, then a legally enforceable right to those services may not have to be provided. It is the argument that providing for them is limited by 'the inevitable conditions of human life, and the general interest' (2008: 199–200).

This is the argument that the government made in saying that society as a whole could not bear the cost of providing such services. To provide the services would be to burden the taxpayer too much or lead to an unacceptable reduction in public provision of other services.

Under the Disability Act, there is a legal entitlement to an independent needs assessment for each individual, as well as entitlement to complaints and appeals procedures. A person with a disability also has legal entitlement to be represented by a personal advocate to work on their behalf for the provision of services. However, there is no automatic legal entitlement to have the actual services themselves provided, services which have been determined to meet the assessment of needs. For health and education needs, provision is subject to regard for 'the practicality' of providing the services as well as regard for meeting the cost within the year's overall financial allocation for services. In effect, instead of getting services for identified needs as of right, people with disabilities will get them subject to resources and where practicable. The same limiting factors of cost and practicability also apply for the legal entitlement of people with disabilities to have services provided for them by public bodies in ways that meet their special needs, services such as making information available in media which they can access.

Achieving Equality Rights for People with Disabilities

An important factor, which Mill points out, is that the argument from social expediency is not set in stone. It is an argument that has always been made against granting to people what they claimed were their rights, and, for a time, social expediency stood in the way of something becoming a right that eventually did become a right.

> The entire history of social improvement has been a series of transitions, by which one custom or institution after another, from being a supposed primary necessity for social existence, has passed into the rank of a universally stigmatized injustice and tyranny.
>
> Mill 2008: 200

Mill cites slavery and discrimination on the basis of colour, race and sex as examples of practices once considered necessary for the public good which, over time, came to be seen as a denial of a right. An example from recent history is the right of women to the same pay as men for similar work.

This point is of particular relevance for advocacy. It means that, through advocating for a change in public opinion and attitude, disability services can move from being granted subject to resources, as at present, to being granted automatically as of right to ensure the disabled do not suffer injustice (see Conaty 2005).

One argument made against people with disabilities, and people with welfare needs in general, having an automatic right to be provided with services is that it clashes with the right that others claim they have to be entitled to their wealth and not have it taxed in order to pay for those services. In Chapter 11 on social justice we will see that Nozick makes this argument in relation to welfare services generally.

If the argument is accepted that being provided with services is an equality right, then it should trump other considerations, such as cost. This is because it can be argued equality rights have an importance that is too basic for their realisation to be left open to an indefinite future. The then Irish Human Rights Commission observed that, while the progressive realisation of economic and social rights is 'a necessary flexible device which takes account of the realities of economic life', greater priority needed to be given in the Disability Bill of 2004 to realising these rights:

> The Bill does not go far enough in putting in place an innovative mechanism of the provision of resources and services which would effectively guarantee the progressive realisation of the rights of persons with disabilities. Further statutory expression of the concept of 'progressive realisation' of the relevant rights is required.
>
> Irish Human Rights Commission 2004: 10 and 2

Exercise 6. 1

Questions to Consider and Discuss

From a human rights perspective, consider and discuss the following examples of treatment of older people, which are based on complaints received by the Health Service Executive:

1. A woman recently discharged from hospital who received no home help visit, despite having been approved for a visit for two hours a day, and as a result was left in bed for two days and three nights. A 'breakdown in communication' was given as the cause.
2. A man suffering from the disabling effects of a stroke who was told by the home care worker that he would have the number of showers he was given reduced to 'at most two a week', after he raised his voice with anxiety

while the care worker was moving him with a hoist.

3. A woman with arthritis who had three heart operations who reported she
    was finding it difficult to cope with daily activities after she had her home
    help service withdrawn. Her case was seen to be 'of a low priority'.

Source: Duncan 2003

Exercise 6. 2

Question to Consider and Discuss: Are the Human Rights of Asylum Seekers in Ireland Being Met?

The former Ombudsman for Ireland, Emily O'Reilly, raised human rights concerns regarding restrictions experienced by families awaiting a decision on their application for asylum in Ireland. She argues that the State may not be meeting its human rights obligations to asylum seekers under the Constitution and international agreements. Asylum seekers are catered for under a policy of direct provision of accommodation which includes provision of meals and a payment of €19.10 a week per adult and €9.60 per child. Her article gives details of the restrictions entailed by the policy, such as the exclusion of asylum seekers from social housing and taking up employment. She states that 'they have almost no personal income, no control over their food and general living conditions and are, in effect, excluded from normal society'. She outlines the difficulties faced by one family, in particular by one child who was suicidal. She also highlights the effect on the childhood of children living under the conditions laid down by the policy, which can be up to five years or more in some cases due to delays in receiving a decision. Read her article, then consider and discuss whether there is a moral obligation on Ireland to do more to try to meet the needs of asylum seekers on the basis of human rights. (See O'Reilly E. 2013 'Dealing with Asylum Seekers: Why Have We Gone Wrong?' available in *Studies: An Irish Quarterly Review*, Summer 2013, Vol. 102, No.46.)

Exercise 6.3

Check out the websites of Amnesty International Ireland and the Irish Human Rights Commission and/or literature for examples of documented human rights issues and cases. Select one example of an abuse and, drawing from your understanding of human rights, explain why the abuse is morally wrong.

CASE STUDY 6. 1

Case Study: Darren's Development

Analyse the case study below by addressing the following questions:

1. What are the ethical issues involved?
2. What are the factors that have contributed to the issues? (Include consideration of further likely background factors.)
3. What care action would you recommend?
4. Drawing from a philosophical understanding of human rights, how you would justify your care action?

Nineteen-year-old Darren has a mild intellectual disability. As part of the development services provided by the day centre he attends, staff try to find work placements for service users who are interested in obtaining work experience. A placement was found for Darren in the local branch of a big supermarket chain where he stacks shelves and checks stock levels. Darren works there unpaid for one day a week. From feedback Darren's care worker has received, she knows that he works very hard to prove that he is capable. She also knows from speaking to Darren that he wants to have his own money so he can buy things for himself, such as his own clothes, and go out more and enjoy himself by socialising in the town with the friends he has made through his work placement.

The supermarket found that it needed more staff, and the manager decided he had better ring the care worker first to see what she would think of Darren working full-time for the going rate of pay. The care worker is delighted for Darren and tells him the good news regarding the offer of full-time work. However, she noticed a slight look of concern on Darren's face, but she did not dwell on it because she was so certain the job would be of great benefit to him. Darren was still living at home, so she rang his parents to let them know what she took to be good news. However, Darren's mother said they did not want Darren working full-time. They were very afraid that if he had his own money that this would lead to him doing more for himself, that he would be going out in the world and placing himself at greater risk, that he had a right to be kept safe, and that she and her husband had a right to peace of mind. She also said that, as Darren's parents, they had a right to decide what was in his best interests. The care worker tried to explain the benefits that working full-time would have for Darren's development, but his mother would hear none of it. In fact, she started to blame the care worker for 'putting notions' in Darren's head that he could do things that he was not able for, and she insisted that his work placement cease. To spare Darren's feelings, she said that the care worker should tell Darren he was being let go because the supermarket now had less need for staff. However, from talking to Darren's father, the care worker feels that he may be more open to the idea of Darren working full-time, but that he tends to go by whatever is wife says.

CASE STUDY 6. 2

Case Study: Young, Vulnerable and at Risk

In the first decade of the twenty-first century, 18 of 37 children who died while in the care of the State died from unnatural causes, which included suicide and drug overdose. Also, 84 of the 151 young people known to social services to be in need of care died of unnatural causes. (Health Service Executive, cited in O'Brien 2010.)

From a human rights perspective, consider and discuss the circumstances of the following young person and his family, together with the shortcomings, requirements and difficulties in providing them with adequate care. The case described is made up for study purposes. (For some details of other cases, see O'Brien 2010; 2008; and 2011; and 'Report into Deaths of 23 Children Raises Concern over Impact of Under-staffing', *The Irish Times*, 15 November 2013.)

As a young social care worker from a loving and well-off family, Betty's eyes were opened to the reality of the lives of people in need of care on her first assignment, which was to work with a senior social worker on a case of suspected parental neglect of fourteen-year-old Jimmy. Before setting out to make contact with Jimmy and his mother, Betty had read the case file and the social worker had briefed her on the family's circumstances. Jimmy's mother had been taken into state care from a young age when her own parents were unable to look after her. She had spent most of her life in different foster care placements, some of which had not worked out and she had run away. In the last year before she turned eighteen, she had been in residential care when she became pregnant with Jimmy. She had been delighted to find she was pregnant, the social worker said, and was determined to give Jimmy the kind of normal childhood she had missed out on. When asked about the father, she had said she did not know who he was, as she'd 'been sleeping round', and she was insistent she wanted to rear Jimmy herself, as she had bad experiences of verbal and physical abuse from her own father. Social services had enabled her to get set up in independent living in a flat. After that, there was no further contact with her or Jimmy until yesterday when the headmaster in Jimmy's school reported to social services that he had not been attending for weeks. Then this morning the gardaí had been in touch with social services to report that Jimmy had been caught robbing and buying drugs from a known dealer.

When Betty asked the social care worker why there had been no follow-up contact over the years, he said the problem is that child care services are stretched by lack of resources, staff shortages and social workers having large caseloads which they cannot cope with. He brought Betty over to his filing cabinet and opened a drawer to show her a row of thin files, all of which he said were reported cases of suspected neglect or other abuse which he had not yet investigated. He said that it was the same for other social workers in child care services, and that they were constantly trying to get management to provide extra staff. Over two hundred extra posts had been promised by the minister, but no recruitment had yet taken place. He said his time, and that of his colleagues, was taken up with emergency cases which came to their notice. As a result of the calls from the headmaster and the gardaí, the senior social worker had approached the section manager with the case, and they decided they had to give priority to checking out Jimmy's home circumstances and putting in place a care plan for him.

Jimmy's last known address was at his mother's flat in an inner city complex where Betty noticed the lifts did not work, there was ugly graffiti on the concrete walls of the stairwell and used syringes for injecting drugs on the landings. Jimmy was not in the flat when they called. His mother looked stressed and nervous, as if she had something to hide, and Betty wondered if she had a drug habit because she looked skin and bone and avoided eye contact. She said she could not remember when she had last seen Jimmy, that it could have been a week ago or maybe longer, and that he tends to come and go when it suits him but never stays long. When told of Jimmy's absence from school and of the call from the gardaí, she broke down and cried. She said that she had always tried to do her best for Jimmy, and that he was a 'really good kid' who 'loved life', despite all she had not been able do for him. She said he was 'easily led', and she feared for him the influence of bad company. Then she started complaining about a problem with blocked sewerage in the pipes and the damp patches on the bedroom walls. She said, 'I don't blame him for not wanting to live here. Look around.' Betty could see the damp on the walls, broken furniture and remains of meals that had not been cleaned up and disposed of.

When Betty and the social worker met up with Jimmy after making enquiries of young homeless people in the area, she was surprised by his happy-go-lucky manner. But on reflection, she could not help feeling he was putting on an act, trying to show that he was streetwise and could look after himself, but that underneath he was scared. When the social worker suggested he go back and live with his mother and resume school, he protested: 'Me Ma has her own life to live and what's the point in going to school – getting jeered and fighting.' They arranged emergency hostel accommodation for Jimmy as a temporary measure. 'He really needs secure residential care or foster care', the social worker said. 'An emergency hostel is no solution. Young people accommodated there have to leave the premises early after breakfast and can't go back in until the evening, and they are left hanging about the streets all day, with little or no money. It's not surprising they get involved in robbing and drinking and drug-taking to ease the pain and for something to do. But it won't be easy to get a place for him, and even then it may not work out, as some young people can still find it difficult to cope. They need the ongoing support from psychological services to help them face early childhood experiences that are affecting their present behaviour, but they can be waiting months to be seen by a psychologist given the waiting list and the shortage of psychologists in social services.' 'The really sad thing', Betty said, 'is that he doesn't seem to realise how vulnerable he is. It's as if he had accepted his life on the street is normal. He has no expectancies for anyone to do anything for him.'

CRITICAL EVALUATION

Are Rights Natural?

A crucial point about rights is the claim that natural laws exist which provide a basis for how people should behave, and rights can be seen to follow from the existence of such natural laws. But is it true that there is something called natural law which lays down basic features of human living that people find naturally good and other features naturally bad? Is it a step too far to give certain basic human characteristics the status of law, i.e. something that underlies and directs how people should live? You can argue that to derive the status of law from some basic features is to put a construction on them which they do not naturally have. Aquinas, for example, as we have seen, claims that it is self-evident to reason that there are basic natural human inclinations to preserve life, form a family and live in society, and that laws naturally follow from this obliging people and governments to support practices and behaviours which accord with such inclinations as naturally good, and to also rule out other practices and behaviours as naturally bad which undermine these inclinations. It is claimed, then, that natural rights follow from the self-evidence of these basic inclinations which indicate natural laws. Such rights include a right to have your life preserved and not left at preventable risk, a right of families to protection, and a right as an individual to be treated equally with others in society. It is some version of this argument which underlies the claim that natural law exists from which there are natural rights. But is natural law self-evident to reason in this way?

While people can certainly be considered to have basic inclinations arising from their nature, this does *not prove* they have a resulting set of rights. For some philosophers natural rights are not self-evident. Vardy and Grosh (1999: 198) make the point that if natural rights existed 'it would be as if each infant were born with an indelible stamp on his or her forehead indicating the list of rights which must not, in any circumstances, be interfered with because they were implanted there by Nature.' Clearly this is not the case. There is not the same physical or empirical evidence (i.e. evidence from any of the five senses) for natural rights as there is for the brain and heart we are born with. Rights in this sense are not self-evident.

In addition, if rights are self-evident, then you would expect they would be readily respected. However, the actual behaviour of people and governments throughout history down to the present day has often flown in the face of a recognition that human beings have natural rights. This is cited as evidence that there are no such things as human rights, or at least that if there are such rights that they are far from being self-evident from nature. d'Entreves (1964: 74) makes this point when he says that the history of human behaviour is 'the stumbling block of all natural law theories' and, as we have seen, the main philosophical source for the existence of rights is natural law. However, you could argue that violations of human rights don't disprove the existence of human rights as derived from nature. All that the violations show is how weak and imperfect human beings are morally.

Nevertheless, the reason of lack of self-evidence for the natural existence of rights led Bentham to dismiss the notion of natural rights as 'nonsense' and the notion of absolute natural rights as 'nonsense on stilts' (cited by Almond 2004: 266). Also, for MacIntyre 'there are no self-evident truths', and 'natural and human rights then are fictions' (1985: 69–70).

Neither Bentham nor MacIntyre are arguing against treating people in a way that having human rights suggests. All they are arguing is that the existence of human rights cannot be justified philosophically.

Essential Interests and Rational Agency Theories

Both theories certainly identify basic, desirable features of human life which strongly suggest that everyone should be entitled to them. But do they actually prove that we have a right to them? They also seem to be based on accepting some account of human nature, of accepting some features or qualities of being human as natural, and which make a set of rights rationally justifiable. In effect, they are also arguing that it is somehow self-evident to reason that rights follow from the basic features of being human. However, as we have seen, it is not necessarily self-evident to reason that rights follow from basic human needs and interests, and philosophers take issue with the idea that there is a basis in nature for rights. Put slightly differently, while there are certainly basic natural interests and requirements, rights themselves are not part of nature, and it could be that we impose them on nature, for understandable reasons, rather than being able to justifiably derive them from nature.

Are Rights Universal?

It is also argued that to regard people as having natural rights is a particular Western way of thinking which is not found in the same way in other traditions and cultures. Irish political philosopher Edmund Burke (1729–1797) was among the first to criticise the universality of natural rights. For him, a person does have rights, but they are not the same rights for everyone universally. Instead, they arise out of, and are particular to, a person's cultural tradition, and it remains open for rights to be regarded differently within different cultures. From an historical perspective, the idea of natural, individual rights emerged out of a particular Western tradition of thought, and proponents of universal rights are sometimes criticised for not having enough respect for different cultural traditions, such as in some Eastern countries, where values of fitting into a community by, for example, living according to what people believe to be God's law can be given more importance than individual rights. But whether the fact that rights have a particular Western origin and have not the same appeal in other parts of the world is an argument against regarding rights as having universal validity is open to debate (see Langlois 2009).

Legal Acceptance of Some Rights

Despite the difficulty of proving that rights naturally exist, there is a definite sense in which rights *do exist* – this is as part of international agreements and covenants (Vardy and Grosh 1999: 199). Here they are known as human rights, and the reference to them as 'natural' is dropped. Almond also makes this point (2004: 261) when she says, 'The practical discussions of rights . . . are likely to involve what are today called human rights. The justification of rights of this sort is essentially ethical, although the international community, in attempting to enshrine them in law, seeks to convert their justification into a matter of fact and practice.' It is for this reason that instead of reference to 'rights', the phrase *legally protected interests* is sometimes used.

Does Lack of Proof Matter?

Does it matter if it cannot be proved that each person has certain human rights? Can we not just take it that it is highly desirable to look on people as having rights? Well, of course we can. However, the point is that the lack of a clear and universally accepted theoretical justification for human rights may be seen as making it easier for people and governments not to provide for rights in practice. If rights are provided for specifically in law, then they can be enforced through legal action. The problem is that if human rights in practice are viewed only as a product of international agreement, then the level of moral compulsion that agreements can afford is not as strong as it would be if rights could be proved to exist morally. Also, lack of clear and compelling moral proof for the existence of rights makes it easier for governments to avoid providing people with their rights. It makes it easier for them to postpone implementing rights agreements and to break agreements. If there was clear and compelling proof, it would underpin the understanding for rights to be provided in practice. (See Buckle 2004: 168.)

Rights as Expansive and Individualistic

Blackburn raises concerns about the lack of limits to the rights which people could assert they have. He wonders how far the state is obliged to go to meet all the possible rights which could be asserted. For example, the UN Covenant commits governments to provide for a person's 'economic, social and cultural rights indispensable to his dignity and free development of his personality'. This could arguably include people being seen to have a right to extensive lists of services, and he raises a concern that in requiring governments to be responsible for extensive rights we may be taking away from people the responsibility for their own development.

Also, for Blackburn, emphasis on the language of rights tends to lead to a cultural climate in which people look out for their own individual needs. This takes away from a communal climate of people living together and supporting each other. He sees people asserting their own entitlements, regardless of the effect that this will have on others (2002: 103–7).

REVIEW

The idea that people have rights has proved an effective moral justification for bringing about social and political improvements. There is a philosophical difficulty proving that people actually do have rights. The claim that it is self-evident that people have rights from the existence of common natural tendencies is open to challenge. However, rights have become incorporated into international agreements and domestic law. Whether viewed as rights or legally protected interests, they can provide legal force for provision of certain welfare services. At the same time, services do not have to be provided automatically in full unless there is specific legal requirement to do so, but under international agreements they must be progressively realised.

FURTHER READING

Banks, S. (2006) *Ethics and Values in Social Work*, 3rd ed., Palgrave Macmillan (check Chapter 5).

Fagan A. 'Human Rights', *Internet Encyclopaedia of Philosophy* available at www. iep.utm.edu/ (accessed 17/07/2013).

Norman, R. (1998) *The Moral Philosophers: An Introduction to Ethics*, 2nd ed., Oxford University Press ('Rights-Based Ethics' pp. 185–189).

The Peter McVerry Trust at www.pmvtrust.ie.

REFERENCES

Almond, B. (2004) 'Rights' in *A Companion to Ethics*, P. Singer (ed.), Blackwell.

Aquinas, Saint Thomas (1998) *On Law, Morality and Politics*, W. Baumgarth and R. Regan SJ (eds.), Hackett.

Blackburn, S. (2002) *Being Good: A Short Introduction to Ethics*, Oxford University Press.

Buckle, S. (2004) 'Natural Law' in *A Companion to Ethics*, P. Singer (ed.), Blackwell.

Carolan M. (2007) 'Rights of Disabled Travellers Breached', *The Irish Times*, 23 May 2007.

Conaty F. (2005) 'A Missed Opportunity to Advance Equal Rights', *The Irish Times*, 29 April 2005.

Copleston, F. (1957) *Aquinas*, Pelican Books.

d'Entreves, A. (1964) *Natural Law: An Introduction to Legal Philosophy*, Hutcheson University Library.

Duncan, P. 2003 'Home Is Anything but a Safe Haven for Some Vulnerable Elderly Citizens', *The Irish Times*, 4 June 2013.

Finnis, J. (1980) *Natural Law and Natural Rights*, Clarendon Press Oxford.

Gewirth, A. (1982) *Human Rights, Essays on Justification and Applications*, University of Chicago Press.

Irish Human Rights Commission (2013) 'Features of the European Convention on Human Rights Act 2003', available at www.ihrc.ie (accessed 15 July 2013).

Irish Human Rights Commission (2013) 'Observations on the Disability Bill 2004', available at www.ihrc.ie (accessed 15 July 2013).

Jeffers J. (2003) 'The Fate of Natural Law in Irish Constitutional Jurisprudence: Dead or Alive?', available at www.nuigalway.ie (accessed 9 July 2013).

Lally C. (2013) 'St Patrick's to Close over "Very Disturbing" Conditions', *The Irish Times*, 4 July 2013.

Langlois A. J. (2009) 'Normative and Theoretical Foundations of Human Rights' in *Human Rights: Politics & Practice*, M. Goodhart (ed.), Oxford University Press.

MacIntyre, A. (1985) *After Virtue*, Duckworth.

McClelland, J. S. (2002) *A History of Western Political Thought*, Routledge.

Mill, J. S. (2008) *On Liberty and Other Essays*, Oxford World's Classics.

O'Brien, C. (2010) 'Deaths Total, Children Who Died in Care', *The Irish Times*, 5 June 2010. (For some details of other cases, see also O'Brien C. 'Teenager Deaths in HSE Care', *The Irish Times*, 24 April 2010; 'Life and Death on the Streets', *The Irish Times Weekend Review*, 18 October 2008; and 'Children at Risk, Cases Not Being Followed up', *The Irish Times*, 2 August 2011.)

O'Reilly, E. (2013) 'Dealing with Asylum Seekers: Why Have We Gone Wrong?' in *Studies, An Irish Quarterly Review*, Summer 2013, Vol. 102, No. 46.

Reilly, Judge Michael (2013) 'Annual Report of the Office of the Inspector of Prisons 2012', Office of the Inspector of Prisons.

Vardy, P. and Grosh, P. (1999) *The Puzzle of Ethics*, HarperCollins (Chapter 16).

Note: The rights agreements and laws referred to can be accessed on the internet by keying in the relevant title.

7
Greatest Happiness Principle

OVERALL AIM

To explore an influential principle which claims to show that the happiness of everyone is equally important.

LEARNING OUTCOMES

At the end of this chapter you should be able to:

- Explain the basis of the greatest happiness principle in the idea of equality and desire for happiness.
- Describe happiness in terms of avoiding pain and increasing pleasure.
- Explain how happiness is estimated in ethical decision-making.
- Appreciate the role the principle played in the introduction and development of the welfare state.
- Draw from the principle to support reducing hardship by meeting welfare needs.
- Draw from the principle as a guide in providing care in group settings.
- Demonstrate understanding for some of the main criticisms of the principle.

INTRODUCTION

Not everyone does well in society. Some people are said to 'lose out' or to 'get left behind' in relation to their standard of living. They experience unhappiness or misery from poverty. In caring for clients, care workers will frequently come across cases where poverty is a big factor in the reasons why clients need care. They may need direct help with food, clothing, bill payments or housing. The State provides a range of welfare services for those requiring help, e.g. jobseekers' supports, family income supplement and back-to-school clothing and footwear allowance. Also, voluntary agencies such as St Vincent de Paul and the Simon Community provide direct help with basic needs. In some cases clients may not be aware of their legal entitlements to welfare services and care workers can play an important role in helping them to obtain a service.

Poverty remains a significant source of hardship and misery for many people in Ireland. In the chapter on empathy, we saw how poverty is defined in terms of social exclusion from a lack of income and resources; income and resources that people not living in poverty have as a normal part of their lives. There are also certain criteria that show the number of people affected by each of three types of poverty. The numbers are compiled by the Central Statistics Office from a Survey of Income and Living Conditions (SILC), and are updated annually. (The figures cited here are for those in each category in 2011, the latest available at time of writing. For updated figures, check the website of the Central Statistics Office; for other source material on poverty see also the website of the Office of Social Inclusion.)

People at Risk of Poverty

People in this category are those living in households where the income is 60 per cent of the median or middle point of the scale of all incomes. In 2011, 16 per cent of people were at risk of experiencing poverty (up from 14.7 per cent in 2010). At-risk-of poverty is also known as relative poverty, relative, that is, to the standard of living experienced by others in Irish society.

People Experiencing Material Deprivation

People in this category are deprived of at least two items in a list of eleven. It is *enforced deprivation*, i.e. not a choice. In 2011, 24.5 per cent – almost a quarter of the population – experienced material deprivation (up from 22.6 per cent in 2010). They are unable to afford:

1.   Two pairs of strong shoes.
2.   A warm waterproof coat.
3.   New (not second-hand) clothes.
4.   A meal with meat, chicken or fish (or vegetarian equivalent) every second day.
5.   A roast joint or its equivalent once a week.
6.   Heating at some stage in the last year.
7.   Keeping their house adequately warm.
8.   Buying presents for family or friends at least once a year.
9.   Replacing any worn-out furniture.
10.   Having family or friends for a drink or meal once a month.
11.   Having a morning, afternoon or evening out in the last fortnight for entertainment.

People in Consistent Poverty

This is also known as the *combined income-deprivation measure*. People whose income is below the at-risk-of or relative poverty line of 60 per cent of the median and who also lack two or more items from the deprivation list are regarded as living in consistent poverty. The figure in 2011 for those experiencing this form of poverty was 6.9 per cent of the population (up from 6.3 per cent in 2010).

Groups Most Represented in Poverty

Those who are represented the most among people experiencing poverty are children, the unemployed, lone parents, people with disabilities and the elderly.

Some Effects of Poverty

Poverty is a contributory factor for a range of personal and social problems. It is linked, for example, to child neglect, addictions, homelessness, substance abuse, poor health, domestic violence and crime. Of course, not everyone who is poor experiences personal and social problems as a result, but for some it is a pressure in their lives which makes it more likely that they will go on to experience a problem.

Child poverty is a particular care need in Ireland. It is linked to a range of problems which children go on to experience, such as educational under-achievement, welfare dependency and crime. In 2012 there were 6, 249 children in the care of the State. A minority are taken into care for reasons of physical or sexual abuse. For the majority, the causes relate to neglect due to poverty and the inability of parents to cope. Some children also experience homelessness, where they are living in temporary accommodation, such as B&Bs or with relatives, with or without their parents, or street homelessness, where they are exposed to a range of risks to their safety and health. (For information on child poverty in particular, see Barnardos Ireland website, which includes the report 'Measuring Children's Perception and Experiences of Deprivation' produced by Trinity College's Children's Research Centre. Information on the policy for tackling poverty in Ireland can be found in the 'National Action Plan for Social Inclusion' available on Office of Social Inclusion website.)

In this chapter, we will look at a moral theory that supports the requirement for as much as possible to be done to help people in need, in particular those who experience poverty. The greatest happiness principle relates to providing the greatest happiness for the greatest number of people, and it sees the happiness of everyone as equally important. The theory from which the greatest happiness principle comes is known as utilitarianism.

UTILITARIANISM

Two Basic Features

The utilitarian view is based on accepting that there is:

- A basic equality and freedom of all citizens in a democratic society.
- A desire for happiness on the part of each person.

In this sense, equality means a basic equality of worth or importance which *all* citizens have, independent of actual economic or social position. Since all are equal and have an equal right to happiness, Mill claims that it follows from this that everyone's happiness should be catered for as much as possible. He believes that 'society between equals can only exist on the understanding that the interests of all are to be regarded equally' (Mill 2008: 165).

First, a more basic question needs to be answered: why should we, or society, be concerned about the happiness of others? Why not just suit ourselves? Being concerned with the happiness of others is called 'altruism'. Mill claims that being concerned about the happiness of others is its own good and has its own benefit. He gives three reasons why we should look out for others or be altruistic.

1. Altruism is Part of Human Nature

He speaks of 'the desire to be in unity with our fellow creatures, which is already a powerful principle in human nature'. He adds that 'the social state' is 'natural' and 'necessary' and that a direct impulse to promote the general good may be one of the habitual modes of action in every individual (2008: 149). At the same time, Mill is realistic in recognising that people normally act from mixed motives, which include satisfying their own interests (2008: 145). This is a view similar to Aristotle's – that human nature is essentially social.

2. Altruism is Pleasurable

We can learn from experience that caring for others is a pleasure. Mill refers to people who are lucky enough to be able to satisfy their own pleasures to the extent they desire, but who remain dissatisfied. He says the reason they remain dissatisfied is because if they are caring for nobody but themselves, they miss out on one pleasure essential for anyone's happiness, which is the pleasure that comes from acting in the interests of others (2008: 144–5).

3. Altruism Proves Itself in Practice as the Meaning of Ethics

Mill appeals to the psychological facts of experience when he holds that the more we have a society working on the basis of people co-operating to provide for the interests of each other, the more this will become confirmed in people's minds as the overall meaning of ethics. In other words, we will recognise that to behave altruistically is the right way to behave (2008: 165–6).

The Principle

We have seen that utilitarianism accepts that everyone has a basic equality and desire for happiness. To form the principle, these two elements are combined into one statement. The principle was first put forward by the founder of utilitarianism, Jeremy Bentham (1748–1832). It is the principle that the good is that which provides for the greatest happiness of the greatest number of people. He named it in short 'the Greatest Happiness Principle'.

This principle provides a criterion for judging actions. The criterion is that an action is good as far as it produces more happiness than unhappiness for the greatest number of people and it is bad as far as it produces more unhappiness or misery than happiness.

Mill (1806–73) begins his essay 'Utilitarianism' by stating the basic principle laid down by Bentham: 'The creed which accepts as the foundation of morals, Utility, or the Greatest Happiness Principle, holds that actions are right in proportion as they tend to promote happiness, wrong as they tend to produce the reverse of happiness' (2008: 137).

Meaning of Happiness: Utility, Pleasure

But what is happiness? The first thing to strike anyone about the question is that happiness can mean different things to different people. We have seen how it means *flourishing* for Aristotle. Bentham, however, takes a basic, practical view of the meaning of happiness to try to ensure it accommodates everyone's view. To start with, like Aristotle, he regards happiness as what everyone desires. At the most basic level, he says we desire to avoid pain and increase our pleasure. 'Nature has placed mankind under the governance of two sovereign masters, *pain* and *pleasure*. It is for them alone to point out what we ought to do, as well as to determine what we shall do' (Bentham 1988: 1). In addition, Bentham did not make any distinction in quality between what gives people pleasure. It is a matter of whatever appeals to the individual.

Mill agrees with Bentham in identifying happiness with pleasure. 'By happiness is meant intended pleasure, and the absence of pain; by unhappiness pain and the privation of pleasure' (2008: 137). We desire things for our happiness, either because they give us pleasure or they are a means to obtaining pleasure. We avoid them because they cause us pain or are a means of avoiding pain (2008: 137). Pleasure is understood in both its physical and emotional senses. Mill points out that the term 'utiltarianism' comes from 'utility', i.e. that which is useful, and what is useful includes whatever agrees with us or gives us pleasure (2008: 136). For Mill, also, happiness refers to the interest of every individual (2008: 148). Everybody seeks to have their preferred interests satisfied as well as possible, and, instead of 'happiness', some utilitarians today use the term 'satisfaction preference'.

Higher Pleasures

For Mill, what gives us pleasure is not confined to the satisfaction of our bodily desires for good food, wine or sex. He provides what he sees as a more refined understanding in claiming that some activities enable us to enjoy higher pleasures. 'Human beings have faculties more elevated than the animal appetites, and when once made conscious of them, do not regard anything as happiness which does not include their gratification' (2008: 138–9). Higher pleasures include enjoyment of music or nature or company.

Mill is sometimes accused of being high-minded in claiming that pleasures of the intellect or spirit are higher than those of the bodily senses, but he says it is simply a fact of human experience that people find such pleasures indispensable to their happiness once they get to know them. It is 'an unquestionable fact that those who are equally acquainted with, and equally capable of appreciating and enjoying, both, do give a most marked preference to the manner of existence which employs the higher faculties' (2008: 139). So, he is not imposing a high-minded view of pleasure by having recourse to some moral authority such as human reason – he is not trying to lecture us on what is good for us. Instead he is leaving it up to people to decide from their own experience the kind of things that give them pleasure and constitute their happiness once they are 'qualified by knowledge' of both types. People themselves are 'the only competent judges'. There is 'no other tribunal to be referred to' (2008: 141).

The Equally Deserving Happiness of All

The key point of utilitarian ethics is that judgments about good and bad or right and wrong relate not just to my own preference for happiness, but also to the preferences of others who may be affected. The theory requires us to treat our own happiness as no more important (but no less either) than their happiness. This means that in making judgments about how best to behave, we must regard ourselves 'as strictly impartial as a disinterested and benevolent spectator' (2008: 148).

However, as individuals in our ordinary daily affairs, we can't literally take everybody's happiness into account – this is beyond our capacity. Realistically, we can take into account only the happiness of those few with whom we are involved, but in doing so we are playing our part in contributing to the greatest happiness of the greatest number. Those, however, who engage in forming public policy and making the law are in a position to take decisions for the happiness of everybody. Therefore, they should always take into account the preferences not just of some, but also of all (2008: 17–18). If this can be done by reducing the great misery of a few at little cost to everyone else, then this is the morally right policy. In the next section we will try to make clear why this is required by the principle.

Not Necessarily Majority Preference

A utilitarian is not saying that right and wrong depends solely on what the majority see as their happiness. It is not a matter of *counting heads* or simple democracy. The greatest happiness principle has sometimes been misinterpreted in this way. The principle requires us to produce the *greatest happiness* of the greatest number. This means that if a particular decision produces a larger amount of happiness for a minority (say through relief of misery) compared to a small reduction in happiness for the majority, then that decision is justified if it produces the greatest happiness overall. In making a decision, all the amounts of happiness produced for individuals have to be added together (aggregated) and set against the amount of loss in happiness others may experience from the decision to see which is the biggest: the increase or loss in happiness. If there is a bigger loss in happiness than there is a production of it, then the decision is wrong. But if there is a bigger production of happiness overall than a loss, then the decision is morally right. For example, if instead of spending money on a new state-of-the-art sports stadium, which would bring some happiness to a lot of people, the government could bring more overall happiness by using the money to provide a care service such as long-term accommodation for the homeless, then using the money for the care service is the morally correct decision even though it would benefit relatively few people. Once the benefit to the minority results in the greatest overall amount of happiness, then it is justified.

Estimating Consequences: Giving Weight to Subjective Factors

For Mill, as we have seen, pleasures differ not just in quantity but also in quality. This means there is a huge difficulty in being able to measure the quality of one pleasure with another. The same problem arises in measuring the extent of hardship people suffer due to their particular conditions. To be able to accurately measure pleasure and hardship, we would need to be able to isolate people's subjective experience of them in relation to some highly variable factors, such as intensity and duration. It is simply not possible. Thus, for Mill, instead of any actual measurement, all we can do is come up with our best estimate. This is done by considering the consequences our decision will have for ourselves and others.

Consequentialism

If the consequences of our decision to act in a certain way, *in so far as we can know those consequences*, produce more happiness over unhappiness, then the action is morally right. If the consequences produce more unhappiness, then the action is morally wrong. The only relevant factor in making the estimation is consequences (2008: 151). For this reason, utilitarian theory is often called 'consequentialism'. Phrases that express the consequentialist approach to ethics include 'for the greater good' and when we advise against an action because it will do 'more harm than good'.

Steps in Estimating Consequences

To try and estimate consequences of an action in terms of the pleasure or harm it will bring for people is difficult. If it's to be done accurately and thoroughly, we may often need to:

1. Map out the different courses of action which we could decide on as a response to an issue or problem.
2. Estimate the consequences each course will have for all concerned, and link those consequences to our estimation of people's preferences and the extent to which they will bring them pleasure or pain.
3. Treat everyone's preference for pleasure or happiness, our own included, as of equal value.

Rule and Act Utilitarians

As a help in estimating which consequences will generally produce the most happiness, some utilitarians believe we should follow rules. Rule utilitarians claim that we should not decide on which *particular* act is the best, but which *type* of act, if done by most people, would produce the greatest happiness of the greatest number. They advocate sticking to certain rules as the best way of achieving the happiness of everybody. They say we can learn what these rules should be from experience of the type of actions that tend to cause unhappiness or happiness. For example, they argue that there should be a rule requiring everybody to tell the truth and not tell lies because experience tells us that lying generally causes more unhappiness than happiness. Mill is a rule utilitarianist. However, he does not believe in following rules at any cost. He recognises that the complicated nature of human affairs will always throw up justifiable exceptions to the rules (2008: 157). Mill's allowance for exceptions is quoted in the critical evaluation of Kant's ethics in Chapter 3.

Act utilitarians, on the other hand, hold that each act has to be examined on its own merits. In other words, we have to keep an open mind and not decide in advance on which act will produce the greatest happiness of the greatest number. Moral decisions have to be made on a case-by-case basis. For example, an act utilitarian would say that we should be truthful and honest about a particular matter only if it can be shown that this brings more happiness to all concerned than unhappiness.

GREATEST HAPPINESS PRINCIPLE AND SOCIAL CARE

Inclusion of Others on an Equal Basis

The principle is directly related to social care since it requires people to be concerned with the happiness of others at least as much as with their own happiness. In addition, since governments are in a position to make decisions affecting the happiness of everyone, it requires social policies to provide for the happiness of everyone where everyone is treated as having an equal desire for happiness.

Guide for Decision-making in Casework

Situations frequently arise in care work where the behaviour of a client is having a negative effect on other clients in care. As a result, care teams have to make hard decisions about the happiness of both the particular client and the other clients. Estimating the greatest happiness produced overall by a particular decision can be *one way* they could morally justify a particular decision. Here it is important to emphasise again that giving priority to an individual client who has particular needs may produce the greatest happiness overall – on the other hand, it may not. This is what has to be estimated, and a judgment made.

Gives Priority to Reducing Suffering

In general, the theory regards relief of suffering as the main way in which the most happiness can be provided overall. In other words, it takes the view that more happiness is likely to come from relief of suffering than from providing additional pleasure to those who are not suffering.

Social Policy Influence

In devising his utilitarian theory, Bentham was motivated by the need for social reform to end poverty. In particular, he wanted to end the position in which the wealthy and powerful in British society at the time enjoyed privileges which gave them an advantage over everybody else. His aim was to provide an overall ethical principle to guide political decision-making, especially in the way that those decisions are enshrined in law.

For Mill, too, deprivation of one kind or another was the only real obstacle in the way of bringing about happiness for almost everybody (2008: 145–6). He believed that 'all the grand courses, in short, of human suffering are in a great degree, many of them almost entirely, conquerable by human care and effort' (2008: 146).

Education to Empower Citizens to Make Informed Choices

In particular, Mill saw a need for education. Through education, people can also come to realise what is of value or worth for their happiness or pleasure. He especially believed that education would enable people to appreciate the higher pleasures that contribute most to a happy life. Through education, people can also come to realise better how their own interest is bound up with the interest of others. Education, too, he believed, is central to developing in people a sense of individual freedom, which for him is a core value. The realisation of personal freedom is necessary to ensure that people can determine their own lives and not have authority imposed on them. His classic essay, *On Liberty*, is one of the foundational pieces of writing in support of liberalism.

GREATEST HAPPINESS PRINCIPLE AND IRISH BANKING CRISIS: CASE STUDY EVALUATION

Background Sketch

During a period of about ten years up to 2008, Irish society experienced an economic boom. Effectively, there was full employment, high wages and easy access to loans from banks. The rapid economic growth proved unsustainable and collapsed dramatically in 2008 due to a crisis in the banks. The government stepped in to save the banks by giving a blanket state guarantee that it would support the banks with taxpayers' money, in particular, by paying the banks' liabilities to institutional investors (i.e. bondholders).

The Irish crisis had its roots in an international financial crisis, which began in the US, where banks had been issuing loans, called 'sub-prime' mortgages, on a wide scale to people who were at risk of being unable to repay them. The lender banks packaged the loans into financial products and sold them on to other banks around the world. When many of the original borrowers defaulted on repaying their loans, the financial system suffered a crisis. Banks no longer trusted each other's creditworthiness and stopped lending to each other, which resulted in the flow of money drying up.

One of the roots of the lending practices, which led to the crisis, lies in the idea that it is considered a good thing to allow banks have more freedom from government regulation to develop and sell financial products and make investments. For Tony Judt in his book *Ill Fares the Land*, one source for this idea came from an argument made by Friedrich Hayek. He had argued, in his book *The Road to Serfdom* (first published in 1944), that people need maximum freedom from government management of the economy to provide a safeguard against the re-emergence of extreme left-wing and right-wing dictatorships which had been a feature of the first decades of the twentieth century.

Hayek also argued that morality is, in essence, a matter of personal freedom and responsibility, and that when moral requirements are offloaded into political programmes which provide for the social good, our sense of morality loses touch with its roots. Where morality becomes lodged in the implementation of ideas for the common good, it is placed at a remove from its connection to personal responsibility, choice and voluntary self-sacrifice (Hayek 1993: 156–7). These ideas are said to have influenced Milton Friedman and other economists of 'the Chicago School'. Their ideas found favour with the governments of Thatcher and Reagan in the 1980s, who deregulated the financial markets to give financial institutions more freedom from government (see Judt 2010: 97–106).

Before the crisis, Irish banks had easy access to borrowing on the international markets, money that they then lent out to property developers in particular and to home and commercial property buyers. It was this money in large measure that funded the property boom during a period when Ireland became known for having what was called a 'Celtic Tiger' economy.

The crisis resulted in the government borrowing €67.5 billion from a 'troika' of international lenders (the European Union, European Central Bank and the International Monetary Fund) to keep the Irish banks and country going. Economically and socially, the crisis led to a sharp deterioration in people's living circumstances. Consequences included wage cuts, businesses closing, high unemployment, personal debt (particularly mortgage debt on houses bought for inflated prices, which they were believed to be worth at the time), and high emigration. The crisis also led to cutbacks in government spending on care and other services through 'austerity budgets', as part of the means of servicing the borrowing from the troika and restoring the country's finances. So, what went wrong?

Some Findings in the Honohan and Nyberg Reports

Domestic Responsibility

Two government-commissioned reports, known as the Honohan report (2010) and the Nyberg report (2011), include an examination of the conduct and practices of people in senior positions in the institutions central to the development and management of the crisis.

Nyberg found that the international roots of the crisis 'did not in themselves cause the crisis in Ireland though they helped precipitate it' (ii). He refers to a background in Ireland during the boom years of 'a national speculative mania', which was 'centred on the property market' (i). In a similar vein, Honohan refers to 'construction frenzy' (1.30). He found it characteristic in such a mania for 'households, banks and public authorities' to be 'willing to let the good times roll on until the very last minute', though in Ireland's case this 'may have been exceptional' (ii).

Nyberg found that the mania could have been resisted, and that some of the causes of the crisis lay in 'domestic Irish decisions and actions' (ii). For Honohan, 'there is *prima facie* evidence of a comprehensive failure of bank management and direction to maintain safe and sound banking practices' (1.30). He found also that, 'In an important sense, the major responsibility lies with the directors and senior managements of the banks that got into trouble' (1.6).

Bank Practices and Conduct

The main practice that got banks into trouble was 'risky borrowing and lending behaviour' (Honohan 1.21), as they sought to maintain and increase their share of the property market in competition with one another and increase their profits. The larger banks 'tolerated a gradual lowering of retail standards' by, for example, advancing 100 per cent mortgage loans in some cases (1.20) and not ensuring they kept adequate loan documentation (1.10). Honohan also found that financial incentives, which banking staff and mortgage brokers were given to sell loans, probably contributed (1. 6). Nyberg found a 'willingness of banks to accept higher risks by providing more and shockingly larger loans' (ii). Honohan also says that 'the banks were naturally prone to over-optimism, and even (later) denial' (1.17). Nyberg also found 'groupthink' and 'herding' significant causes of bank failures. In groupthink people think alike; they are focused on the same goals and the same means of achieving them, with little or no critical discussion or evaluation of what they are doing. Herding is where people automatically follow each other by moving in the same direction, as Nyberg found the main banks did in pursuing profits through giving out increasingly risky loans, to property developers in particular (iv). Both reports also found that few people were prepared to challenge the consensus view, and that there was pressure to conform. Contrary views were unwelcome and discouraged and could have career costs for individuals (Honohan 1.16; Nyberg iii).

Government

Honohan found that factors which contributed to 'the unsustainable structure of spending in the Irish economy' included government policies which boosted the construction sector. The government also increasingly relied on the sector and 'other insecure sources' for tax revenues (1.3). On the government's blanket guarantee of the banks' liabilities, which led to such costly economic and social effects, Honohan outlined that there were enough warning signs of failing banks for the government to have been better prepared during the previous year, before making the fateful decision taken under pressure on the night of 29 September 2008. He found that while some form of guarantee would still have been necessary, it need not have been as extensive as it was. If it had been less extensive, it would have left open more options for assisting the banks which could have reduced the cost to the State (1.25).

For Nyberg, the core problem about the guarantee was a lack of accurate information. Decisions were made on 'the erroneous assumption that all banks were and would remain solvent' (ix). With more consideration of the implications of the interruption in the flow of foreign funding, which was then occurring, a link to the fact that the banks were insolvent 'could perhaps have been uncovered' (viii), and had it been uncovered, the government would have been in a position to consider other, less costly options. Also, Honohan found that state authorities charged with oversight of the banking sector, the Central Bank and the Financial Regulator, had 'an unduly deferential approach' in their dealings with the banks (1.13).

Ethical Evaluation

Nyberg made the point that it was characteristic of 'the mania' that 'traditional values, analysis and rules could be less observed … because their relevance was seen as lost in the new and different world' (i). So, what were the traditional values and rules that became 'less observed'? We will look at two here: the greatest happiness principle and the social value of virtue. But it is important to recognise first that it was far from the case that everyone was caught up in the 'national speculative mania' to which Nyberg refers. It was not the case that 'we all partied', to quote the then Minister for Finance Brian Lenihan in November 2010. Many young couples and others were simply buying a family home, and in 2007 there were still many people suffering from the hardship of poverty and other social problems. (See first edition of this book for some examples.)

Clearly, the practices outlined in the previous sections are not in keeping with the greatest happiness principle, in either a strict form where people's interests are regarded as equal, or in a lesser form where at least some account has to be taken of other people's interests. The practices were focused on the banks' own short-term interests as they saw them at the time. By providing loans that people wanted, they were of course providing an economic and social service, and the country appeared to be doing well. However, there is no indication they were behaving from a deeper awareness that it was in the best interests of everybody, in particular with concern for the longer term consequences. In the end, the practices were also shown to have been against their own interests as well as the interest of society at large, which indicates the extent to which providing for the greatest happiness of the greatest number of people was not a guiding principle.

Also, since government has particular responsibility to rule in the best interests of everybody in the country, there is no sign either that it was conscious of trying to follow a greatest happiness principle. For both banks and government, the finding that criticism of their practices and policies was discouraged indicates their unwillingness to look deeper into whether the benefits of their practices and policies were ultimately in everybody's interest.

For Aristotle, too, as we saw earlier, it is because of the naturally existing ties we have to family, friends and community that any decision we make for our own good should take account of the effect it will have on others to ensure their well-being is given its due and is at least not adversely affected.

Traditionally, banking (and good government) is understood to be based on practising the virtue of prudence. Prudence is behaving in a cautious way and with forethought. In particular, it is seen as necessary to underscore a bank's responsibility for the safekeeping of other people's money, both in their investors' interests and in the interests of the wider society. Prudence is also required for careful scrutiny of loan applications to ensure that borrowers will be able to repay them, and that a bank has sufficient security in the event of a default. Prudence is also seen as essential in the bank's own interests to maintain their customers' trust. For Aristotle, prudence is one of the virtues, i.e. a rational choice of the midpoint between extremes of excess and deficiency where the excess is recklessness. Nyberg makes the point that the extent to which prudence was lacking was reflected in the end by the extent of the losses suffered by each bank and financial institution (v).

Self-restraint and moderation are also virtues. They are rational responses to desire, and it was desire for higher profits, salaries and bonuses that contributed to the risky lending. 'Hubris' is a word that has been much used in commentary on the banking crisis. It refers to a type of behaviour Aristotle would have recognised, for it was portrayed in Greek dramas performed in amphitheatres in his day. 'Hubris' is having a sense of overweening pride in one's achievements, accompanied by having blind spots for what could go wrong, and which eventually does go wrong and brings about a person's downfall. In general, a person is blind to their own flaws and to how fickle fate can be in a complex and changing world.

The causes of the Irish banking crisis and the factors behind the government's guarantee are of huge public interest and controversy. An Oireachtas inquiry has been established, and further findings of relevance to an ethical understanding are likely.

CASE STUDY 7.1

Case Studies: Individual Behaviour in Group Care Settings

Having regard to the greatest happiness principle, consider the response of a care team to provide appropriate care to overcome the difficulties in caring for both the individual and the group in the following examples. For example, what might be the consequences of excluding the individual from participating in the group in the short term? What might be the consequences of allowing the individual to remain? If your view of the appropriate decision includes a need for more resources or services, consider how the greatest happiness principle might support their provision. To consider more particular examples of the general ones mentioned below, include details relating to a possible client and his/her background.

1. A hyperactive child in a child care setting who appears to have strong attention-seeking needs.
2. An autistic adolescent in a group care setting whose behaviour is disrupting care activities for other clients.
3. A seriously troubled youth in a secure detention centre.
4. A man in a hostel for the homeless who breaks the hostel rule that people drinking alcohol on the premises will be asked to leave.

Exercise 7.1

Questions to Consider and Discuss: Means and Ends

Does the end always justify the means where the end succeeds in providing the greatest happiness of the greatest number? Can you think of examples where you can argue that it does not justify the means because the means go against other values that are more important than the greatest happiness of the greatest number?

Exercise 7.2

Question to Consider and Discuss: Increasing Overseas Development Aid

In each of the five years since 2008 when the country experienced an economic downturn, Ireland's overseas development aid (ODA) budget was reduced. It has gone from 0.59 per cent of GDP (gross domestic product – a measurement of the country's economic performance) to 0.47 per cent. In money terms, there was a fall from €920m to €628m in 2012 (McGee 2013).

In light of the greatest happiness principle, and the suffering experienced by the world's poorest people, should Ireland increase its budget for ODA, even if by doing so it would mean spending less on services at home, or increasing taxes on those who are better off financially? By raising ODA to achieve the level recommended by the United Nations (0.7 per cent of GDP), Ireland would be signalling it believes better-off countries have a moral obligation to do more to help those in greatest need.

CRITICAL EVALUATION

Provides an Ethics Inclusive of People's Preferences

Under the greatest happiness principle, morality is not imposed. It is a matter for individuals to decide what is good and bad for their happiness. The theory respects the authority of each person to know his/her own best interest. It then provides for decision-making based on trying to accommodate everyone's best interest as far as possible.

Difficulty Estimating Consequences

There is difficulty in having accurate knowledge of what people prefer for their happiness as a basis for making good ethical decisions. Also, there is difficulty accurately estimating the amount of happiness an action will produce overall. The problem is compounded when short-term and long-term consequences have to be included in the estimation.

Also, since estimating the amount and quality of pleasure has to take into account everyone's preferences, there is no reason *in itself* for giving priority to relieving poverty. For example, suppose you could show that more happiness would in fact be produced for more people by building a sports stadium than by using the same money to provide long-term accommodation for the homeless – this would then indicate a moral requirement to use the money for the stadium. The spirit of utilitarianism is directed toward relieving misery in society as a priority, but unless this can be shown to produce the most happiness overall in a particular action, then there is no moral justification for doing so.

Difficult Not to Give Priority to Own Happiness

Another difficulty with utilitarianism is that it underestimates the priority people feel they are entitled to give to their own happiness. For example, it would seem that if a disabled person's desire for independent living causes more unhappiness for his family than the happiness it would bring him/her, then s/he has to bow to the interests of his/her family as the morally right response. The same would apply in the case of a person who wants a divorce.

In his essay 'Famine, Affluence and Morality', utilitarian philosopher Peter Singer gives a striking example of the principle that we must regard the general happiness as overruling our own desires where the two are in conflict. Singer argues that because our happiness counts no more than other people's happiness, and because world hunger is a condition of extreme misery, then people in the affluent Western world are morally obliged to do whatever it takes (including, if necessary, drastically reducing their standard of living) in order to provide for the greatest happiness of the greatest number.

But it appears to go against a natural intuition to say that our own happiness counts for no more than the happiness of others. It is said to be 'counter-intuitive'. Certainly, in practice, people generally have always felt they have a natural right to give priority to their own happiness.

No Allowance for a Distinction between Acting and Omitting to Act

Since the happiness of all is the sole criterion, the theory also claims that we are just as responsible for the harm we can prevent (if we don't do anything to relieve it when we could do so) as we are for the harm that we directly cause. Utilitarians don't make a distinction between omitting to act and acting when it comes to having moral responsibility. However, most people would say that while we may have *some* responsibility to act to prevent others experiencing harm, such as famine victims, it is not the same responsibility we would have if we actually caused the harm.

On the other hand, regarding the question of moral responsibility to end poverty in developing countries, one of the arguments made is that policies of developed countries on trade, debt repayments and arms sales contribute directly to causing poverty-related harm. On this issue, some argue strongly that more developed countries have at least some direct responsibility both to end existing poverty in developing countries and to change their policies so that they don't contribute to causing harm.

No Allowance for Motive as Morally Relevant Factor

A further criticism made is that utilitarianism excludes motive or intention in assessing the morality of an action. Assessment is based solely on consequences. Yet in law, for example, intention is taken into account. It matters significantly if the killing of another person was intended, for then it is murder, whereas if it was unintended it is manslaughter. If a care team's decision to place a client in foster care produces more unhappiness than happiness for the client and foster parents, it is clearly relevant to assessing the action morally that it was the care team's intention to produce happiness. At the same time, Mill recognises that while utilitarianism does not see motive as relevant to the morality of an action, it is very much relevant to considering the worth or character of the person who acts (2008: 149).

Assumes Good Equals the Greatest Happiness

Mill accepts that he has not proved by logic that the greatest happiness principle is true – he says that he cannot. Any theory, he believes, has to start by assuming its first principle is true, and utilitarianism is no different (2008: 168). Nevertheless, he argues that the basis of utilitarianism is 'psychologically true' and that is all the proof that is needed (2008: 172). He explains this as shown below.

> No reason can be given why the general happiness is desirable, except that each person, so far as he believes it to be attainable, desires his own happiness. This, however, being a fact, we have not only all the proof which the case admits of, but all which it is possible to require, that happiness is a good: that each person's happiness is a good to that person, and the general happiness, therefore, a good to the aggregate of all persons.
>
> Mill 2008: 168–9

Benn points out that this view, which is the basis of utilitarianism, can be criticised. This is because it is claiming that, in one way or another, we always act to obtain pleasure for ourselves. But is this true? For Benn, the reason we get pleasure from obtaining what we want may not simply be because it satisfies our desires, but because we regard what we desire as having a fundamental value. For example, the pleasure we get from helping a friend is not just because it satisfies our desire, but because we recognise an independent value in friendship as something good in itself. As Benn puts it, 'The pleasure of getting what we want often comes because we attach an independent value to the things that we want, and manage to get' (Benn 1998: 69). Mill, though he does not seem to realise it, implicitly attaches an independent value to the higher pleasures. He is strongly implying that they are good, not just because we desire them once we have experience of them, but that there is something good about them regardless of whether we desire them or not.

REVIEW

The greatest happiness principle is a simple, practical response to the problem of understanding what good should mean. It is also supportive of social care in its view that everyone's desire for happiness is of equal value and should be provided for as much as possible. Even though it can be criticised on many grounds, it is a common sense view of ethics. In addition, it is likely that in practice it is the view of ethics that many people accept, at least in part, whether they are explicitly aware of doing so or not. This is because the consequences of our actions for others are a major factor in our view of what we consider to be the right thing to do.

FURTHER READING

Banks, S. (2006) *Ethics and Values in Social Work*, 3rd ed., Palgrave Macmillan (section on 'Utilitarian Principles' in Chapter 2).
Benn, P. (1998) *Ethics*, UCL Press (Chapter 3).
Norman, R. (1998) *The Moral Philosophers: An Introduction to Ethics*, 2nd ed., Oxford University Press (Chapter 7).

REFERENCES

Benn, P. (1998) *Ethics*, UCL Press.
Bentham, J. *The Principles of Morals and Legislation*, Prometheus Books.
Central Statistics Office 'Survey on Income and Living Conditions (SILC) 2011', available at www.cso.ie (accessed 17 November 2013). (For other source material on poverty see the website of the Office of Social Inclusion.)
Hayek, F. A. (1993) *The Road to Serfdom*, Routledge London.
Honohan, P. (2010) 'The Irish Banking Crisis, Regulatory and Financial Stability Policy 2003–2008, A Report to the Minister for Finance by the Governor of the Central Bank', available at www.bankinginquiry.gov.ie (accessed September 2013).
Judt, T. (2010) *Ill Fares the Land*, Allen Lane.
LaFollette, H. (ed.) (2002) *Ethics in Practice: An Anthology*, 2nd ed., Blackwell (Singer's essay 'Famine, Affluence and Morality').
Mill, J. S. (2008) *On Liberty and Other Essays*, Oxford World Classics, OUP.
Nyberg, P. (2011) 'Misjudging Risk: Causes of the Systemic Banking Crisis in Ireland', Report of the Commission of Investigation into the Banking Sector in Ireland, available at www.bankinginquiry.gov.ie (accessed September 2013).
McGee, H. (2013) 'Government Seeking to Stabilise Overseas Aid Budget', *The Irish Times*, 13 September 2013.

8
Diversity

OVERALL AIM

To explain some sources for understanding why people have different moral beliefs, with a view to recognising the value of accepting moral diversity in society.

LEARNING OUTCOMES

At the end of this chapter you should be able to:

- Explain why morals can be considered relative to a person or culture (relativism).
- Explain how moral relativism follows from Moore's view that the meaning of moral goodness cannot necessarily be identified with any quality, such as well-being, which leave it open to being interpreted differently.
- Explain the arguments for relativism from egoism and cultural difference.
- Relate a relativist view to the value of accepting moral difference.
- Show understanding that relativism itself is open to challenge as an adequate basis for understanding moral values.
- Recognise that there are limits to practices that can be considered acceptable.
- Recognise that under relativism, the basis for providing social care is a matter of personal or cultural belief rather than an independent moral requirement.

INTRODUCTION

People are diverse in many ways because of gender, nationality, ethnicity, language, religious affiliation, secular beliefs, as well as political and philosophical views. Acceptance of moral difference contributes to a society in which all people are valued equally and in which members of all cultural groups are integrated into society and feel they belong. It is a value that shows respect for people's independence and right to live in accordance with the values they see as appropriate for them. Ireland's population includes many diverse cultural groups as a result of people who have come to live and work in the country from all parts of the world, many of whom have become Irish citizens. Yet many retain the values and beliefs of the culture in which they were born and brought up in, and in which they bring up their children, whether, for example, it is East European, African, or Middle or Far Eastern. The difficulty some people have in accepting cultural difference as a value has been, and continues to be, an issue in society. Acceptance of difference in relation to the Travelling community and culture has been an issue in Irish society going back many decades. At an extreme, non-acceptance of the value of difference can manifest itself in racism, which includes the attempt to denigrate people on the basis of their difference through verbal or physical abuse, or through discriminatory practices. Cultural difference is only one feature of diversity. The Economic and Social Research's 'Annual Monitoring Report on Integration 2012' found 'worsening attitudes towards migrants in recent years' than had existed before the economic recession began to impact in 2008. It reported that 'Discrimination across a variety of life situations, ranging from shops, housing, pubs and transport, is a serious issue that needs to be addressed.' (See the report under 'Publications' on the Economic and Social Research Institute website; see also Crosbie 2013.)

For people working in care, an important value is to have the same regard for all people, including those who belong to minority groups whose values differ in certain respects from the values held by the majority. In providing care services for families from different cultural backgrounds, care workers will come across examples of practices that reflect different value systems to those of Irish society, for example, in relation to the authority and role of fathers and mothers and in relation to different expectancies for male and female children. Gender equality, which is an important value in Irish society, may not be reflected to the same extent in the relations some cultures value between men and women. Value differences can sometimes become an issue in getting service users to accept and implement care plans where they see measures in the plans to be at variance with their values. For example, they may see measures that promote independence and autonomy as a threat to adhering to the authority of their religious beliefs.

In this chapter we will look at some reasons why we should accept other people's values even though we may disagree with them. First, it is accepted that people have a universal human right to their cultural beliefs and practices. They have the right to manifest their religion or belief alone, or in community with others, in public or private. This is acknowledged in both Article 18 of the UN Declaration and Article 9 of the European Convention on Human Rights. So, the philosophy behind human rights and their legal status are the main sources for understanding the acceptance of diversity. One other main source of justification for moral difference which we will look at is moral relativism. Moral relativism is the view that there is no common set of values which can be shown to apply to everyone. Instead, values are relative to an individual or culture, and this provides justification for why values can vary.

If relativists are right and people can validly have their own morality, this provides a reason for the value of accepting people's moral beliefs where they differ from our own. We cannot prove our values are superior, nor can they for their values – so acceptance of difference is justified.

RELATIVISM

Objective and Subjective Truth

Moral relativism is the view that a common ethical basis for everyone cannot be established. Instead, our morals are always related to something from which they come, such as our feelings, ego, culture or society. In this way, morals are said to vary between individuals and between social groups. In general, moral relativism is the view that morals are not *objectively* true. That is, they cannot be shown to be true by any independent evidence which would make them compelling for everybody. Instead, morals are merely *subjectively* true, i.e. true only for the person who holds them in relation to their own thoughts, feelings, time in history or cultural upbringing.

Moral Authority

One way of understanding relativism is to see that there is not a single moral authority which everyone accepts as binding. For many, the authority lies in the teachings of their particular religious belief, while for others it is the norms of their society, and for others again it is their own individual feeling or viewpoint or their conscience. More likely again, the source for the authority is felt to lie in an unclear mixture of these influencing factors. In any event, there is not a recognisable single authority which everybody accepts.

Origin of Relativism

The view that morals can be considered relative has been recognised for a long time, but it wasn't until the twentieth century that it has become a common ethical position. The ancient Greek philosopher, Protagoras (480–411 BC), expressed a relativist position when he said, 'A human being is the measure of all things . . .' (Woodruff 1999: 292). Applied to morals, this means that it is up to each person to decide on what has value and what does not. Wong (2004: 433) speculates that Protagoras is likely to have been led to his relativist view from contact between his own culture and others from which he learned that different cultures have different moral beliefs.

Modern Relativism

Interpretation is a word often used now when people disagree about moral issues, and it indicates recognition of relativism. Often when we disagree with someone over whether a particular practice is morally right or wrong we may say, 'Well that's your interpretation, but it's not mine.' In doing so, we are recognising the subjective nature of viewpoints. In the nineteenth century, Nietzsche claimed that no actions are good or bad in themselves – it is only our interpretation of them that makes them good or bad: 'There is no such thing as moral phenomena, but only moral interpretations of phenomena' (1989: 91).

The publication in 1903 of G. Moore's book, *Principia Ethica*, did much to make a relativist position common. This was because he pointed out that there was no way anybody could ever really know what good and bad are. If good cannot be known, this leaves it open to people to associate good with nothing at all or with whatever they want. Moore's ethics is famous for an insight known as 'the Naturalistic Fallacy' (1962: 10). He pointed out that it is a fallacy (an error) to think that good can be defined by something in particular such as pleasure or well-being which are natural, desirable features of human experience. In the next section we will look at the fallacy as a means of understanding why it leaves the question of good and bad open to being understood in different ways.

Relativism is quite a common position for people to hold today. It is associated in particular with individualism. This is the idea that each individual is his/her own moral authority and there is no authority which can bind us to common moral standards.

MOORE'S INSIGHT: MORAL GOOD AS INDEFINABLE

For Moore, disagreement between philosophers about ethics is based on confusion. This is because philosophers have always assumed that the subject of ethics – the good – can be defined. But this is a false assumption. If something is able to be defined, then it can be broken down into parts in which the essential part unique to it is identified in the context of its other parts, which it may share with other things. For example, a pen can be defined by a nib or ballpoint that enables a person to write, while at the same time it shares having ink and tubing with other objects. In this sense *pen* is a complex object and can be broken down into its parts to define exactly what it is. But *good* is not like this at all. It cannot be broken down into anything else (1962: 7–8). Good is simply good. 'If I am asked, "What is good?" my answer is that good is good, and that is the end of the matter' (1962: 6). Actually, for Moore it is not quite 'the end of the matter' since he had a lot more to say about it! Moore calls good 'a simple notion' (1962: 7). You simply know what it means. It cannot be defined or explained. He says we have an *intuition* of good, but it is an intuition that draws a blank. It is an intuition through which we can realise there is nothing we can put our finger on which corresponds exactly to the meaning of what is morally good.

Moore emphasises that we have no intuition of some mental content or mysterious substance which could be substituted for the good. As he puts it, 'there is nothing whatsoever which we could substitute for good, and that is what I mean when I say it is indefinable' (1962: 8).

Relativism Arising from Moore's Insight

If Moore is right, then, in practice, it makes morals relative to whatever a person sees good to be. Since good is not anything that can be defined, and since our only knowledge of good consists of this recognition through a blank intuition, it is, if you like, up to each person to fill in the blank intuition of what good means. This, then, will make morals relative to people's intuitions.

Moore did not put forward a specifically relativist position, but it is a consequence of his view. He believed that in practice we could, and did, have intuitions of certain things as good. He also suggests we all have the same intuition of what things are good in practice. He called them 'practical goods'.

The main thing our intuition of practical goods relates to is 'the pleasures of human intercourse' or 'personal affection' (1962: 188). He claims this is something we can all recognise. In practice, this means having a civilised society (1962: 158). So, a rule against murder is an obvious example of a rule we need. Other rules that help make life pleasurable for everyone include 'industry, temperance and the keeping of promises' (1962: 157).

However, Moore still sticks to his view that we have no means of knowing, either by reasoning or feeling or willing, that these practical goods which he mentions are good (1962: 141). We are faced with having to accept that things we recognise as good are so from self-evidence, which is always open to challenge by other people as not self-evident to them. The result is that, while Moore's list of things that are good may appeal to us, we don't have to accept them. We could still validly give priority to fulfilling our plans and activities as the main good for us without regard to the effect doing so may have on others. Moore's intuition of what good is in practical terms is *only his intuition*. However much his intuition may appear to make sense, other people could validly have a different intuition of what good is. From his insight that good is indefinable, he provides understanding for a relativist view of morals.

TWO FURTHER ARGUMENTS FOR RELATIVISM

These are:

- Psychological egoism.

- Cultural difference.

Psychological Egoism

This is the argument that all of our acts are done to satisfy our ego, that they have self-interest or self-regard as their primary motive. Egoists point to the prevalence in society of people acting primarily to satisfy their own interests and desires, such as for wealth, power or pleasure. In our interpersonal relations, egoists say we are always suiting ourselves in one way or another.

Psychological egoists in particular argue that even if we think we are acting for the sake of some ideal or principle, such as concern for others, we are either deluding ourselves or being hypocritical. They are not saying we always act in an obviously selfish way. However, they are saying that in every act there is a self-regarding element, and that this is the element for which we do the act. They claim they can always identify a self-regarding motive. For example, they will point out one of the following reasons why we are kind to others:

- To increase our chances of receiving kindness in return.
- To feel good about ourselves.
- To avoid feeling bad or guilty.
- To ensure others think well of us or to earn praise.
- To feel satisfied from living up to our beliefs.

If we protest that none of those self-regarding reasons explains why we want to act kindly, they will simply say that it must be for some other self-regarding reason.

In a similar way, they argue that the person who risks his/her life for others does so because they have been conditioned by their upbringing to admire heroic actions, and the thought of being considered a hero appeals to their ego. Psychological egoists would also argue that parents who make sacrifices for their children do so because they get pleasure from seeing them develop, or because it is socially expected of them, or because having and supporting children is deeply instinctive behaviour.

If egoists are right, then there is invariably a self-regarding reason behind our behaviour. We may find this unappealing, but for egoists it is the reality and, as such, we should accept it for what it is. Psychological egoism is mainly taken to be a *descriptive* ethics as distinct from a *normative* ethics, i.e. it describes a belief about people's motives for behaving in an ethical way, while stopping short of advocating that this is how people *ought* to behave. However, egoism has also been turned into a prescriptive guide for how we ought to behave. As such, it has as its main principle that we should always act to satisfy our self-interest unless by acting in the interests of others we are serving our own self-interest for the better. We should consider the interests of others only when it suits our interest.

How, then, does psychological egoism lead to the value of acceptance of difference? Well, if the theory is right and we always act out of self-interest, it means we have understanding for why people may justifiably differ in the values they hold because they see it to be in their self-interest to hold those values.

Cultural Difference

This relativist argument claims that ethical requirements are *nothing more than* those that happen to be part of our particular culture. The justification for ethics, in other words, can be reduced to the views that members of a culture have about certain practices. Morality is no more than the conduct that happens to be approved of, or disapproved of, in one culture or another.

In secular liberal cultures, for example, gender equality is an important moral value, understood as men and women having equal rights. However, in some Islamic cultures and traditions, people value a different relation between men and women. Muslim communities vary in the practices they consider acceptable for expressing the relationship and some are more liberal than others. But, in its stricter forms as practised in Saudi Arabia, for example, women are not allowed to drive. They are also expected to be looked after by a male relative, and not to travel on their own or mix freely with other men besides male relatives. Women also have to dress modestly in a loose robe (abaya) and head cover (hijab); a face veil (niqab) is optional.

Also, within Western culture, there are different groups who hold different moral beliefs. For example, within the gay and lesbian community, the right to have a sexual relationship (and option of marriage) with a partner of the same sex is a morally important value. By contrast, within the Catholic cultural tradition, it is morally wrong. Also, within the secular liberal tradition the right to personal choice is an important value, and for many it includes, in certain circumstances, both the right of women to choose to have an abortion, and the right for people to choose euthanasia or assisted suicide. By contrast, both practices are regarded as morally wrong by many others, in particular by members of religious cultures. Cultural difference also includes the acceptability of the death penalty for murder in many non-Western countries and some US states, whereas it is viewed as unacceptable in EU countries where it is banned.

Parekh makes the point that it is 'an obvious fact' that our culture shapes us in 'countless ways'. Our culture holds out to us particular ways of life and attachments as well as developing in us particular 'moral and psychological dispositions' (2000: 11; 110). From our culture we learn which practices are acceptable and unacceptable, as well as how people can differ in their moral attitudes (2000: 156). Cultures express human capacity in different ways. Parekh cites the example of how Buddhist and Hindu cultures respect and care for the natural environment and for all forms of life, which for them are important moral values. In contrast, in Western cultures in the past people generally considered their relations to the natural world to be outside the sphere of moral concern (2000: 144; 215). (This view has been changing as a result of growing recognition that we are engaging in practices that cause environmental damage which adversely affects our well-being. There is now a branch of moral philosophy known as environmental ethics.)

As a result of cultures expressing human capacities in different ways, Parekh takes the view that no one culture's value system can be privileged over another's. In particular, he argues that Western societies should allow for the participation of the values and practices of minority cultural groups whose values relate to their particular culture, and not require them to be confined to the private sphere. Parekh argues the case for a fully multicultural society where the values of minority cultures and their value practices are accepted and included, along with liberal values and practices as part of society's operative public values.

Relativist Argument from Moral Change

To add to their argument that values are relative, relativists point to the fact that many moral beliefs within cultures change over time. They argue that if a practice was acceptable at one period in time and then becomes unacceptable, or was once considered unacceptable and then becomes acceptable, then this also shows that morals are the kind of things that vary and differ.

Many examples can be given to illustrate how moral views of certain practices have changed over time. For example, many white people in the southern states of the US up until the 1960s, and in South Africa until the 1990s, considered apartheid morally acceptable. In Ireland, up to the early 1970s it was considered morally (and legally) acceptable to pay women less than men for similar work. In the public service, women had to give up their jobs on marriage. Into the second half of the twentieth century, under Catholic moral practice it had been considered acceptable (by some) to punish young girls and women who were perceived to be engaged in prostitution, or who gave birth outside marriage, by effectively confining them to hard work in institutions known as *Magdalene Laundries*. They were also required to give their babies up for adoption. (In 2013 the State apologised to women who had worked in the laundries for its role in the wrong done to them.) Also, for many people in Ireland moral attitudes toward sexual activity have changed significantly over the last fifty years in relation to sex outside marriage, single parenthood, contraception, and gay and lesbian relationships.

It is because of such variations in moral beliefs between cultures, and because of variation over time, that relativists argue there is no set of moral requirements that can stand up as common for everyone.

Cultural Difference and Limits to Acceptance

While it is now a generally accepted value that it is a good thing to have acceptance for the values of other cultures as well as to develop appreciation for them as part of the recognition and celebration of cultural diversity, it is difficult to accept that all practices that have value for people within a culture are morally valid. Tolerance, in practice, does not require a person to be tolerant of everything. André Comte-Sponville makes this point strongly in a chapter on the virtue of tolerance (2002: 157–83).

A problem with accepting cultural relativism *fully* as grounds for acceptance of difference is that it would mean having to accept practices which we find unacceptable. A strong example is the practice of female circumcision or genital mutilation, which is still an accepted ritual practice, particularly in some African cultures and in parts of Asia and the Middle East. From the perspective of other cultures, and human rights especially, it is considered to be a violation of an individual female's bodily integrity which inflicts irreparable harm. It can take different forms, which include cuts to genital organs. The practice dates from far back in history and one of the reasons for it is to contain women's sexuality, in particular to preserve virginity until marriage. It is inflicted on babies as young as a few weeks, but usually on girls between four and fifteen. It has severe physical, psychological and sexual health consequences and can result in death. To ensure that the practice is officially specified as a criminal offence in Ireland, the Female Genital Mutilation Act was made law in 2012.

People outside the particular cultures in which it is practised, and who do not accept it, are adamant that they are right, i.e. no girl or woman anywhere should ever be subjected to such treatment. In other words, such examples give rise to conviction that there have to be some moral absolutes, i.e. practices considered wrong or right in themselves regardless of what is acceptable in certain cultures. Another way of putting this is to say that we pack a lot of emotional conviction into our disapproval of certain practices, and that the source for this disapproval must come from somewhere other than what is, or is not, culturally acceptable.

While Parekh takes the view that we get our values from culture, he does not accept the full relativist position that values consist only of particular cultural beliefs. For example, he does not accept female circumcision or genital mutilation or gender inequality (2000: 277–284). He believes values come from interplay between culture and human nature to provide for different forms of the good life. Two of the basic features of human nature are that we each have 'a distinct self-consciousness with an inescapable inner life' and a need and desire for well-being (2000: 132–3). We have, then, to be able to show rationally that particular cultural practices, if they are to be acceptable, serve as valid expression of support for these features of human nature as opposed to damaging or suppressing them.

DIVERSITY AND SOCIAL CARE

Relativism provides understanding of why people have different values and related value practices. In doing so, it provides understanding of why the value of diversity in how people live and behave is justified within limits. In particular, it helps us to understand why narrow moralistic judgment of other people's behaviour is not justified or acceptable in social care.

It also helps provide understanding for cultural integration, which is important for a cohesive society in which all people can feel they belong and play their part. It helps to show that there is no moral basis for such practices as hate speech, racism and groups becoming ghettoised. It also helps to show there are no moral grounds for treating people unequally just because they have different values to the prevailing ones in society.

Acceptance of diversity is not always an easy value to practise, in particular for those who hold strongly to their own moral beliefs as being the true ones. Comte-Sponville makes the point that there is an inevitable tension between 'truth' and tolerance. People who believe that their political, religious or secular liberal beliefs are *the truth* can find it difficult to have tolerance for practices incompatible with their truth. This is because, strictly speaking, the only value consistent with truth is acceptance of the truth and all that goes with it. This can set people against views other than their own. There is always a danger that conviction about being in possession of *the truth* can lead to intolerance and even fanaticism (2002: 163–5).

A further point about relativism, which has a social care implication, is that it supports the view that there is no compelling reason for people to have a moral obligation to care for others unless it is their personal choice or the belief of their culture which they accept. One version of relativism that has grown to have a lot of influence on society is individualism. Individualism supports the entitlement of each person to fulfil his/her own needs without any particular obligation to help others unless it is their choice. We will consider this viewpoint more closely in Chapter 9.

So far, I have been making the case for the relativity of values and for the way in which this can be taken to underlie the value of acceptance of moral difference within limits. In simple terms, who is to say who is right when it comes to morals? However, the relativist position is open to what can be considered valid criticisms, and we touched on one of them in dealing with the difficulty in accepting a fully relativist position which would mean having to accept practices we consider seriously wrong. We will look at these criticisms in the critical evaluation section.

Exercise 8.1

Think of your own examples of how morals have differed over time and how they differ between cultures. Consider what that tells you about ethics.

Exercise 8.2

Question to Consider and Discuss: Providing for Equality and Diversity in France

At the start of 2005, the French government brought in a law banning the wearing of prominent religious symbols, including the Muslim headscarf (hijab), in public schools and public service employment. The government was concerned to maintain the secular nature of French society. Then in 2011 a French law came into force which banned the wearing in public places of the burka and niqab veil and other clothing or gear that fully covers the face. Reasons for the law included the view that people should be immediately identifiable in the interests of security and social connection. Also, the French Republic is based on a clear separation between the state and religion. People's religious beliefs and practices are seen as a private matter. Some who support the ban argue that in the interests of showing equality between men and women, and between all citizens in the public sphere, religious beliefs should not be seen to mark people out as different. They argue that the wearing of the symbols emphasises difference to an extent that takes away from the core value of equality. Also, they regard the practice of women having to cover up their bodies with clothing as a symbol of oppression, as it can be required of them from the beliefs of their culture whether they agree with the practice or not. They see the ban as being in the interests of women and as protecting French values and tradition. Some who oppose the ban argue that it is contradictory to believe in liberal values such as the equal right of all citizens to personal freedom and the right to choose how to live life, while at the same time preventing people from having the freedom to practise their cultural beliefs and display their religious affiliation in public. In 2013 the French government was considering extending the law to prohibit people who work with children in private crèches from wearing religious symbols.

With reference to this issue, and the strong attachment people can have to their cultural values and practices, consider and discuss cultural moral relativism as a basis for justifying acceptance of diversity in society. (For further material, see Chrisafis 2013 and Arthur 2003.)

CRITICAL EVALUATION

The Limitation of Moore's Logical Approach

It is true that moral goodness cannot be defined as having essential and recognisable parts. But Moore's approach to understanding the meaning of goodness is abstract. It is disengaged from the strong attachment to a view of good which people experience, whether as pleasure, virtue, or some other value. The practical reality is that we experience goodness in connection with certain behaviour and practices we find of value, and badness in connection with other behaviour and practices we find objectionable. Moore's view is based on general assumptions about what counts as meaningful. But you could argue that even though you cannot define good it is every bit as meaningful as something we can define. Perhaps the experience of goodness is especially meaningful precisely because we cannot define it in the normal way we can define other things, and because it retains an element of mystery.

Psychological Egoism: Difference between Personal Desire and Self-regard

The argument for psychological egoism can be faulted. Bond (2001: 7–20) argues that it rests on a confusion. He points out that yes, there is a strong personal element to why we act because all our acts are done to satisfy some desire that we have. But this does not have to mean that all our acts are done for a self-regarding motive. An act done for a personal desire can be a personal desire for the good of others; it can be done primarily for the sake of others. This is different from doing it for a self-regarding motive. Of course, we may be kind to others for a self-regarding motive, but we can still act out of a desire for the good of others regardless of the amount of satisfaction it brings us. Bond says egoists have confused the statement 'all acts are self-regarding' with the statement 'all acts are done out of personal desire'. Not all acts are self-regarding because we can have as our own personal desire a desire for the good of others.

Baier finds fault with egoism in a similar way to Bond. He says that even if we do have an egoistic motive for our actions, that 'does not make it the operative one' (Baier 2004: 199). In other words, our effective motive can be our desire for the well-being of others even if, mixed in with it, we also have the motive of satisfying our own needs in some way.

Cultural Difference: Distinction between Morals Being Part of Culture and Consisting of Culture

Some argue that because we are inevitably cultural in our viewpoint, we can never

be in a position to make culturally neutral value judgments about cultural practices, and that we therefore have to respect people's practices no matter what those
practices are. They argue that no one can transcend his/her own cultural background to make judgments from on *high*, as it were. In his essay 'Multiculturalism'
Arthur gives Fish's view as follows: 'we cannot make "objective" judgments about
cultures, but rather only ones from our own cultural vantage point' (2003: 430).
However, this is not necessarily the case.

It is true that moral views about the same practices differ between cultures
and also that within cultures some moral perceptions have changed radically
over time, particularly in Western cultures. But this does not have to mean that
morality is *only* about what is culturally acceptable and unacceptable at a given
time. There is a difference between saying that morality *arises for* people within
their culture and saying that morality only *consists of* particular cultural attitudes.
(See Bond 1996: 21–43 for more on this point.) If we accept that morality consists
only of cultural attitudes and practices, then we would be obliged to accept those
attitudes and practices because that would be all that morality meant. It would
mean we should be able to have no problem accepting and following the practices
of other cultures when we visited them. We would have to accept the old advice
that 'when in Rome, do as the Romans do'. If we lived in ancient times and visited
Rome, we would have to accept their practice of feeding Christians and criminals
to the lions. But the reality is that we don't morally accept the practices of other
cultures where those practices conflict with our moral view.

In addition, changes in moral attitudes considered for the better in any culture
come about because people feel that current attitudes are unacceptable and voice
criticism. This, too, indicates that people have a sense of morality that does not
always coincide with that of their time in history or culture. If morality consisted
solely of what happened to be acceptable in our culture, why would anyone be
activated to bring about change? So, against the relativist argument that moral
change over time justifies the view that morals are relative to a culture at a certain
time, we can argue that the demand for change indicates a source for morality that
is not reducible to a culture's beliefs at any particular time. We could argue that
over time we are becoming clearer about what is morally acceptable and what is
not, and the reason for this transcends people's personal views or their cultural
practices.

The Relativist Position in Practice

In practice, few, if any, relativists will go so far as to accept or advocate the full
implication of their ethical position, which is that a free-for-all in morality is
justified. They tend to accept a version of Hobbes's social contract view of ethics,
which we will look at in Chapter 10. This is the view that as a matter of social
convenience, we should all agree that certain behaviour is right or wrong. It is

a view of ethics based on what is called *collective* or *enlightened* self-interest. It supports the value of providing at least some care for those in need so that society will be better for everyone through having fewer social problems.

At the same time, relativism can – and does – contribute to a climate of scepticism about the existence of *higher* standards which have to be followed. This can result in not according much, if any, weight to moral arguments that go beyond self-interest for why an action should or should not be taken. This is notably the case in international relations where one theory known as *realist* stresses that a country's self-interest is the best basis for dealing with other countries.

Relativist Position as Self-contradictory

Finally, there is an old philosophical argument that some find convincing as a means of disproving the relativist position. The argument goes like this: relativists say no one is in a position to judge that the morals of a person or culture are better than any other because morals are always relative. In other words, there is no general truth that applies for everybody where morals are concerned.

However, this statement *itself* amounts to at least *one* general truth, i.e. the truth that morals are always relative. So, if the relativist's statement of its own position can be true in universal application, there is no reason why other claims about morality could not also apply universally.

Put another way, by insisting that there are only various partial truths, relativists are insisting on this as a general truth. Thus they are contradicting themselves. In any event, if we can only have relative or partial truth from the perspective of our own culture, how can we be so sure that there are no general truths applying to all cultures? There still could well be general truths; the possibility is not ruled out, even if we can't prove it.

REVIEW

Relativism is the view that there is no common morality. Instead, morals are relative to a person or culture. This view provides understanding for differences in moral beliefs among people in society, especially a society shared by people of different cultural traditions. A relativist understanding is one way by which the value of acceptance of other people's values and practices can be supported. It also supports an integrated society in which people of all cultural backgrounds are treated equally and have equal opportunities. Criticisms of relativism also show that it is limited in providing a complete account of people's moral experience.

FURTHER READING

Benn, P. (1998) *Ethics*, UCL Press (Chapter 2).
Comte-Sponville, A. (2002) *A Short Treatise on the Great Virtues: The Uses of Philosophy in Everyday Life*, Heinemann (Chapter 13 on 'Tolerance').

REFERENCES

Arthur, J. (2003) 'Multiculturalism' in the *The Oxford Handbook of Practical Ethics*, H. La Follette (ed.), Oxford University Press.

Baier, K. (2004) 'Egoism' in *A Companion to Ethics*, P. Singer (ed.) Blackwell.

Bond, E. (2001) *Ethics and Human Well-Being: An Introduction to Moral Philosophy*, Blackwell.

Chrisafis, A. (2013) 'France's Headscarf War: "It's an Attack on Freedom"', available at www.guardian.co.uk (accessed 22 July 2013).

Crosbie, J. (2013) 'The Growth of Intolerance', *The Irish Times*, 29 June 2013.

Comte-Sponville, A. (2002) *A Short Treatise on the Great Virtues: The Uses of Philosophy in Everyday Life*, Heinemann.

Fish, S. (2003) cited in 'Multiculturalism' by John Arthur in *The Oxford Handbook of Practical Ethics*, H. LaFollette (ed.), Oxford University Press.

Moore, G. (1962) *Principia Ethica*, Cambridge University Press.

Nietzsche, F. (1989) *Beyond Good and Evil*, Prometheus Books.

Parekh, B. (2000) *Rethinking Multiculturalism: Cultural Diversity and Political Theory*, Palgrave Macmillan.

Wong, D. (2004) 'Relativism' in *A Companion to Ethics*, P. Singer (ed.), Blackwell.

Woodruff, P. (1999) 'Rhetoric and Relativism: Protagoras and Gorgias' in *The Cambridge Companion to Early Greek Philosophy*, A. Long (ed.), Cambridge University Press.

9
Social Well-being

OVERALL AIM

To show the connection between the practice of virtues and providing for the well-being of everybody in society.

LEARNING OUTCOMES

At the end of this chapter you should be able to:

- Explain the crisis MacIntyre claims exists in ethics because of individualism or 'emotivism'.
- Explain the effect of emotivism on the way people relate to each other and on the growth of social problems.
- Explain why people need to practise virtues to have a society in which there is social well-being.
- Define virtues as the means needed to obtain the goods internal to social practices.
- Give examples of the goods or social benefits that come from practising virtues such as caring for others, courage and justice.

INTRODUCTION

One of the consequences of relativism is that it has given rise to a view that when it comes to what people should, or should not, do, they can suit themselves. However, if people behave on this basis, then it will have negative effects on social well-being. For social well-being, society needs people to practise virtues such as restraining their own needs and desires in the interests of others. In caring for others, care workers can come up against the lack of practice of virtues due to self-interested behaviour. For example, a range of social problems from family breakdown to serious crime can be considered to owe their existence in some part at least to self-interested behaviour. Parents may pursue their own desires to an extent that they neglect their children, resulting in the family needing support.

A young person may satisfy his immediate desires by discharging his frustration in anti-social behaviour, or in offences such as joy riding, vandalism or theft. In each case, the problems their behaviour caused could be avoided by the practice of virtues of restraint and consideration for the interests of others. This is not to say that lack of the practice of virtues is the simple cause of social problems. Factors such as poverty, lack of parenting skill and negative peer pressure make the lack of practice of virtues understandable and their practice difficult. The consumerist climate of society can also make it difficult for people to practise the virtues. Consuming is one of the main prevailing patterns of social behaviour. Also, material success is often admired above other values, as is celebrity. Down through history the understanding that placing too much emphasis on having and enjoying material goods can lead to the loss of attention to matters of the soul or spirit has been part of religious teaching. In the twentieth century two non-religious writers in particular – Vaclav Havel and Eric Fromm – wrote about the increasing power of market forces having a negative effect on the kind of society we live in, and about the kind of responses we have to our own lives and the lives of others. They describe a society driven by the market forces of selling and buying in which, in practice, people value to greater or lesser extent satisfying their needs and desires through consumption and acquisition of material goods, along with achieving socially recognised status.

For Fromm, the power of the market is such that it has come to have a certain unacknowledged 'authority' over how a lot of people behave, an authority that takes away from their sense of individual freedom and capacity for evaluative thinking. The market forces lead to 'a market orientation' in which people become more acquisitive and competitive. This affects social relations by making people more inclined to look on others to see what they can get from them or how they can gain from them, rather than appreciate them for who they are in their person (see Fromm 1982: 67–82; 1994:105–6; and esp. 1991: 76–185). One example is the way different social groups are inclined to look out for their own interest in competition with other groups, in particular for how they can benefit from government decisions, rather than seeking decisions that would benefit everyone. Another example is where elderly people are taken advantage of financially by family members.

Havel, too, saw people's over-involvement with market inducements as alienating them from 'living in truth' as authentic individuals by narrowing their horizon of interests to immediate material satisfaction. He describes how this can lead to a person becoming 'demoralized' (Havel 1989: 62).

Neither writer is arguing against the need for a market society and the benefits it brings. There is a need for a thriving sustainable market in which people can make purchases so that the moral good of employment-related growth can occur to combat unemployment and poverty. Moreover, as MacIntyre observed, external goods are perfectly natural objects of desire. No one can despise them without 'a certain hypocrisy' (MacIntyre 1985: 196). Nevertheless, as part of their analysis, both Havel and Fromm saw a need to be aware of the negative effect that living in a market society can have so as to protect and develop moral sensibility as an essential dimension of being human.

Another factor that affects the social climate and makes it harder for people to understand why they should practise virtues is the example of the narrow pursuit of self-interest by some in business without due regard for the wider social implications of their activities. In Chapter 7 we looked at some of the practices found to have been at work in leading to the Irish banking crisis in 2008, and many commentators have pointed out that bankers neglected traditional banking virtues of prudence, responsibility and trust, and replaced them with greed, irresponsibility and recklessness in pursuit of ever bigger profits and salary bonuses during the 'Celtic Tiger' years.

Corruption in politics and business is also a factor which, in the bad example it sets, has a negative effect on social well-being. It erodes the public's trust and confidence in fairness and can influence people to look out for their own interests to the exclusion of looking out for the interests of others. Since corruption charges against individuals can be difficult to prove, there is also a negative effect on social well-being from the perception among the public that corruption is occurring and that people are not being held responsible for it under the law. Cronyism also contributes to cynicism about politicians serving the public good and has a knock-on negative effect on the climate of social well-being. With cronyism politicians are seen to favour friends or supporters, for example, by getting them appointed to positions, such as on the boards of state organisations, rather than seeking out the best person suitable for the appointment on merit alone.

Care workers come up against lack of resources to meet care needs, especially resources such as staff or increased services. If there was more practice of the virtues of caring for others and justice in political decisions on behalf of society as a whole, this would lead to more resources being made available. However, this is unlikely to happen to the extent needed unless people in general practise virtues, and also unless they want and expect politicians to provide for care as a priority in managing the distribution of monies available. For MacIntyre, a particular virtue that is needed for social well-being is the courage to speak out and act against indifference and opposition to the social good (1985: 91–2).

As we saw in Chapter 2, Aristotle brings out the interrelation between personal and social well-being. In his 1985 book, *After Virtue*, MacIntyre restated and developed Aristotle's view in the light of the growing trend he saw for people in modern Western societies to ignore the need to practise virtues in order to provide for social well-being.

There are many social practices that are good for people, such as family life, business and sport. MacIntyre points out that we need to practise the virtues if we are to obtain the goods internal to such social practices. One overall social good to which better practice of virtues would contribute is a society with fewer social problems, in particular related to crime. Another good it would give rise to is a strong sense of community as opposed to division. Thus for MacIntyre, virtues have the status of being much more than good qualities which people may or may not have – they are social needs on which society depends if it is to function well.

DEFINITION OF VIRTUE

MacIntyre gives the following definition of virtue:

> A virtue is an acquired human quality the possession and exercise of which tends to enable us to achieve those goods which are internal to practices and the lack of which effectively prevents us from achieving any such goods.
>
> MacIntyre 1985: 191

CORE VIRTUES

MacIntyre points to three core virtues needed to obtain the internal goods of any social practice. They are:

1. Justice; this includes, as an aspect of fairness, recognising the part played by others in the success of a social practice we are pursuing, for example in business or sport.
2. Courage; this includes taking on the challenges, demands and risks of the practice.
3. Honesty, i.e. facing the facts and not overlooking awkward ones that are inconvenient. Honesty includes self-honesty in not deceiving ourselves about efforts needed to improve.

To illustrate why we need to behave virtuously if we are to obtain the goods of social practices, MacIntyre uses the example of the social practice of a child playing a game of chess. To obtain the goods internal to chess, a child needs to play honestly and not cheat. By playing honestly, the child develops certain capacities which are goods in the sense of being beneficial to him/her for his/her fulfilment in life and also beneficial for the community to which s/he belongs. MacIntyre identifies three goods internal to the social practice of chess:

1. Analytic skill, i.e. being able to break down a situation or problem into the component parts in order to work out the best response to it.
2. Strategic imagination, i.e. being able to plan ahead to achieve a desirable goal.
3. Competitive intensity, i.e. being able to stand up to a challenge or adversity and to do one's best to overcome it.

To these internal, self-development goods can be added the satisfaction that comes from having tried to do one's best and from the social enjoyment of the game. We can see that they are real goods. By having them, people benefit themselves and each other. They are internal goods which enable a person to live well in managing life's demands and opportunities. The important point here is that these goods are only obtainable provided a person plays honestly and does not cheat. The person who cheats may get the external good of winning, but s/he is ultimately defeating himself/herself by losing out on the internal goods (1985: 88). The same can be said of the sportsperson or the businessperson who cheats in the social practice of sport and business. Trust, for example, is central to business. If investors cannot trust that companies are trustworthy, they will be less inclined to invest. This will result in a slowdown in economic growth, growth that provides the goods of employment for people and tax revenue for government to use for the well-being of society.

In a similar way, goods internal to the social practice of family life include a feeling of belonging (in contrast, perhaps, to loneliness and isolation) as well as feelings of security and solidarity. To obtain such goods, the practice of the virtues of loyalty and helping out are necessary. We forfeit such goods through being uncaring and selfish in our family relationships. Without virtues, engaging in social practices is 'pointless except as a device for achieving external goods' (1985: 191). MacIntyre has no objection to external goods. External goods, which include money and property, are perfectly valid goods. They are natural objects of human desire. In addition, the wealthier we (and society) become, the more we are able to be effective in practising certain virtues such as generosity and justice (1985: 196). However, if external goods are obtained dishonestly, then a person cuts himself/herself off from internal goods.

SOCIAL NATURE AND VIRTUOUS PRACTICE

MacIntyre is not simply arguing that there is a payback from practising the virtues in having a society with fewer social problems. On a more fundamental level, he is arguing, as Aristotle did, that virtues express our human nature and provide us with the good life. Our human nature as social beings means that our own good is inseparable from the good of society, and to achieve our good requires the practice of virtues. This provides a common basis for understanding ethics (1985: 54–55). However, to the extent that people may have realised this in past societies, it is realised less now. He points out that the historical trend in the Western world has been for people to move away from practising virtues to benefit from social practices and, instead, to behave more in ways that suit themselves as individuals.

THE DECLINE IN VIRTUE AND THE CRISIS IN ETHICS

Drawing from Homeric poems and ancient Irish and Icelandic sagas, and from studies about them, MacIntyre presents a picture of people at the time whose lives were bound up in their expected social roles, through their family, work and social positions. He sees them as recognising the vital role that practising virtues played in their well-being, for example in producing the goods necessary for living, in providing support for each other to overcome hardship and adversity, and in defending the society against external attack. Virtues instilled in them included courage, loyalty and consideration for others. Furthermore, to have let people down meant experiencing a sense of dishonour or shame (MacIntyre 1985, see esp. Chapters 10 and 11). In broad terms, up to the European Enlightenment period in the seventeenth and eighteenth centuries, the understanding of good and bad was closely bound up with living out a good life in accordance with religious belief and with maintaining social bonds of family and community.

A number of developments contributed to the change from a social to a more individual understanding of ethics. For example, all the practical benefits that have come from science and technology have served to emphasise how much we are at the centre of a world we have made for ourselves, and of how much we are capable of doing for ourselves, without needing to rely so much on social bonds and religious belief.

Also, the growth of the market economy resulted in many more people than before having money over and above the amount needed for spending on necessities, which they could then spend on lifestyle choices. This resulted in people being able to do more to provide for the kind of life they wanted for themselves separate from the community. Third, the growth of democratic rule and individual rights meant that society came to be seen as serving the individual's needs rather than the individual serving the needs of society. These and other developments brought about major advances in human well-being which we experience today. However, they all contributed to positioning the individual at the centre of his/her life. MacIntyre points to a downside in the way this has led ethics to be seen as a personal matter.

Once people had a greater sense of themselves as individuals it led to a growth in the tendency to feel restricted in how they wanted to live by a moral authority that bound them to social obligations and religious belief. It led to an increase in the numbers who felt oppressed by demands made on them for the good of the community or the good of their soul. These demands were seen as preventing the individual from pursuing his/her own fulfilment.

Placing emphasis on the individual as a moral authority resulted in greater liberation from external authority. However, for MacIntyre, it has led to a loosening of ties between individual and community well-being. Increasingly in ethics, people began to see that it was up to them to decide on their own morals. It has given rise to the view that morals are a matter for ourselves and that there is no common authority we have to accept. Morals became relative to a person's own views rather than related to some accepted common authority. This has adversely affected the well-being of society as a whole. The price paid for greater personal liberation was the loss of *any* generally accepted authority. This has resulted, MacIntyre claims, in a crisis in ethics whereby the well-being of society has suffered.

Characteristics of Ethical Individualism (Emotivism)

MacIntyre calls the movement to an ethics based on individual authority *emotivism*. Emotivism is the view that ethical values and principles are expressions of personal attitudes, preferences and choices (1985: 33–4). The common phrase 'look after number one' expresses the emotivist attitude. It is the attitude whereby a person feels entitled to indulge his/her interests and desires without social obligation. For example, an emotivist attitude allows people to feel free to change their mind if they want to and break a promise. Another example is the attitude summed up in the phrase 'greed is good', a view expressed in an address to his company's stockholders by Gordon Gekko, a wealthy and ruthless business character in the 1987 film *Wall Street*.

MacIntyre describes three general types of behaviour common in Western societies that characterise the emotivist attitude (1985: 24–31). They indicate patterns of behaviour that have replaced an acceptance of shared values. He believes many people now in Western societies have come to behave in accordance with these patterns to a greater or lesser extent.

Three Types of Emotivist Attitude

Bureaucratic Manager

This is where for reasons of economic gain a person ignores or downplays the adverse consequences of their actions on others. For example, management of a company make their workers redundant and relocate their factory to a country where wage costs are lower. Management claim that their decision is morally neutral; they are merely using means (money, material and people) efficiently to achieve the goal of making greater profits. But this type of behaviour is not morally neutral. It puts profit before people. It involves, in effect, manipulating people without feeling any moral requirement of loyalty to provide for their well-being.

Sometimes the ethical implications of decisions are ignored for economic reasons. Other times they are considered, but set aside in favour of economic gain. A clash between ethical and economic considerations occurs regularly. Remember the film *Jaws*. Sheriff Brody wanted to close the beach after the first shark attack, but the mayor wanted to keep the beach open because of its attraction for holidaymakers whose spending in the local town was important for the livelihood of its citizens. Economics took precedence over ethics: the beach stayed open and more people were attacked by the shark. While there is also ethics on the economics side, such as protecting the good of people's livelihoods, decisions dictated by economic interests can be detrimental to the well-being of others, and this can get ignored or is not taken into account sufficiently. For example, a manager in a care organisation who faces a challenging decision to stay within budget may simply decide that this means needed services have to be cut, regardless of the consequences for those who rely on them. Alternatively, s/he could see if there is a way to over-spend temporarily, or reduce spending on other services where the need is less great, or seek authorisation for a budget supplement based on the importance of meeting the care need. Whichever response s/he takes will depend a lot on his/her attitude as a manager.

Materialist/Pleasure-seeker

In general, this is the practice of disregarding obligations to others with whom we relate in order to pursue individual interest or pleasure. An example would be a person who gets a divorce in order to marry a much younger, more attractive partner. His/her action is not morally neutral because it has consequences for his/her former spouse and children. Neglect of children or dependant adults can often occur for the reason that those with responsibility for looking after them are taken up by their own interests.

Therapy Seeker

People who are well-off often still feel unhappy and discontented with their lives. Discontent and mild depression are common, and a practice has arisen for some people to go into therapy for treatment for their unhappiness. However, MacIntyre sees that this may be a symptom of their preoccupation with themselves and their own needs. In addition, through therapy they may be encouraged to give even more attention to themselves and their needs. People do, of course, have psychological and related difficulties for which they need therapeutic help, and he acknowledges this. However, what people who are unhappy often need more than anything else is to recover the realisation that their happiness is achieved in and through engaging with others as members of a community. This, in turn, means they need to see that they can only become happy through practising virtues such as honesty, loyalty and consideration for others since such virtues sustain beneficial social engagement.

Taylor also refers to the growth in the practice of individuals seeking to find a means to satisfy their own happiness needs through therapy (1989: 508).

Emotivism and Breakdown in Trust

One effect of the emotivist attitude is that, in the absence of shared ethical understanding, people compete with each other to have their point of view accepted. People regard themselves as a separate, isolated individual entitled to their own views and desires, and they are determined to get them accepted and met. When their attitude conflicts with that of another person's, judgments and advice about right or wrong have lost their power to be valid. This is because people regard only those outcomes as morally valid which they want for themselves or that suit them. Since we know that other people are trying to suit themselves, just as we are, this leads to people distrusting each other.

MacIntyre goes so far as to claim that the emotivist attitude leads to people trying to manipulate each other to get their way. In the absence of an accepted common social basis for ethics, we find no way open to us to project our own viewpoint 'except by directing toward others those very manipulative modes of relationship which we try to resist others imposing on us' (1985: 68).

At the same time, MacIntyre points out that we still use moral language to appeal to others to behave in ways we consider acceptable. We make statements such as 'You shouldn't have done that' or 'That is morally wrong' all the time. But the problem is that, having lost touch with a common basis in our human nature as social beings to which these statements could refer, such appeals are often ineffectual.

MacIntyre argues that by behaving in accordance with an emotivist attitude, we are hurting ourselves as much as others. The emotivist attitude prevents us from obtaining the good things that are available to us when we engage with others in social practices.

Institutions and the Challenge to Virtue

No social practice can survive for any length of time without being institutionalised to some degree. Institutions such as sports clubs, business organisations and churches emerge to promote the practices of sport, business and worship. MacIntyre points out that because of their nature, institutions are characterised by power, status, competitiveness and acquisitiveness (1985: 194). As a result, members can come under pressure to give priority to maintaining and furthering the institution's power and status. In particular, they may try to protect the institution's reputation from scandal. In 2009, for example, one of the findings in the Murphy report, into the handling by the Catholic Church and state authorities of complaints and suspicions of child sexual abuse by priests in the Archdiocese of Dublin between 1975 and 2004, was that the Archdiocese, at least until the mid 1990s, was pre-occupied with 'the maintenance of secrecy, the avoidance of scandal, the protection of the reputation of the Church, and the preservation of its assets. All other considerations, including the welfare of children and justice for victims, were subordinated to these priorities' (Commission of Investigation 2009: 1.15).

When people working in institutions give priority to protecting the institution's reputation against criticism, it can result in them ignoring the need to respond through virtues such as honesty, accountability, and consideration for people who have been harmed. 'In this context the essential function of the virtues is clear: without them, without justice, courage and truthfulness, practices could not resist the corrupting power of institutions' (1985: 194).

Life Story According to Virtue (Narrative Ethics)

For MacIntyre, virtues not only tend to enable us to benefit from social well-being but also are, as they were for Aristotle, the means by which we live out the purpose of our life. So the extent to which our behaviour is in accordance with, or deflects from, our practice of virtues is the main indicator of how well we are leading our lives. Virtues, or the lack of virtues, become the key ethical references points about our life in terms of how we are for ourselves and how we will be seen by others. Narrative ethics places ethics in the context of each person's life considered as an individual's story. It is the story of the difficulties, challenges and opportunities life has given us and how we have responded to them. This ethics is based on the recognition of our intentions as the driving force in our life. We intend to do this or that and try to accomplish our intentions as best we can within our circumstances. In this way, we project ourselves into our future. We have intentions for both the short term, such as to get through the day or week by doing certain things, or for the long term, such as to get a job or see the world, or to live our whole life in a particular way (1985: 206–208). By the way we live out our intentions we become identified by the story of our life, both to ourselves and to others. We have a narrative identity, and our narrative identity makes sense only because of its relation to the stories of others in the community (1985: 221–3). One way or another, we are indebted to the wider society for giving us the basis for the meaning we see in what we do and for our self-image. This underlying dimension can often be overlooked and serves to show how connected we are to others in what we value in ourselves.

What should guide our intentions if they are to be morally good? For MacIntyre, it is (no surprise!) the virtues. We give our life its pattern by how well or how badly we practise virtues such as self-honesty and courage (1985: 145). Virtues also form our character (1985: 124). The more we practise virtues with constancy and integrity, the ethically stronger the narrative structure of our life becomes (1985: 203). Narrative ethics has particular relevance as a guiding approach to assess and justify the care needs of individual clients. Looking on narrative ethics from a social care perspective, we can recognise how clients may have come up against great obstacles in being able to shape their lives. People in need of care include those who have had a traumatic past and face a challenging future. This can be the case with asylum seekers, for example, and with unaccompanied minors, whose lives may have included fleeing a war zone and witnessing people being killed, perhaps even a parent. It is clearly important for care workers to assess and provide for their needs by learning their individual stories. For example, they may need professional counselling. Narrative ethics points toward understanding people in the full light of their circumstances. It also points us toward the value of nurturing virtues, such as trust and courage, in clients who may need it in order to cope.

Social Care and the Value of Social Well-being

A society in which there is more recognition of virtue as a social need, and in which virtues are practised to a greater extent at all levels, by people as individuals in their personal and family lives as well as in their work in organisations, institutions and politics, would be a society in which there is more well-being generally and in which care needs would be better catered for. Giving a helping hand has always been important to the social fabric. It is a social practice from which everyone benefits in different ways and at different times. Apart from the benefit of receiving practical assistance, there are the benefits of living in a society with fewer and less serious social problems and with strong community ties. Whether it is recognised in this light or not, such benefits depend on people's consideration for others, kindness and generosity.

For the social care advocate, this understanding of social well-being can help justify the case for more state provision of services for those in need. Of particular relevance is MacIntyre's point that arguments which emphasise certain action, or lack of action, on the basis of economic considerations are not morally neutral because they can have direct implications for the well-being of others. This point of view supports the social care advocate's argument that economic considerations to do with lack of funding should not necessarily hold sway over a moral requirement to provide for care needs, and that providing for those needs strengthens the public good understood as social well-being.

Also, in many different ways, best practice in case work includes, in effect, encouraging people to engage with virtue-led behaviour. For example, a client may need to be encouraged to practise persistence in sticking to a care plan, or family members or others involved in the client's life may need encouragement to practise giving greater consideration to the client and providing practical and emotional support. For the care worker, an understanding of ethics based on the client's life story requires the practice of empathy in particular.

Exercise 9.1

Question to Consider and Discuss: How Healthy Is Social Well-being in Ireland?

From your knowledge and experience of Irish society, identify examples of behaviour and practices that support social well-being, for example, volunteerism, and examples that take away from it, for example, different kinds of anti-social behaviour. Relate the examples to the presence or absence of the exercise of particular virtues.

CASE STUDY 9.1

Case Study: Fergus and Edel's Social Well-being in Older Age

Analyse the case study below by addressing the following questions:

1. What are the ethical issues involved?
2. What are the factors that have contributed to the issues? (Include consideration of further likely background factors.)
3. How would you have handled the issues?
4. Drawing from the philosophical understanding of the ethical value of social-well being, how you would justify your approach to handling the issues? Draw also on other values or principles as you see fit.

Fergus and Edel are in their late 70s and have lived together since they married in their early 20s. They are devoted to each other and, as they do not have children or close friends or relatives, depend a lot on each other for company and support. After a life in which they had both worked and enjoyed active leisure pursuits, they had been managing well in their retirement until Edel had a minor stroke which affected her mobility and speech. She was no longer able to wash and dress without help, which Fergus was able to provide. However, a neighbour reported to the HSE that she had noticed Edel 'wandering around the garden in her nightgown'. She said she had concerns about Edel's well-being and did not think Fergus was capable of looking after Edel given that he was old himself, and he would not know about Edel's needs or be able to meet them properly.

A care worker from the HSE visited the couple and observed their circumstances. She raised with them the option of nursing home care and said it would give Edel 'a new lease of life'. When Fergus expressed doubts, she told him he would be able to visit her every day and stay as long as he liked. She reported back to her supervisor that she thought that Edel would be better off in a nursing home where she would get all the help she needed. She said that she had concerns that Edel might be showing signs of early Alzheimer's disease. Her supervisor told her to continue to try to persuade Edel that her best interests would be served by nursing home care. The supervisor added that she should adopt this policy because if Edel came to any harm the HSE could be held responsible for not taking necessary action to protect Edel's health and safety.

Fergus and Edel considered their options and, in view of what the care worker had said, decided, reluctantly, it would be best for Edel to go into the nursing home. On visiting Edel, Fergus found that the nursing home rules meant that he had to leave by 8 each evening. Also, he found that he and Edel had no privacy, as the only place they could meet was in the day room where there were other residents and visitors and two TVs which were kept on all day. Also, Fergus failed an eye test which he needed to pass to retain his driving licence. As a result, he could no longer drive and could afford a taxi to and from the nursing home only two or three times a week. The care worker suggested that he consider entering the home himself. She said he and Edel would then be together. Fergus asked her about being able to work in the garden, as he had a keen interest in gardening. She said she was sure that wouldn't be a problem as the nursing home had a large garden with plenty of flower-beds that needed tending.

When Fergus entered the home he found he was given a separate room to Edel. He had understood that by 'being together' the care worker meant he would share the same room as Edel. They had slept together in the same bed for nearly forty years. Also, when he enquired about working in the garden, he was told that was for the ground staff, but that if he asked them 'nicely' they might give him some small jobs.

Also, Fergus was dismayed to find that Edel's bed had been taken away and replaced by a cot with side-rails which were raised each night when she went to bed. Edel told him that staff simply said it was necessary to prevent her falling out of bed in her sleep and injuring herself. When Fergus complained to the Nursing Home manager he was told that their policy was 'safety first', and that they could not take the risk that Edel might roll out of bed in her sleep and injure herself. He said the rails were for her protection. When Fergus objected, pointing out that Edel was able to get up in the night and visit the bathroom, the manager said that anyone at her age, especially when they have had a stroke, is at risk, and that Edel has only to press the buzzer and night staff will come and help her to the bathroom. He said that Fergus should prepare himself for a time when he may also need a cot.

CRITICAL EVALUATION

Virtue and Personal Freedom

MacIntyre is credited with reviving recognition that virtues are not just for *do-gooders*, but are a social necessity. Without them, individual fulfilment, which is bound up with social engagement, will suffer. So, too, will the public good, since without the recognition of the social necessity of virtue, people will be pulling against each other to get their preferences met rather than with each other to achieve their fulfilment as social beings.

At the same time, it can be argued that MacIntyre underestimates the value of personal freedom. Some people argue that making a success of their plans and activities or talents enables them to lead fulfilling lives. They may accept that society needs people to be virtuous, but not that it is central to personal fulfilment. This idea of the autonomous individual doing his/her *own thing*, the idea of what is called *expressive individualism*, is well-established in our society as an operative value for many. At the same time, this value co-exists in varying degrees of influence in guiding behaviour with the value of concern and care for others, in particular for family and friends.

Also, personal freedom is a crucial value in enabling people to act against restrictive social practices where they have acceptance as the norm. By emphasising the need for virtue to maintain social practices, there is the danger that the virtues may act to prolong existing practices that are unjustified. For example, if women had not criticised the social practices that required them to be subordinate to men and, instead, remained in an inferior economic and social position through the practice of such virtues as obedience, loyalty and humility expected at the time, the unjust social practice would not have been challenged, at least not to the same extent. It is partly through giving value to the desire for personal freedom that moral change occurs, often against much initial opposition from society, but which in retrospect is regarded as having been valid and necessary. MacIntyre is not arguing against the value of personal freedom or against the necessity for changing unjust social practices. However, there is a tension in his account between practising the virtues to benefit from the goods of social practices and practising them to change those practices where change is justified.

REVIEW

An individualist ethics is understandable in giving more power and authority to people to make up their own minds about what values they want to have. However, there is a danger that it will lead to people suiting themselves and losing touch with their social nature, as well as with the need to behave in accordance with virtues to obtain the benefits of social practices.

REFERENCES

Commission of Investigation (2009) 'Report by Commission of Investigation into the Catholic Archdiocese of Dublin', available at wwww.justice.ie (accessed 1 August 2013).

Havel, V. (1989) 'The Power of the Powerless' in *Vaclav Havel: Or Living in Truth*, Faber and Faber.

Fromm, E. (1982) *Man for Himself, An Enquiry into the Psychology of Ethics*, Routledge & Keegan Paul.

Fromm, E. (1991) *The Sane Society*, Routledge & Keegan Paul.

Fromm, E. (1994) *Escape from Freedom*, An Owl Book, Henry Holt & Company.

MacIntyre, A. (1985) *After Virtue*, Duckworth.

Taylor, C. (1989) *Sources of the Self: The Making of the Modern Identity*, Cambridge University Press.

10
Social Contract Ethics

OVERALL AIM

To explore the ethical basis for two contrasting views about a social contract which the people would agree to for how they would like to be ruled, along with the purpose and type of social policies which follow from each contract.

LEARNING OUTCOMES

At the end of this chapter you should be able to:

- Give an account of how the social contracts of Hobbes and Rousseau derive from their view of how people would behave in a state of nature.
- For each contract, show how particular ethical requirements follow, which inform the purpose and direction of social policy.
- Connect the ethical requirements for peace, security and individual self-interest under Hobbes's social contract with conservative or neo-liberal social policies.
- Connect the requirements for freedom, equality and common interest under Rousseau's contract with labour or social democratic social policies.
- Evaluate the merits and weaknesses of the ethical basis behind the purpose and the direction of each type of social policy.

INTRODUCTION

Social care work takes place in the context of social conditions and care workers constantly come up against these conditions when providing care. There is a range of such conditions relating, for example, to levels of wealth and poverty in society and employment and educational opportunities. There are more specific conditions such as eligibility for social housing and housing waiting lists, and availability of developmental services for people with learning challenges. These conditions influence the type and extent of the care needs which people come to have.

One set of ethics which influences the viewpoint people have toward social conditions is known as social contract ethics. Social contract ethics places emphasis on people's membership of society. It is our membership of society, these theories claim, which is the most important thing about us when it comes to understanding ethical requirements.

What constitutes the social good has been the subject of much debate over the centuries. This debate is about the big question of the purpose of society. One way of addressing the question is to ask: 'What kind of social conditions do we all agree the state should aim to provide for us?' As we shall see, the question has been answered in two basic and contrasting ways. These two ways gave rise to the idea of two different types of contract between the people and the state, with each having different implications for the kind of social policies that will provide for the social good.

Hobbes (1588–1679) claims that, if we were asked, we would want the state to provide us with peace and security and the conditions to pursue our own self-interest as much as possible. Since these are the things we would want first and foremost, they should inform and direct the government's policies. Also, Hobbes claims we would all agree on this, and so it forms the basis for a contract between ourselves and the government. Rousseau (1712–78), in contrast, claims that, if we were asked, we would want the government to provide us with freedom and equality above all, and we would want it to provide for the common interest more than our individual self-interest. Rousseau, too, claims we would agree on this and so it should form the basis of a contract between ourselves and the government.

The ideas in each contract have had a big influence on understanding the role of political rule in providing for the social good and they continue to have influence. From Hobbes's contract comes the idea that the state has little requirement to provide directly for the welfare needs of citizens. This view stresses that individuals have responsibility for providing for their own needs. Broadly speaking, in politics, this is the view which conservatives or neo-liberals take to a greater or lesser extent to justify their social policies. From Rousseau's social contract, on the other hand, comes the idea that the state has a large responsibility to provide directly for the welfare needs of all citizens. Generally, in politics, this is the view that lies behind socialist, social democratic and labour social policies to a greater or lesser extent. It's important to emphasise that neither type of party bases its social policy directly or exclusively on the ideas of Hobbes or Rousseau. In addition, party members would not necessarily agree fully with their ideas. The ideas are only one broad, background influence that has contributed to what is called a party's *ideology*. A number of other ideas from political theory also exert influence. Also, in practice, the policies of the different parties can differ in important respects from what Hobbes's and Rousseau's ideas suggest. This is due partly to the demands of practical politics, in particular to the influence of social conditions that prevail at a given time and the influence of the views of the public. At the same time, the parties can be considered to be guided broadly by the two different perspectives which the ideas provide.

HOBBES'S SOCIAL CONTRACT

Hypothetical Nature of the Contract

The first thing to make clear about the social contract for both Hobbes and Rousseau is that there never has been an actual contract, nor is there ever likely to be one. The idea is hypothetical. It is supposed or imagined – but for a very real purpose. This purpose is to understand what type of public good people would sign up for in a contract so that it could then be provided for in reality. Ideas we find convincing – and thereby win our agreement – form the basis of the contract, which justifies it as a guide to social policy.

The Desire for Power

Hobbes's social contract is based on his bleak view of how people behave. He says people act to satisfy their desires in competition with each other, and that they seek power above all in order to be able to satisfy their desires as much as possible. Furthermore, this behaviour provides the basis for understanding what is meant by good and bad. For good is simply whatever people instinctively desire and bad is whatever they have an aversion for (1968: 120). There is nothing else to good and bad other than a perpetual pursuit to satisfy desires. It is the meaning of happiness (1968: 129–30).

In trying to satisfy their desires, people act in isolation from each other, looking after themselves first and foremost. This gives rise to competition and conflict over the means of satisfying desires. As a result, people desire power above all in order to be able to hold onto and increase their capacity to satisfy their desires. 'I put it for a general inclination of all mankind, a perpetual and restless desire for power after power, that ceases only in death' (1968: 161).

State of Nature

Hobbes imagines what life would be like in a state of nature where there is no *common power* in the form of society as we know it and, in particular, no enforceable laws. Life in a state of nature would be 'a war of every man against every man' (1968: 188). He is not saying that people would actually be engaged in physical aggression and defence all the time, although he believes it would be common. He includes in his idea of war the fear of aggression, which he believes would be constant. It is fear from knowing that people will of their nature attack you if they feel they need to in satisfying their desires (1968: 185–6).

In this state of nature there are no common conveniences because they require co-operation and people do not co-operate – there is no industry, no culture and only 'a continual fear, and danger of violent death'. Hobbes follows this with a description of life that has often been quoted since, though it is sometimes forgotten that he is referring not to life as it is in society, but only to how it would be in a state of nature. He says that in a state of nature 'the life of man' is 'solitary, poor, nasty, brutish, and short' (1968: 186). He accepts that this never was the actual condition for all mankind, but believes that it would have been for some peoples at certain times and that in his time it continued to be in some places (1968: 187).

For Hobbes this is the type of behaviour people exhibit because of their nature. He is not decrying it or deploring it. He is simply accepting it as the reality on which any view of social good will have to be based if it is to win agreement. As we shall see in the next section, this account of the reality of human behaviour gives rise to the need for a particular type of social contract. Consequently, he argues the contract can be justified because, if given the choice and knowing the reality of how people behave, we would agree on it for our own interests.

From the State of Nature to the Social Contract

Hobbes then points out that living in a climate of fear and aggression is to no one's advantage. This is because he believes people are roughly equal in strength of mind and body, so no one will really be able to gain at the expense of others through force. In any event, those who do succeed will still always be in fear of having whatever advantages they acquire taken from them by others who are weaker but who combine forces (1968: 183). In other words, a state of nature is not a state conducive to *anyone* being able to satisfy their desires because they need peace and security to do so. This is why the idea of a social contract for the whole of society arises. Through a social contract, people look to society to protect them. 'Fear of oppression disposes a man . . . to seek aid from society: for there is no other way by which a man can secure his life and liberty' (1968: 163). Put simply, a contract makes good sense. It is prudent.

The Social Contract

In a state of nature each person has a *right of nature* to use his own power to do whatever it takes to preserve his own life. Self-preservation is an absolutely fundamental right. So, under the contract, people agree to transfer this natural right to look after their own self-preservation to a ruler, for the purpose of peace and security. Each person gives up that amount of his natural liberty as is necessary to ensure peace (1968: 189–90). It is this 'mutual transferring of Right' to the state which gives rise to the social contract (1968: 192). Since we transfer our right to preserve our own life to the state, it then becomes the main job of the state to protect our lives for us. It becomes the job of the state to protect everyone through laws and their enforcement so we can all go about our business in peace and security. This, for Hobbes, is the principal item in the contract because it is the only item on which people would be sure to agree. We can see, then, how it follows from this contract that the state has only this limited or minimal role of providing for whatever is necessary to maintain peace and security for everyone.

> **Historical Note**
> Hobbes lived in a time when a sovereign or king had absolute power over people. But, as you can imagine, the idea that the only justifiable society is one based on a contract agreed between the people and their ruler threatened the power of the king. Hobbes's idea was a force in history that led to modern democracy, which allows for a government to be elected by agreement.

Morality under the Contract

Morality under the contract relates solely to behaving in ways that maintain the peace. Thus, respect for the laws designed to provide for peace, and respect for the independence and freedom of everyone under the law, are high on the list of moral requirements.

Hobbes is sometimes represented as saying we have no moral obligations to others except the more negative one of refraining from harming them through observing the law, but he lists other more positive requirements. They are an important part of his theory, but not often emphasised. These more positive requirements have for him the status of moral laws. He says we should treat everyone as equal and be fair in our dealings with them, as well as showing them gratitude and mercy. However, we should not do so because we know these are good ways to behave in themselves (we don't know that they are). Instead, we should practise these traditional virtues only because they help to avoid social conflict and provide for social harmony. There is no other reason or justification for them.

At the same time, Hobbes goes so far as to say that there is a moral requirement on the state to provide welfare for people under laws if through no fault of their own they are unable to work. Social welfare, at least for the unemployed, is a good thing. Assisting them should not be left to private charity alone. But, again, the only reason why the state should provide this element of welfare is to avoid poverty becoming a cause of social conflict. Also, significantly for Hobbes, state welfare is charity. Welfare is not something due to people as a right for their self-preservation (1968: 387).

The crucial thing for Hobbes is that these moral laws are derived entirely from the recognition of the need for peace. They have no other foundation (1968: 216), and they have no other call on us either. Putting it another way, we invent morality as a rational response to conflict with others by identifying it with laws and practices that are in our own interest. Morality under the social contract is only a necessary device – a device to provide for what is called *enlightened* self-interest.

HOBBES'S CONTRACT AND SOCIAL CARE

State's Limited Role

For Hobbes, the social contract provides understanding for the idea that the state is required to provide for the public or social good. However, the state's responsibility for the social good is limited to providing for peace and security for all. These are clearly basic and important care needs for everyone, but people have many other care needs besides peace and security, however broadly peace and security needs may be interpreted. For example, people in poverty need care even though they are never a threat to social order through using force as a political means, or by engaging in criminal or anti-social behaviour. Of course many people in need are clearly not a threat to social order, such as young children and the very old. Under Hobbes's contract there is no obligation on the state to provide for their needs. Instead, it is left up to people to provide for their own needs and the needs of their dependants from their own resources.

The reason, for Hobbes, that the state's power is limited to providing peace and security is to allow us the most freedom possible to pursue our own self-interest, to which we have a natural right, since this is how we would behave in a state of nature. This gives rise to a society characterised by *possessive individualism* whereby each individual seeks to advance his own interests (MacPherson 1962). It is a society in which there is no requirement or expectancy on the state to do more than some necessary minimum to help people, through providing them directly with the services they need.

Political and Social Policy Implications

In politics, conservatives generally, and neo-liberals in particular, take the view that a small, limited role for the state in providing for people's care needs through social welfare is the most that is justified. They maintain that individuals have a natural right to do what they want for themselves without interference by the state. Thus they argue that low taxes and low spending to provide for care needs are justified for the sake of supporting both the right and responsibility of individuals to look after themselves.

Also, conservatives and neo-liberals today usually make the economic argument that self-interest is the driving force for creating a wealthy society, which ends up not just being for the benefit of a few, but also for the benefit of all. They point out that if the state puts curbs on individual freedom through high taxation, then this creates disincentives for individuals to use their freedom to pursue their self-interest in creating wealth, with the result that society as a whole suffers from lack of wealth creation. They argue that to provide the maximum incentive to work is the best way of ensuring wealth will be created, wealth that will then spread to others through its owners investing it productively to create more wealth, thereby leading to a need for more people to be employed. This is the *rising tide lifts all boats* argument. It is also sometimes called *the trickle down effect*.

In addition, if a society is doing well economically, then even with low taxes the government will be getting a bigger tax take than otherwise. This means it will have more money to spend on care services if it chooses to do so. In this way conservatives and neo-liberals might argue that their approach can lead to the means to provide for more and better care services. At the same time, they believe in the value of providing for self-interest more than in the state providing people with services, so it is not central to their philosophy that money raised from taxes should be spent as a priority in developing services which provide directly for everyone's welfare needs. A labour or social democratic view is that without direct state assistance, many people who are living in difficult circumstances will be unable to improve the material quality of their lives by their own efforts. They argue that the state needs to spend a lot on providing directly for their needs, in particular through giving them the opportunity to do more for themselves by, for example, securing employment and coming off social welfare payments.

A Divided Society

Critics have questioned Hobbes's basic point that there is an equality of strength between people. In reality, people differ considerably in their levels of both physical and mental capacity. This means a contract which provides for only the limited social good of everybody's physical security suits those who will not need social care more than it suits those who will need it. It will certainly not suit people who have a disability or mental illness. Also, because of the overriding importance Hobbes places on a right to self-preservation, as long as people are not endangering the peace, there is nothing to restrict them from pursuing their self-interest to become wealthy and powerful, if they so desire, and then using their position to maintain and increase their advantage with little obligation to others. Hobbes's contract can be criticised for giving society a structure in which there is a deep division between those who manage to do well materially and those who find they cannot.

Morality as Mutual Convenience and Charity

In Hobbes's ethics care is provided either for the practical reason of helping to hold society together or out of charity. It is not required from a sense of justice as something good in itself. In practice, therefore, state services for people in need will always be insecure and uncertain. They will depend either on the charitable disposition of rulers or on their judgment about the extent to which poverty may be a threat to social order.

ROUSSEAU'S SOCIAL CONTRACT

State of Nature

In contrast to Hobbes's view of how human beings would behave in a state of nature, Rousseau believed people would have had a natural sympathy toward each other. In addition to looking out for themselves, they would have recognised that hardship was common. Particularly in the early stages of emergence from a state of nature into social organisation, the need to provide for basic necessities as well as coping with illnesses and natural disasters would have nurtured in people a spirit of co-operation and mutual aid (Cranston 1972: 20–21).

At the same time, life in Rousseau's state of nature is *precarious and uncertain*. This is because if other people tried to take advantage of us, we would need *physical strength* to defend our freedom and possessions. Also, in a state of nature people are not so much free as independent and separated from each other (Rousseau 1972: 77), so it's no ideal state. Only by forming into society can we fully realise our freedom by uniting with each other for our mutual benefit. If we want to be free, we have to join with others in following rules for our own good and the good of others. Ethics arises fully in the need to establish rules and abide by them (1972: 64–5).

Rousseau's Criticism of How Society Developed

The problem, as Rousseau sees it, is that the way society developed did not lead to freedom for everyone. This is expressed in the famous opening two sentences from *The Social Contract*: 'Man was born free, and he is everywhere in chains. Those who think themselves the masters of others are indeed greater slaves than they' (1972: 49).

How did conditions in which people lack freedom come about? Rousseau says it came about through competition among people for possessions and power, in particular through people acquiring and increasing ownership of property. This did not lead to freedom and equality, but to restriction and inequality. It led to a society in which there was a class division between rich and poor. It led to inequality and exploitation, which in turn led to both the threat, and occurrence, of civil disturbance and violence. It led to a society in which even the wealthy and powerful still had to fear for the security of their possessions and position. (This explains his point that 'masters' are still 'slaves'.) Rousseau makes two interrelated points about this society.

His first point is that such a society is in nobody's best interest. His second point is that it is unjust because it came about without agreement. Therefore, an agreement between people, or a social contract, is needed to provide a morally justifiable basis for society that will be in everyone's interest. 'Since no man has any natural authority over his fellows, and since force alone bestows no right, all legitimate authority among men must be based on covenants' (1972: 53).

Rousseau's Contract

Freedom and Democracy

Rousseau says that the social contract is essentially about building on the natural independence we had in a state of nature in order to provide for real freedom. It is about having a form of social organisation in which natural independence is furthered or developed through being converted into social or civic freedom. In drawing up the contract, the task is

> . . . to find a form of association which will defend the person and goods of each member with the collective force of all, and under which each individual, while uniting himself with others, obeys no one but himself, and remains as free as before.
>
> Rousseau 1972: 60

A society in which people are free in this way is the only one we could envisage getting the agreement of everyone. Since a free person is one who rules himself/herself, so a free society is one in which the people make their own laws and rules which they then follow. In short, the social contract provides for a democratic society.

Historical Note

Rousseau's *The Social Contract* was one of the books that influenced the French Revolution, in which rule of the king was overthrown to be replaced by democracy.

The Problem of Providing for Democracy in Practice

Ideally the social contract should provide for a direct democracy in which all citizens would be directly involved in making the decisions. But Rousseau recognises that a direct democracy is not practical given the large number of citizens in a modern state (1972: 122). A representative democracy in which people elect politicians to represent them is the one we are familiar with. At the same time, he recognises that there is a problem with representative democracy. This is not only because, strictly speaking, people can only represent themselves, but because people will differ on the kind of laws they will want their representatives to introduce. The rich, for example, will want their representatives to introduce laws that favour their own interests, and so also will the poor. The result will be a struggle for power among different sections of society, with the section that succeeds in getting most representatives elected winning.

The 'General Will'

Rousseau's solution to the difficulties with representative democracy is his idea of the general will. The general will is different to the will of all. The will of all is the outcome of agreement about providing for everybody's private desires or interests, but the general will is the common interest (1972: 72). As he puts it, 'the general will derives its generality less from the number of voices than from the common interest which unites them' (1972: 76). In other words, the general will is a psychological bond that unites people, both in their humanity and need for social co-operation. It 'should spring from all and apply to all' (1972: 75). In making decisions about the general will on particular issues, elected representatives have to consider what best serves the interests of everyone as a whole.

> When a law is proposed in the people's assembly, what is asked of them is not whether they approve the proposition or reject it, but whether it is in conformity with the general will which is theirs; each by giving his vote gives his opinion on the question, and the counting of votes yields a declaration of the general will.
>
> Rousseau 1972: 153

What the general will means for a particular matter 'does not always have to be unanimous' (1972: 70). At the same time, 'the general will is always rightful and always leads toward the public good' (1972: 72).

Objectives of the General Will: Freedom and Equality

The main objective of the general will is to bring about the value of the freedom of everybody. Decisions made about society have to provide for it as a priority.

Also, because the general will relates to everybody, it has to relate to everybody equally. Thus, decisions made have to provide for everyone's freedom equally. Acts of the general will should 'make no distinction between any of the members who compose it' (1972: 76). Any form of discrimination is ruled out by the principle of providing for the general will.

Meaning of Equality in Living Standards

But what about differences between people in terms of the standard of living they can enjoy? By equality, Rousseau says he does not mean that everyone has to have the same income or standard of living. Equality for him means ensuring that there are no great differences in income between people. He says that in the interests of the general will, the rich should be moderate in their expectation of having wealth, and the poor should be moderate in desiring wealth.

At the same time, Rousseau accepts that citizens will form into groups, such as those made up of people who have the same occupation, and that groups will seek to influence the elective representatives to provide for their interests rather than the general will. But he believes that if there are many groups promoting their differing interests, they can balance each other out in the influence they exert, and that their influence can contribute to a harmonious society based on the general will (1972: 73–4; 96).

ROUSSEAU'S CONTRACT AND SOCIAL CARE

State Provision of Social Services

Rousseau's contract supports social care directly. This is shown in particular through his idea of equality. In practice, equality means ensuring that nobody is too poor or too rich. People are to have incomes close to each other. In line with this is the requirement that no group, whether older people or those with disability, should be at a disadvantage compared with the rest of society where the state is in a position to remove that disadvantage. Catering for the needs of disadvantaged groups through legal provision is in keeping with consideration of the general will, with the common bond that unites all people.

COMBINED INFLUENCE OF BOTH TYPES OF CONTRACT

In practice, in democracies today, some combination of the general perspective afforded by Hobbes's and Rousseau's ethical ideas for a social contract tends to influence the overall direction of social policy rather than one to the exclusion of the other. However, one more than the other will be emphasised and have more influence depending on the type of political party in power.

Exercise 10.1

Question to Consider and Discuss: Role of Government in Providing Support Services

From your knowledge of Irish society, do you think the government has a moral obligation to do more to help families by providing, for example, improved social housing, amenities, and educational supports, and families whose members, in particular young teenagers, are at risk of engaging in practices that lead to social problems, such as addictions, anti-social and criminal behaviour, and organised crime? Relate the obligation you think the government has to the level of contractual obligation Hobbes and Rousseau consider a government has under their social contract.

Exercise 10.2

Question to Consider and Discuss: No Such Thing as Society

Do you agree with Margaret Thatcher's view, expressed below? Relate her view to both Hobbes's and Rousseau's views on the extent to which the state should be expected to help people. Think of examples of particular social policies, for example, in relation to social welfare benefits, which would follow from her view and those that would not follow from it.

> They're [i.e. the people constantly requesting government assistance] casting their problems at society. And, as you know, there is no such thing as society. There are individual men, women and their families. And no government can do anything except through people, and people must look after themselves first. It is our duty to look after ourselves and then, also, to look after our neighbours.

Source: From an interview published in *Woman's Own*, 23 September 1987. Quote available online from wikiquote under 'Margaret Thatcher'.

CRITICAL EVALUATION OF HOBBES'S SOCIAL CONTRACT

No Actual Contract

One criticism that can easily be made is that there never was, nor is there ever likely to be, an actual social contract. Therefore, the kind of contract people would agree to is, at best, only plausible speculation.

Unlikely to Win Agreement of All

Would Hobbes's contract be one which those in need of care would willingly agree to, since it makes them dependant on charity? Hardly. It won't serve their interests as equal members of society. The problem is that under Hobbes's theory people are seen as having only an equality of approximate strength. They are not accorded an equality of moral status. This is a point made by Kymlicka (2004: 189–91).

Contract Open to Being Broken

A problem with Hobbes's view is that, in practice, the need for peace and security is unlikely to provide *of itself* a sufficient moral reason to prevent people harming others. The thing about a contract is that it can be broken. People may well feel tempted to break it if they feel they can get away with it and avoid punishment. There is no other moral requirement stopping them, since morality has meaning and value only from being bound up with the contract.

Provides Justification for the Value of Individual Freedom

At the same time, Hobbes's contract supports the value of individual freedom. In other words, for him the common good, which the contract provides for, is precisely to allow for maximum individual freedom. It can also be argued that by facilitating individual freedom you are facilitating human nature, and that this is the best way of ensuring society will work for the benefit of all.

Realistic View of Human Nature

Some would argue that Hobbes provides a realistic account of how people are naturally inclined to behave by seeking power to satisfy and advance their own interests, either individually or by joining with others who can help them. There are many examples from history in business, politics and international relations which bear out this view.

CRITICAL EVALUATION OF ROUSSEAU'S SOCIAL CONTRACT

Unrealistic View of Human Nature

We can see how Rousseau has a very different idea from Hobbes about how the social contract serves the social good. For Rousseau, the contract is not a practical necessity for our self-preservation so much as a moral requirement to underpin and provide for relations of freedom and equality among people. However, the main problem with Rousseau's social contract is making it work. It would seem to be expecting too much of people that they would set aside their private interests and be guided only by a notion of the general will.

Vagueness of the General Will

Freedom and equality can be expressed in tangible ways as manifestations of the general will, for example, by a minimum wage and high-quality social services. At the same time, the general will remains a vague notion. People have to look into their own souls, as it were, to see what is in the best interests of everyone. But this is quite a subjective process, and people could understandably reach different conclusions.

Contradiction in Forcing People to Be Free

There is the danger that an idea like the general will would be abused by some people if they attained power. There is a notorious passage in which Rousseau raises the question of what is to happen to a person who refuses to obey the general will. His answer is that in the interests of ensuring that the will has force, such a person 'shall be constrained to do so by the whole body, which means nothing other than that he shall be forced to be free' (1972: 64). Putting it another way, people are not allowed to live in accordance with their own good, as they see it, where it conflicts with the general will. They have to be made to comply with the requirements of the general will. This, as you can imagine, could easily lead to the suppression of people's individual freedom.

Rousseau himself is not advocating any form of tyranny. As we have seen, individual freedom is, for him, of the first importance. However, in order to try to secure freedom in society for everyone, he ends up suggesting that the freedom to live according to your own interests can be suppressed where it is not in accordance with the rulers' interpretation of general will. Furthermore, in history, his idea of the authority of the general will has provided justification for others, who believed they knew what the general will was, to impose laws on the people restricting their freedom. It has been done in the name of the *general will* or the *common good* or simply *the people*. This happened in the twentieth century, particularly in the totalitarian communist states of the former Soviet Union. However, this form of state rule was influenced much more by the ideas of Karl Marx.

> **Brief Note on Marx's Ideas**
>
> Marx argued that the structure of the capitalist economic system inevitably gives rise to injustice and oppression for a section of society that has little capital and power. Those who own a lot of capital use their wealth to ensure the political process and public policy maintain and increase their advantage over those who own little. Marx's solution involved public ownership and control of resources, property and production of goods and services in the interest of providing a just society for all. With the collapse of the communist system in the former Soviet Union and countries of Eastern Europe at the end of the 1980s, Marx's ideas lost much of their influence in the West. China has a communist one-party system which draws from Marx's ideas.

REVIEW

Social contract ethics is about the social good that follows from regarding society as based on an agreement between members about the overall purpose of political rule. Two different types of contract have been put forward as justified, with different views following from each about what the social good requires by way of social policy. Under Hobbes's contract the state provides for peace and security so that people can pursue their own self-interest as they choose. Under Rousseau's contract the state provides for the general will, understood as the freedom and equality of all in practical terms such as material well-being in the common interest. Hobbes's type of contract represents one broad background influence on the social policy of conservative or neo-liberal parties and Rousseau's on the policy of labour or social democratic parties.

FURTHER READING

Benn, P. (1998) *Ethics*, UCL Press (Chapter 5).

REFERENCES

Craton, M. (1972) *Introduction to Rousseau's The Social Contract*, Penguin Classics.
Hobbes, T. (1968) *Leviathan*, Pelican Classics.
Kymlicka, W. (2004) 'The Social Contract Tradition' in *A Companion to Ethics*, P. Singer (ed.), Blackwell.
MacPherson, C. (1962), *The Political Theory of Possessive Individualism: Hobbes to Locke*, Oxford University Press.
Rousseau, J. (1972) *The Social Contract*, Penguin Classics.

11

Social Justice

OVERALL AIM

To explore the role that ideas of social justice have in providing social care.

LEARNING OUTCOMES

At the end of this chapter you should be able to:

- Relate justice to having basic rights.
- Explain Aristotle's idea of justice as balance.
- Explain Rawls's idea of justice as fairness.
- Explain Nozick's idea of justice as entitlement to keep what you obtain voluntarily.
- Relate each idea of social justice to differing types of social policy.

INTRODUCTION

Justice is a powerful idea. Injustice arouses strong feelings. People have fought and died to achieve what they believed to be justice. Mill says the reason why people are so affected by justice is that it bears directly on their means of survival and security. They feel it is something they cannot be without. This is why demands for justice are seen as the strongest of ethical demands. The feeling is not merely that justice *ought* to be provided, but that it *must* be (2008: 190).

Justice is something people feel should lie at the foundation of their relationship with each other, at the foundation of their society, and indeed at the foundation of the world's economic and social order. But what exactly is it? As we shall see in considering the theories of Rawls and Nozick, some people can see certain economic and social conditions as just, while others see the same conditions as unjust. People dispute what justice means in practice. Arising from different ideas of what social justice means are different implications for the kind of polices that serve justice. Mill identified three general features which people associate with justice.

Moral Right

The easiest way to identify features of justice is to look at why some conditions are regarded as unjust. For Mill, apart from wrongful exercise of power over another person, injustice is either withholding from people or taking away from them something to which they have a moral right (2008: 185). Also, we say that justice is something which people *deserve*. So, social justice is something people *deserve as of right*.

Legal Entitlement

Justice is also connected with law (2008: 189). If certain social arrangements are considered just and deserved as of right, then people expect that they will be provided for in law. This puts the provision of justice on a much stronger footing than, say, generosity. We don't say of people that they have a right to generosity, let alone a legal entitlement to it (2008: 185) – but we do say this of justice.

Equality

But what kinds of things do we have a right to expect from society as a matter of justice? First and foremost, justice relates to the right to be treated equally. For example, it relates to the right to be treated equally under the law. Equal pay for equal work regardless of gender or ethnicity is another example of justice as equality. In general, if people are being treated less favourably than others for no understandable reason, then we say they are being treated unjustly. An understandable reason would include 'some recognised social expediency' (2008: 200). A social expediency might include government financial inability to provide for the equality. In social care practice, care workers may come across cases where some children in a family are being treated less favourably than others, perhaps because of disability or gender.

SOCIAL JUSTICE

This relates to the overall arrangements that should be provided for people in terms of their living standards. The first view holds that there should be a relatively equal arrangement of wealth in the interests of the common good. The implication of this first view is that the wealth in society should be shared out or distributed. The second view holds that a just arrangement of wealth is one in which people provide for themselves. The implication of this second view is that people are entitled, in justice, to keep the wealth they acquire even though this results in a great disparity of wealth in society. For some, this view includes the idea that it is unjust for wealth to be taken off people through tax and given to others in welfare payments and free or subsidised public services.

Aristotle and Rawls argue, for different reasons, that for the state to provide a greater level of equality in income and living standards is morally just. Nozick argues that it is morally unjust because people have a moral right to keep what they have acquired.

ARISTOTLE: SOCIAL JUSTICE AS BALANCE

For Aristotle, justice is a key virtue because the just person is constantly disposed toward the good, not only toward his/her good but also toward the good of others. For him social justice refers to the way money or other material benefits should be divided or distributed among members of a community. Remember, a virtue for Aristotle is the midpoint between extremes of excess and deficiency. This means that an unjust society and world is where there is an excess of wealth alongside a deficiency. Social justice is the mean between extremes of having a lot of wealth and of having little. In practice, this requires providing for a greater level of equality in living standards with no big gap between those who are rich and those who are by comparison poor. The just is *a right proportion* or balance, and the unjust is a violation of that proportion (1998: 122–4). The traditional emblem of justice, weighing scales in balance, expresses this idea.

But how do we decide what is the right proportion? Broadly speaking, the *right proportion* is judged on what people deserve in terms of their contribution to society, and in terms of the needs they have for which they may require assistance if they are to achieve well-being. So you can argue, for example, it is just to apply a higher rate of tax on incomes above a certain level since people on such incomes have more than provided for their own needs, while at the same time it would be unjust to tax them unduly given their efforts. Also, you can argue that those who are unable to provide for their own needs deserve, in justice, that society provides for them.

Aristotle accepts that, in practice, it is difficult for anyone to judge precisely what the right proportion is that people deserve to have. But he maintains it is an essential pubic task and virtue which people (politicians especially) should practise. A just society and world are ones in which everybody can flourish.

Aristotle also wrote an influential book called *Politics*. In his *Ethics* he points out that political activity has greater importance in contributing to the flourishing of everybody than people's individual efforts (1998: 2). The main way that politics does this is through an elected government having the power to redistribute the wealth of society justly from the money it raises in tax.

ARISTOTLE'S SOCIAL JUSTICE AND SOCIAL CARE

Aristotle's meaning of social justice is probably the one that accords with most people's understanding. That is, a just society and world are ones in which there are no big gaps between rich and poor. Governments are frequently criticised for being unjust where their policies result in widening the gap. In particular, budget tax and welfare changes can be judged on the basis of their net overall effect on narrowing or widening the income gap between welfare recipients, or those on low pay, and high earners.

Also, by the extent to which the Irish government tries to grow the economy to provide jobs and have job-creation measures, and also by the extent to which it implements an effective, adequately funded National Action Plan for Social Inclusion, it can be regarded as seeking to provide for greater justice in Aristotle's sense. Achieving targets for poverty reduction is one element of the Plan. These are the kinds of measure which fit in with what Aristotle understands it means to provide social justice.

RAWLS: SOCIAL JUSTICE AS FAIRNESS

The Veil of Ignorance Method

Rawls argues that it is only fair that we decide on the principles of justice from behind 'a veil of ignorance'. This means we must imagine we know nothing about ourselves, neither about our economic or social status, nor our abilities and talents. There is a complete blackout on such knowledge. We should not ask, 'What principle of justice would I adopt if I knew what my talents, interests and station in life would be?' Instead we should ask, 'What principle of justice would I adopt if I were ignorant of my talents, interests and station in life?' (2004: 514).

In deciding on social justice 'it is essential that no one knows his place in society, his class position or social status. Nor does any one know his future in the distribution of natural assets or abilities, his intelligence, strength and the like' (2004: 514). The veil requires us to assume we have no way of understanding in advance what sort of person we are or our place in society.

The veil returns us to 'the original position'. This is not some real original position which either we or our ancestors were ever in – it is purely imaginary or hypothetical. Rawls's purpose in asking us to go there in our mind is very practical. It is a method by which we can decide on principles of justice that will be fair because we will all be deciding on them from the same position. They will be fair because we will all decide on them 'in a situation of equality'. In other words, the veil forces us to be fair. This is the reason he calls his theory 'justice as fairness' (2004: 515).

But what's the point, you may still ask, in going there in our mind if it never existed in reality and never will? Rawls's answer to this objection is that the conditions of fairness presented in the original position are 'ones which we do in fact accept' as fair. 'Or, if we do not, then perhaps we can be persuaded to do so by philosophical reflection' (2004: 519).

Two Further Reasons for the Veil

1. Necessary for Agreement

Without the veil, Rawls argues we have no chance of ever getting agreement on principles of justice. This is because those who are wealthy will want to hold onto their wealth, while those who are poor will want to improve their position through society giving them more benefits. Since the wealthy will regard the money they make as their own, they will select a principle that regards it as unjust for them to have to pay taxes to support those less well off. Those less well off, on the other hand, will feel entitled to regard it as just that the wealthy contribute to improving their living standards by arguing, for example, that since everyone is a member of society by birth they are entitled to a decent share of society's wealth. By getting rid of bias (we would need to know our actual position to be biased), the veil makes possible agreement on principles of justice which provide for everyone's interest (2004: 518).

2. Minimises the Influence of Luck

As things stand, luck plays a huge part in influencing a person's prospects in life. This is because so much depends on the circumstances we are born into, which are a matter of luck or 'natural chance' (2004: 514). We could be born the son or daughter of wealthy, caring and happy parents, or of parents mired in poverty and personal problems. However, deciding on living conditions from behind a veil means that our position will not depend so much on luck, but on the arrangements agreed by everyone for everyone. These arrangements will be, as we shall see in the next section, to provide for the best possible social arrangements and wealth for everyone.

Making a Rational Choice

Imagine that you – and everyone else – gets the opportunity to provide the basic design for the way society will be. What are the main features of the design you will choose? Rawls argues that the rational thing to do would be to decide on a society which will give you the following two main features: civil liberties and as much wealth as possible.

Rawls argues that the position we would choose coincides with what is rational and, because it is rational, it is just. In general terms we would want the best possible position for ourselves. This is a rational choice. It is not just our choice, it is everyone's rational choice. So what, then, does *best possible position* mean in practice as the rational choice? He says that rationally we would want to choose two things for this position, and that as a result of these two things there are two principles of justice.

1. Civil Liberties

Our first choice, Rawls says, would be to have social arrangements that provide for the maximum amount of individual freedom. Without freedom, some people would have power over others without their consent – no one would want to choose this. It would make no sense. Maximum freedom means freedom of thought and speech, of elections and of the press as well as freedom to own property.

These are known as civil liberties and are essential for any just society. These freedoms are so basic and important that they cannot be sacrificed to provide for a more equal distribution of wealth. Therefore, it is the first responsibility of government to provide for a just society by guaranteeing equal civil liberties for all citizens. Since this would be everyone's first choice, Rawls claims it gives us the first principle of justice. 'First, each person is to have an equal right to the most extensive basic liberty compatible with a similar liberty for others' (2004: 520). From this principle come principles of equality. For example, it rules out discrimination, and the equality principle rules in the right to equal opportunity. So, for example, in a just society people who have equal ability and motivation should have equal chance of success no matter what their background.

2. Highest Possible Wealth

Once civil liberties are provided, we will then want to choose our economic and social position, or, in simpler terms, choose how much wealth we would like to be able to have. Here again, guided by the rational choice, everyone would rationally choose the highest amount possible. This means there will be an equality of wealth with everyone getting the highest. Rawls says 'the sensible thing' would be to choose an equal distribution of wealth so you would not lose out (2004: 522). This choice both suits ourselves and ensures that no one does better than us by their choice. In this way, everyone wins by getting the highest possible income which will be the same.

However, Rawls says there is no reason why this result of actual equality should be final, provided it can be bettered. This leads him to the view that if, in practice, inequalities in positions give rise to an improvement in the circumstances of some people who otherwise would be worse off if those inequalities did not exist, then those inequalities are justified (2004: 522). Put simply in financial terms, if *highest possible income* means €500 a week where everyone gets the same and it means €550 for the lowest position where there is inequality, with some getting €600 and others €650, etc., then inequality is justified because it has brought up the best possible position for those getting least.

In practice, Rawls argues, if 'various incentives' succeed in producing a wealthier society overall that improves the position of the least well-off while resulting in income inequality, then that inequality is justified (2004: 522). It is justified because it is something we would choose. We would see this as a rational choice to make. It is the choice that, in practice, will result in the *wealthiest possible position*.

So, if I set up my own business and make a lot of money for myself but by doing so employ staff and pay taxes, taxes that contribute to the wealth of others who do not benefit as much as me, then this is just because I have improved their starting position. We are all better off than we otherwise would have been because of this arrangement. Even if we end up in a position of having the least wealth, we cannot argue that we have lost out because the inequalities are justified only if they improve the least position from what it would be under equality. So, 'there is no injustice in the greater benefits earned by a few provided that the situation of persons not so fortunate is thereby improved' (2004: 516). From this line of reasoning, Rawls gets his second principle of justice.

This is that everyone should gain from the way positions in society are arranged. 'Second: social and economic inequalities are to be arranged so that they are both:

- reasonably expected to be to everyone's advantage, and
- attached to positions and offices open to all' (2004: 520).

His principle emphasises that 'while the distribution of wealth and income need not be equal, it must be to everyone's advantage, and at the same time, positions of authority and offices of command must be accessible to all' (2004: 520).

In effect, this means that economic and social policy should aim to do two things simultaneously: maximise the overall amount of wealth while making sure that the least well-off benefit as much as possible. The least well-off should be catered for as much as possible in a way that is consistent with having incentives to provide for the wealthiest society. So, if asked to decide what justice should be from behind the veil, we would choose maximising the advantage of the least advantaged because it is the rational choice. It ensures we get the best possible position for ourselves. To choose otherwise would be to risk losing out, and this would be irrational.

His principle of justice does allow some people to have more than others, but only if the effect of some people having more results in the well-being of the least well-off being promoted. It is a principle that guarantees that even the most disadvantaged members will have a decent standard of living, i.e. the best they could reasonably expect.

RAWLS'S THEORY AND SOCIAL CARE

Rawls's theory claims to prove why we are morally obliged to have a society that is directed toward improving the living standards of the poor. The poor deserve to live in a society that is organised to improve their circumstances, not out of charity, but on the basis of principles of justice that are logical and rational. Since these principles constitute a rational understanding of what justice means, governments and other institutions must be guided by them in deciding social policy in relation to tax levels and welfare benefits and so on (2004: 523). Governments are morally obliged to provide adequate care services to ensure that the position of people in need of care is the best possible one they could reasonably expect. The veil ensures that if it turns out that we are born with autism or some other disability, we have chosen a society which will provide the best possible services for us. As such, his theory represents a strong argument that advocacy requests for improved care services should be met as a matter of justice.

His theory also helps us understand why all have a right to equal opportunity, and that conditions in society in which some people are held back by practical obstacles such as poverty or lack of facilities infringe their right.

NOZICK: SOCIAL JUSTICE AS ENTITLEMENT

Introduction

Nozick's theory is a direct response to Rawls's theory, and one that comes to the opposite conclusion. He argues people are entitled to keep their wealth and have no moral obligation to share it with the less well-off. Anything you obtain voluntarily you are entitled to keep or do with it as you please – it is your entitlement. While continuing to maintain its basic thrust, Nozick later modified his view, by accepting a need for a level of co-operation and an ethics of caring. In its original form, summarised here, his view represents some of the main ideas behind a neo-liberal position based on the individual and not on considering society as a whole.

Criticism of Justice Related to Distribution

Nozick criticises the use of the words 'distribution' and 'redistribution' of wealth in deciding what is just. He argues that in using such words we are already assuming that justice relates to having some arrangement for a more equal share of wealth, but there is no reason why justice should have to be about providing for this equality.

No Central Moral Authority

Nozick's main problem with the idea of distribution is that it implies that there is some central power in society *with the moral authority* to share out the wealth. The reality is that there is no power having such moral authority and never has been. He accepts, of course, that there is a democratically elected government, but he says it has no right to take people's wealth off them in tax to distribute to others. 'There is no *central* distribution, no person or group *entitled to* control all the resources, jointly deciding how they are to be doled out' (2004: 527). This is because wealth does not belong to the government, it belongs to the people who have it. Wealth will only belong to the government if people give it to them voluntarily. However, we are not given any choice; governments take money from citizens in tax by force of law.

If there is no body with the moral right to distribute wealth, it makes no sense to talk of redistribution as a way of rectifying unfairness. He says 'we are not in the position of children who have been given portions of pie by someone who now makes last-minute adjustments to rectify careless cutting' (2004: 527).

He says we would find it very unjust if the government decided to distribute our marriage partners to us. We would say they have no right to do that. People are not the property of government. On the other hand, a government does give itself the right to distribute money, money which does not belong to them, but belongs to the people from whom they take it. So, he says, there is no more a right to distribute resources than there is a right to distribute 'mates in a society in which people choose whom they shall marry' (2004: 527).

He does not say the government should take no tax at all. It is reasonable to take some tax to provide common services of benefit to everyone, for example, infrastructure such as roads, policing and defence. His objection is the injustice of using tax to give direct transfers of money to the needy in welfare payments and free or subsidised services. Also, he is not saying that the aim of caring for the needy is necessarily wrong. His point is that it is wrong to do so by the Robin Hood practice of 'taking from the rich to provide for the poor'.

Justice as Entitlement

For Nozick, justice is a matter of being entitled to what you have as long as you got it voluntarily. In this sense he refers to all the things you have as your 'holdings'. What you have, you are entitled to hold. There is 'justice of acquisition' (how we get what we have) and 'justice of transfer' (how people give to others). In both cases justice is solely a matter of 'voluntary exchange'. That is, once it happens without in any way forcing or deceiving others, it is just (2004: 528). Voluntary means of obtaining and transferring wealth, or 'holdings', include such common practices as:

- Pay in return for work.
- Profits from the sale of goods or services.
- Gifts, including inheritance.
- Return on investments.
- Prize winnings.

All such means are fair because they have come about either by the choices you make on your own behalf or the choice other people make to give you money or other valuables. This leads to his principle of justice as quoted below:

From each as they choose, to each as they are chosen.

Nozick 2004: 532

> **Example**
>
> It is perfectly just for a top soccer player to get, say, €150,000 per week, a TV celebrity presenter €500,000 a year, or a top banker even more. They freely accept this (not surprisingly!) in return for offering their skills. Nobody is forced to pay them that amount. In the case of the soccer star, his pay is made up of a free decision by his club to agree to the figure his agent negotiated for him, which in turn is based on free decisions by spectators to buy tickets to matches, by TV companies paying to televise them and by fans buying club merchandise. In the same way, a person who works for low pay freely accepts what is freely offered. This is fair, no matter how high or low a wage he gets.
>
> (adapted from Nozick: 533)

In this way, the just state is the one we end up with as the outcome of the countless free decisions which all the different individuals in society are entitled to make.

The Justice of Making Rectification

However, if a person uses non-voluntary means to acquire his holdings, i.e. the person from whom s/he gets them has not agreed to their transfer, then s/he is not entitled to them. Such means include:

- Theft.
- Fraud.
- Breach of contract.
- Force.

Examples of this arise from history where, for example, blacks and Jews were forced to work against their will. Other examples include the Aborigines in Australia and the Native Americans in the US, who had their land taken from them by European settlers. Nozick accepts that if in the past people gained their present holdings by unjust means, then the justice of entitlement requires that they make amends where possible. There is a valid principle of reparation. It may not be possible to establish the extent, or the beneficiaries, of the injustice if it occurred in the distant past. In 1999, the German government agreed to pay compensation to descendants of Jews used as forced labour under the Nazis.

The Injustice of Patterned Theories

If the state imposes some overall *pattern* to the way people come to acquire and increase their wealth, it is unjust. Nozick sees Rawls's principle that wealth should be distributed to maximise the advantage of the least well-off as an example of an unjust pattern.

Interference in People's Lives

Nozick's main objection to patterns is that they are impositions which interfere with people's lives. The problem with Rawls's principles is that they 'cannot be realised without continuous interference with people's lives' (2004: 534). In addition, he goes so far as to claim that interfering in people's lives by requiring them to pay a certain amount of tax to support the less well off amounts to forced labour and is 'a violation of people's rights' (2004: 535). In taking x hours of a person's earnings in tax and using it to pay for services for others who are less well off, the government is, in effect, forcing the person to work for somebody else's purpose. He argues that if the government was to try to introduce a new law requiring people to work extra hours so their earnings for these hours could be used to pay for services for those who are less well off, people would be justified if they felt aggrieved. But, he says this, in a way, is already happening. He further claims that by requiring people to work to pay tax that goes on services for others makes the government a 'part-owner' of their lives (2004: 573). The government, in effect, is assuming it has a property right over the lives of other people in forcing them to behave as it wants, even if it is for a good purpose, such as alleviating poverty and hardship.

Non-voluntary Nature of Paying Tax for Social Care

Nozick's problem with paying tax to the government to provide for care services is that it is not a free decision which we make. It would be fine if the government sought and obtained agreement from everyone to tax their earnings to pay for other people's needs – then it would be fair. But this has never been done. He says 'everyone above a certain level is forced to contribute to the needy' (2004: 537). He says we are not free to say to the government, 'Don't compel me to contribute to others and don't provide for me via this compulsory mechanism if I am in need' (2004: 537). We can't opt out. The government forces us to comply with their wishes.

NOZICK'S THEORY AND SOCIAL CARE

His theory does not support the spending of public money to provide social care services. He says the minimal state is the only one that is justified, i.e. the state that does the least to help people directly (2004: 527). Therefore, the only way his theory could be considered to support social care is in its support for the view that the best way to care for people is to encourage them to be self-reliant. One of the values of social care is indeed to enable clients to have as much self-reliance as possible, but for many who need assistance, this cannot be achieved (or only after great hardship) without direct state help. What is more, many people needing care have little capacity to become self-reliant even with family support, such as older people and those with significant disabilities.

Exercise 11.1

Questions to Consider and Discuss

1. From your knowledge of Irish society, how just do you think it is in accordance with Rawls's and Nozick's understanding of social justice?
2. Do you think people should be allowed to keep what they earn and pay only the minimum necessary taxes, or should they be required to pay more tax, in particular on high earnings, to provide funds to help those who cannot meet their own needs?
3. Do you think income inequality is necessary to benefit society by ensuring people have the incentive to provide for themselves by finding work and working hard to create wealth? If you agree, how much inequality do you think is fair while still providing incentives? Would it be a lot, a little or some amount in between?

CRITICAL EVALUATION

Aristotle's View

Aristotle's social justice as balance is dependant on accepting his view of human nature as rational and social, and that practising virtues is the way to achieve human fulfilment. As we saw in Chapter 2, this view is open to criticism. Rationality is not necessarily the defining feature of being human. At the same time, his view of social justice is one that is reasonable. For many who are concerned about injustices in society, and in the world, Aristotle has given a reasonable explanation of justice as a balance or fair share in living standards, and injustice as a big divide.

Rawls's View

Hypothetical Nature of Veil Method

Rawls's veil method for deciding on principles of justice is a version of the social contract, which we saw in Chapter 10. It is based on an agreement between all citizens on the kind of society they want. But the social contract is a purely hypothetical agreement. It never actually occurred or is ever likely to occur. Thus Rawls's theory can be criticised on the grounds that we do not know for sure what decision people would actually make if given the opportunity.

More than One Rational Choice

For Rawls's theory to work, he has to assume that all signatories to the contract see the rational choice as the safest one whereby they do not lose out. In other words, Rawls assumes it is irrational to want to gamble and take your chances, but this is not necessarily an irrational act. Where there is no requirement to distribute wealth to bring up the position of the less well off by taxing those with wealth, you might of course end up a lot worse off, but you might do a lot better, for example, by doing more for yourself than you otherwise would. Also, you could argue that another rational choice would be to choose the principle of the greatest happiness of the greatest number which, while it is close to Rawls's principles, is not the same. It seems rational to choose a society based on trying to provide for the greatest happiness of the most people, even if this means a minority may not be catered for as well as they would be under Rawls's principles. Kymlicka also makes this point (2004: 188).

Assumes People are Equal by Nature

Rawls's theory assumes people have a natural equality. This is the reason why he argues that the original position behind the veil is fair. Yet nowhere in his theory does he prove that people do have a natural equality. It's true that a natural equality of moral status between people accords with what most people see as central to any ethics. However, the only way of showing it to be true is to appeal to it as self-evident – and not everyone would agree that it is self-evident. Kymlicka makes this point also (2004: 188).

Nozick's View

Points Up a Legitimate Problem?

Nozick is not necessarily against the idea that it is morally good to provide social care. His point is merely that there is no justification for requiring people to pay for it in tax if they do not want to. It is not justice to require them to do so. Providing the money for care can only be a matter of individual choice – it is not a matter of justice. If he is right, it leaves a huge problem of how social services are to be provided because tax revenue is the main way of paying for them. However, it may be that if given the choice, most of us would agree to pay tax to provide care services. What do you think?

Supports Libertarianism

His view has been, and continues to be, influential in practice. This is because it supports the libertarian view that individual liberty is the most important value, in particular the liberty to earn and keep wealth without undue interference from government. In general terms, the libertarian or neo-liberal approach supports (on moral grounds) policies of low tax on profits and earnings and low spending by government on social services.

Democracy Provides Government Moral Authority

The nature of democracy is the consent of the people to be governed in the best interests of all citizens, not just some. Therefore, it can be argued that this gives the government the moral authority, and obligation, to provide for the interests of those who have valid reasons for not being able to provide for their own needs.

People Are Not Free to the Same Extent

Nozick's theory depends on accepting the view that all actions people take are voluntary. Once they are, then nobody is wronged and justice prevails. However, people are not free to the same extent to make voluntary decisions. As we saw in Chapter 5, poverty restricts freedom of action and of choice. People born into poverty do not have, in practice, the same absence of restriction on them as people who are wealthy. Poverty, disability and old age limit people's choices. It is difficult, then, to see how they can be expected to acquire holdings as freely as people who are well-off. While they may be able to make a voluntary decision, they do not have the same scope in which to do so as others.

Underestimates Interdependence

Work is the main way in which people acquire their wealth, but work needs an environment in which everybody co-operates if it is to succeed. Large elements of this environment, such as providing healthy, educated citizens as well as security and infrastructure are provided by the state. You could argue, as a result, that people have obligations to the state over and above paying for services that directly benefit them, since the state pays for so much on which they depend if they are to become wealthy.

In addition, you can argue that everybody contributes toward society becoming prosperous. For example, the unemployed, disabled and older people perform social roles such as consumers, parents, carers, lovers and loved ones, all of which are either directly or indirectly related to making society prosperous. Nozick, you could argue, takes an unjustifiably narrow view of society made up of individuals as economic units who act in isolation from each other. A more accurate picture is one of a vast web of interdependency in which everyone contributes something to enable the system to work effectively in generating wealth.

REVIEW

Social justice is a key ethical requirement that underpins social care. A difficulty with it is that it can be understood in different ways, which indicate different levels of obligation to provide for those who need social care. For Aristotle and Rawls there is an obligation for social policy to be directed toward providing for the less well-off. Nozick is associated with the view that people are entitled to keep what they have acquired legitimately and not have to pay for the needs of others beyond some minimum necessary level. Political parties support one position or the other in different degrees. Advocacy claims for social justice for those in need of care can be advanced based on an informed and critically evaluated understanding of how social justice can be understood.

FURTHER READING

Nozick, R. (1974) *Anarchy, State and Utopia*, Blackwell.

Rawls, J. (1971) *A Theory of Justice*, Oxford University Press.

Sandel, M. J. (2009) *Justice, What's the Right Thing to Do?*, Allen Lane.

Scally, J. (ed.) (2003) *A Just Society? Ethics and Values in Contemporary Ireland*, The Liffey Press.

Sen, A. (2009) *The Idea of Justice*, Allen Lane.

Stiglitz, J. E. (2013) *The Price of Inequality*, Penguin Books.

Wilkinson, R. & Pickett, K. (2010) *The Spirit Level, Why Equality is Better for Everyone*, Penguin Books.

REFERENCES

Aristotle (1998) *The Nicomachean Ethics*, Oxford World's Classics.

Kymlicka, W. (2004) 'The Social Contract Tradition' in *A Companion to Ethics*, P. Singer (ed.), Blackwell.

Mill, J. S. (2008) *On Liberty and Other Essays*, Oxford World's Classics.

Nozick, R. (2004) 'The Entitlement Theory of Justice' in *Ethics in Practice: An Anthology*, 2nd ed., H. LaFollette (ed.), Blackwell.

Rawls, J. (2004) 'A Theory of Justice' in *Ethics in Practice: An Anthology*, 2nd ed., H. LaFollette (ed.), Blackwell.

12

Abortion, Euthanasia and Assisted Suicide

OVERALL AIM

To present some of the main ethical considerations behind differing views which people have on abortion, euthanasia and assisted suicide.

LEARNING OBJECTIVES

At the end of this chapter you should be able to:

- Describe in brief the legal and social policy positions on abortion in Ireland.
- Identify moral questions central to the abortion debate.
- Describe the general position of three differing views – conservative, liberal and intermediary – in the debates.
- Explain some of the main ethical arguments in support of each view.
- Identify the central moral question in the euthanasia and assisted suicide debates.
- Distinguish between euthanasia and assisted suicide.
- Distinguish between voluntary and non-voluntary euthanasia.
- Describe the general position of three differing views – conservative, liberal and intermediary – in the debates.
- Explain some of the main ethical arguments in support of each view.

ABORTION: INTRODUCTION

Abortion is a contentious issue in Ireland, as it is in some other countries, notably the US. A difficulty in considering the ethics of abortion is to have terms adequate to capturing differing viewpoints. The most commonly used terms to designate different positions which people take are 'pro-life' (or the 'right-to-life' or 'anti-abortion') and 'pro-choice' (or the 'right-to-choice'). However, those holding a pro-choice view would not consider they are anti-life; and those holding a pro-life view would not consider they lack understanding for women with pregnancies that present them with a crisis or serious difficulty. Also, there are those who see their view as not represented by either side exactly, but as intermediary. They find abortion morally wrong in general, but acceptable in certain limited circumstances.

To designate the three differing views, the terms conservative, liberal and intermediary are used. 'Conservative' and 'liberal' are not used in a political sense. A person's support for a particular type of political party may overlap with their view on abortion, but it need not. Questions of abortion, and of euthanasia and assisted suicide, are fundamental questions of life and death, on which it is quite possible for people of different political persuasions to hold a range of views. Also, a person with a conservative view may be strongly opposed to abortion while at the same time accepting that the state may have a law permitting abortion as a choice in accordance with the values of a liberal democracy. The terms are used here to indicate that, generally speaking, a conservative on abortion is a person who is opposed to abortion in all circumstances, and when a termination is necessary to save the life of the mother it is not considered an abortion. A liberal is someone who believes that a woman should have a choice to end a pregnancy when it is presenting her with a serious difficulty, usually relating to her health – physical or mental. Someone who holds an intermediary view is opposed to abortion in principle but accepts there are certain limited circumstances that make it morally permissible, such as in cases of rape. People with an intermediary view are likely to differ on the precise circumstances in which they consider it permissible and impermissible, with some views reflecting a more conservative position and others a more liberal one.

The account given here is not related to studies of psychological or other effects. It is confined to synopses of some of the main philosophical arguments made in applied ethics which represent each position. They are not the only arguments that have been made and are open to critical evaluation. The literature on the morality of abortion is extensive and is not covered here in detail. The synopses are presented for consideration, discussion and further study. (For an overview of the moral arguments and issues, including critical evaluation, as well information on the literature, see Harris and Holm 2003.)

SOME BACKGROUND

The 1983 Constitutional Amendment

The legal basis for social policy lies in the 1983 constitutional provision. It guarantees the right to life of the unborn with due regard to the equal right to life of the mother. It excludes abortion while allowing for a termination when it is necessary to save the life of a mother. It was inserted in the Constitution by a vote of the people in a referendum. 'The State acknowledges the right to life of the unborn and, with due regard to the equal right to life of the mother, guarantees in its laws to respect, and as far as practicable, by its laws to defend and vindicate that right' (Art. 40.3.3).

Influence of 1992 X Case Judgment

The case involved a fourteen-year-old girl who was a victim of rape and who threatened to kill herself if she had to go through with the pregnancy. She and her parents concluded the best course was to obtain an abortion abroad and made contact with the gardaí in relation to procuring evidence from tests on the foetus to help in establishing the identity of the person who had committed the crime. Since the wording of the Constitution requires that the life of the unborn has to be protected, the case led the Attorney General to obtain an interim injunction from the High Court, which restrained the girl from interfering with the right to life of the unborn and from leaving the country for the purpose of having an abortion. The family contested the injunction. The outcome was that the Supreme Court judged a termination of pregnancy is lawful in Ireland under the constitutional provision, if it can be shown, that there is a real and substantial risk to the life, as distinct from the health, of the mother which can only be avoided by terminating her pregnancy, and it found that a threat of suicide can amount to such a real and substantial risk. The Court had heard evidence in the girl's case that she was at such a risk.

As a result of the case, a referendum was held in 1992 to amend the Constitution to allow a right to travel abroad for the abortion services legally available in another country. The referendum also provided for a right to information about abortion subject to regulation. Both of these amendments were passed. A third amendment to reverse (or roll-back) the Supreme Court judgment which held that termination on grounds of suicide came within the 1983 constitutional provision was rejected.

In 2002 a further referendum to amend the Constitution was narrowly rejected. It proposed providing legal means to protect the life of the unborn after implantation in the womb and to reverse the Supreme Court ruling that a threat of suicide could be grounds for a termination.

In 2005 three women lodged a case at the European Court of Human Rights alleging that Ireland's lack of abortion services breached their human rights. In 2010 the Court found in the case of applicant C, in which a risk to her life from cancer was at issue while being pregnant, that her right was breached by 'the uncertainty' arising from the lack of legislative provision to implement the right to a lawful termination in Ireland under the Constitution. The judgment was made under Article 8 of the European Convention on Human Rights, which provides a right to private and family life.

In 2013 The Protection of Human Life in Pregnancy Act became law. It provides legal clarity and regulation for doctors to end a woman's pregnancy when it is endangering her life. It also gives regulatory effect to the Supreme Court ruling that a termination is lawful under the Constitution on grounds of a proven real and substantial risk of suicide. Conservatives opposed the Act on the grounds of providing for direct abortion when existing medical practice already allowed for a termination when necessary to save a woman's life. In particular in relation to the suicide provision, they do not regard a termination as a means of averting a threatened suicide.

In social care work, between the Supreme Court ruling in 1992 and the 2013 Act, there were cases in which the State assisted suicidal girls in its care to avail of abortions abroad, such as in the C case in 1997.

Much public debate has taken place in arriving at the current position, debate that continues, and in which the conservative, liberal and intermediary views are put forward to influence the legal and social policy position.

Moral Questions Involved

Those who argue against abortion and those who argue in favour of allowing it as a choice, in either wide or narrow circumstances, usually differ on two central questions. These are:

- When does the life of the unborn begin to have the moral status of a person with a right to life such that it is entitled to the protection of the law?
- What moral weight should be given to a woman's choice to end her pregnancy in circumstances where it presents her with a serious difficulty, particularly for her physical or mental health?

Conservative Arguments

1. Continuity through Foetal Development

This argument holds that there is no identifiable stage in the development of the organism from conception to birth at which it can be said to have changed from not having the right to life of a person to having that right; therefore, it must be presumed to have that right from the beginning. It points to the continuous process from the fertilisation of the ovum through to birth by way of various stages, such as when the initial zygote implants in the uterine wall and begins to grow. It is formally known as an embryo until the end of the eighth week and after that a foetus. Commonly, 'foetus' is used to designate the organism throughout the process, during which human organs and characteristics appear and develop. Around twenty-four weeks the foetus can become viable, that is, capable of surviving outside the mother's womb with medical assistance.

It is argued that neither the foetus's lack of human capacities and resemblance in the early weeks nor its growing capacities and resemblance make a defining difference to its personhood. There can be no cut-off stage at which it is less than a living person. Personhood therefore must be taken to begin at the moment of conception. It is sufficient for the foetus to be conceived from human parents for itself to be a human person (Noonan 1967). Since it is seriously wrong to end the life of a person, it is also thereby seriously wrong for an abortion to take place before any particular stage. The foetus has the status of the life of a person and is entitled to protection even though dependent on a mother who has a serious difficulty or crisis in carrying it to birth, and for which she wants to have a termination.

2. Presumption of Personhood

This holds that even if there is a doubt that personhood occurs from the moment of conception, it is morally unacceptable to allow that doubt provide a reason for abortion because it is taking an unacceptable risk of bringing the life of a person to an end. Whether or not it has the moral status of an actual person, it is nonetheless a living human individual in the process of becoming a person, and so it *may have* the moral status of a person. Since this is the position, it is not right to act as though it does not have the status of personhood. In other words, it is reasonable to *presume* it is a person to be on the safe side and avoid making a mistaken judgment which would end the life of a person (Grisez 1970).

3. Genetic Code

The fertilised ovum is not a neutral set of cells. It is an organism in which the genetic code prescribing the uniqueness of an individual has been laid down, including, for example, its gender. No new genetic information from which it will develop characteristics is added after conception. So it is said not just to have the potential to develop into a born individual person but also to be already, in essence, an individual person with growing potential, including for rational thought. This argument is made in particular against the liberal argument that the foetus's lack of functioning capacity makes it not yet a person. It is the argument that its human gene structure already makes the foetus in essence a person regardless of its level of development. Its personhood is not dependant on having particular capacities which have not yet developed, such as sensation or a level of awareness (Noonan 1968; Ramsey 1971; see also Reville 2013).

4. Future Like Ours

This argument assumes that the foetus is a person because it has a future, just as children and adults have futures. Children and adults value their future lives, its experiences, projects and enjoyments, either for their own sake or as means to obtaining something valuable, and it is a serious wrong to deprive them of their future by killing them. For the same reason, it is also seriously wrong to end the life of a foetus which is capable of having a similar future. This argument claims it does not have to depend on proving that the foetus is a person. It is enough to claim that to deprive it of a future (which a person can have) is to cause it serious harm which should not be permitted other than in exceptional circumstances (Marquis 2002: 83–93).

5. Double Effect from Saving Mother's Life

This is the claim that the necessary ending of the life of the foetus to save the life of the mother is not abortion, and therefore not wrong. The reason is because the intention and medical intervention are to save the mother's life and the termination is an indirect and unavoidable consequence, i.e. the second or double effect. Even though ending the life of the unborn is foreseen, it is not desired or directly intended, but intended indirectly or obliquely. For the conservative, in particular Catholic view, this is an important argument because they maintain that abortion is always wrong. By this means they hold that ending the life of the foetus when it is necessary to save the life of the mother is acceptable and not abortion. (For the double effect principle, see Harris and Holm 2003; see also *Stanford Encyclopaedia of Philosophy*).

Liberal Arguments

1. Distinction between a Living Human Organism and a Person

The developing embryo and foetus is a living human organism, but is said not yet to be a person, and hence not to have the rights of a person, because it lacks human capacities and resemblance. While the foetus has a special value as a potential person, it is seen not to have rights comparable to those of a person who is born. In support of this argument, Warren, for example, draws a distinction between an organism being human by virtue of its gene structure and having capacities. She identifies personhood with capacities which people have, and lists six: sentience, i.e. the capacity to have conscious experience, including the capacity to experience pleasure and pain; emotion; reason; communication; self-awareness; and moral agency. She accepts that there are problems in precisely defining necessary characteristics of personhood, and in deciding on valid behavioural criteria that give evidence of them. She accepts also that her choice of capacities may not be absolutely necessary for being considered a person, and that it is not necessary to have all six. She recognises, too, that while infants and some older people lack some of these capacities, they are clearly persons with moral rights. Nevertheless, she maintains that the capacities can be recognised as characteristic of what it is to be a person, and that from its lack of development the foetus can be considered to lack them, in particular in its early stages when it is not yet minimally sentient and lacks all of them, and so does not have the same right to life as a person.

She argues, further, that if the equal rights of a person are accorded to the foetus, then, in practice, respecting its right would mean 'severely threatening the rights and well-being of women' who are clearly persons (2002: 73). The foetus's right to equality of treatment would give rise to inequality for women in requiring women to make sacrifices to bring the foetus to term, sacrifices that undercut the right they have to lead their own life. In later stages of pregnancy she accepts that there is a growing moral problem as the foetus gains sentience, which includes a capacity to experience a sensation of pain, and that understandably people can be 'repulsed' at the thought of its needless abortion (2002:79). Nevertheless, she holds that even if the foetus is accorded some right to life, that right does not outweigh the basic moral rights to life, liberty and physical integrity which women have when the two rights are in conflict and which entitles women to a safe and legal abortion (Warren 2002 and 1993).

This argument that the foetus does not have the same right to life as a person lies behind laws in countries that allow for abortion before a certain stage, for if the foetus is held to have the same right to life as a person, then it would require protection under the law. Among EU countries the stage varies; it is usually three months or twelve weeks, or later if necessary for medical reasons, with the UK allowing it for up to twenty-four weeks, which is known as the viability stage, at which the foetus can survive outside the uterus with medical assistance.

2. The Right to Private Choice

Pregnancy is a private matter relating to the reproductive system in a woman's body over which she has a right to full control. No woman should be forced to bring a foetus to full term against her will. The failure to allow for abortion is said to infringe her right to liberty, self-determination and physical integrity. She is entitled to give priority to her physical and emotional health, including what the effects on her would be of having to cope with the consequences of an unwanted birth. Her autonomy has priority. This argument is supported by Thompson. Unlike Warren, she accepts that the foetus is likely to be a human person well before birth, and consequently to have the right to life of a person at some stage. However, she argues that a woman's right to determine her own life outweighs the right to life of the foetus when they are in conflict.

She asks us to imagine, as an analogy, a woman waking up one morning and finding she has been kidnapped and put in a hospital bed hooked up to a famous violinist suffering from kidney poisoning who is being kept alive by a blood type that only she can supply. She cannot now be unplugged from supplying her blood without causing the death of the violinist. If she is told his right to life outweighs her right to autonomy and she must continue to supply her blood for nine months, Thompson imagines the woman would naturally find this an 'outrageous' infringement of her right to her freedom (2002: 64). Her point is that just as no one has a right to avail of the use of your kidneys unless you explicitly give your permission, the foetus does not have the right to benefit from growing in a woman's body unless the woman has consented to it, even when it needs it for its own survival. There are circumstances in which a woman will not have given her consent, for example, in cases where pregnancy occurs by accident or from rape. She considers that even though the violinist has no right to expect another person to supply him with blood, it could be considered 'morally indecent' to cut off the blood supply resulting in his death, in particular if it is at little cost to the person supplying the blood (2002: 69). Nevertheless, neither the violinist nor society has a right to demand that a person complies. In line with her argument, if a person acts voluntarily in full knowledge that pregnancy could result, then this would give the foetus a right to be carried to term, and so there are some such cases when it would be unjust for a woman to choose an abortion (2002: 68).

3. Value of a Woman's Individual Life and Circumstances

This argument emphasises that a woman is an individual involved in a particular life and in particular relationships with others, such as her immediate family. If she goes through with her pregnancy, she can affect her life in ways she has not chosen, and which she finds have serious adverse consequences for her. She may, for example, be very young and have become pregnant by accident, and be unable to carry the foetus to term without losing out in practical ways affecting her future, or be unwilling to face an emotional challenge of giving the baby up for adoption. In other circumstances, a woman may already be in a stable marriage and have children, and may feel that to cope with her pregnancy and with rearing another child will have a serious adverse affect on her physical and mental health. Or the foetus may have a fatal abnormality, from which it will die on birth or shortly after, a circumstance not included in Irish law as grounds for an abortion, and which came to the fore in the debate leading up to the Protection of Life in Pregnancy Act of 2013. Since there is a range of circumstances that can arise in which pregnancy becomes a problem for a woman and is unwanted (see Warren 1993 for further examples), it is argued that the choice to go through with pregnancy or not should be hers, and that her choice should be respected since she is the person primarily affected. This argument also makes the point that failure to allow for abortion is to distrust women being able to make a responsible decision, and that they have a right to be trusted on the need for an abortion as they see it.

4. Consequences for Women of a Ban

This argument draws from the fact that some women choose to have an abortion, and that to have a ban on abortion will put their health and lives at risk if it is not available to them in a legal and regulated way, and when, as an alternative, they choose to have an unregulated abortion. Part of the reasoning behind providing for abortion in countries where it is legal is to prevent unregulated abortions. Irish women who choose to have an abortion that does not fall within the 2013 Act are obliged to travel to another jurisdiction in which abortion is legal and regulated. It is also argued that a ban would, in effect, force a woman to act against her will in carrying the foetus to term, as she is given no other legal choice.

Arguments for Intermediary Position

1. Proportionate Response

Jane English argues that it is impossible to decide on a set of features which the foetus has to have in order to be considered a person, a set that would be universally acceptable, as there is a range of characteristics which are possible. Nor is it possible to decide on some cut-off point at which the developing foetus becomes a person. Nor is it possible to prove that the foetus is a person from the fact that it is human and living, as it does not follow that it has to be taken as 'a human' or 'a human being' (1997: 20), since this is to make a logical jump by simply affirming a consequence that it is a human *person* from the fact that it is living and human. At the same time, she argues that not knowing the moral status of the foetus does not mean the conservative view has to be accepted, which takes conception as the starting point of the life of a person. Nor does it mean the liberal view has to be accepted either, that a lack of some capacity in the foetus means that abortion can be justified for a range of reasons.

She argues that because the foetus is a potential person, and people are valuable, it is wrong to harm a foetus, unless it is necessary. A choice of abortion is sometimes justified and sometimes not: it is justified when going through with a pregnancy has serious consequences for a woman; and it is not when it presents little or no threat to her interests. She recognises that a foetus is innocent, as it is not responsible for causing any harm; nevertheless, she argues that there is a parallel between harming the foetus and a situation in which people are entitled to defend themselves. People are justified in defending themselves with proportionate force only, i.e. the amount necessary. Where the threat is small, they cannot kill or cause serious injury. But they may do so if the threat is large, where they are at risk of being killed or seriously harmed. In this way she argues that people are never justified in treating the foetus as they please. Further, the foetus is more valuable the more the pregnancy advances. She concludes that abortion is justified in early pregnancy to avoid modest harm coming to a woman, and seldom justified in late pregnancy except to save her life or to avoid significant harm (1997: 25–6).

2.Virtuous Course

Hursthouse sheds a different light on abortion to the previous writers by looking at it from the point of view of virtue theory. She sets aside the question of whether a woman has a right to have an abortion and asks, is having an abortion a virtuous act or one that is lacking in virtue? First, she makes the point that even if it is granted that women do have a right, this, of itself, does not make having an abortion a good or right thing to do. When people give priority to exercising their rights in their lives and relationships, love and friendship get lost in ways that cause harm to others as well as themselves. So abortion should be seen in the context of people's actual lives and relationships, which are relevant to forming the right attitude. The right attitude is bound up with how people look on parenthood, family life, and getting old and dying as important parts of their lives, and in which they normally care deeply for their children, family and friends. In this context, for people to look on abortion as 'an incidental means' to getting what they want is 'callous and light-minded, the sort of thing that no virtuous and wise person would do' (2002: 99). She points out that people take seriously the grief felt by a couple when a woman has a miscarriage and react with appropriate sympathy. This is seen as natural and good, and tells us something about the attitude we should have to abortion.

She is not saying that all women in all circumstance are lacking in virtue when they have an abortion. It depends on the circumstances which give rise to the reason for the abortion. It *may* be described as 'self-indulgent, callous and irresponsible', and manifesting 'a flawed grasp of what her life should be about' (2002: 100; 101), but not in circumstances, for example, of poor physical health or exhaustion from previous child-bearing. At the same time, she suggests that even when the decision is made for understandable reasons and is not irresponsible, the fact that human life has been prevented from continuing can be a source of appropriate regret. A woman may feel responsible for not having developed her character in a way that could have enabled her to avoid having an unplanned and unwanted pregnancy.

While the decision is naturally one for a woman to make, Hursthouse also includes boys and men in having responsibility to act with virtue. Their behaviour can show selfishness or regard for life; fear or courage (2002: 102).

3. Life as Sacred

Dworkin finds arguments that the foetus has a right to life unconvincing. Like Hursthouse, but in a different way, he re-frames the question of abortion from a question about rights to one about differing views on how respect for the sacredness of life should be shown. Most people, he claims, intuitively regard human life as sacred, and it is this that exercises them on the question of abortion. 'Almost everyone shares, explicitly or intuitively, the idea that human life has an objective, intrinsic value that is quite independent of its value for anyone, and disagreement about the right interpretation of that shared value is the actual nerve of the great debate about abortion' (1994: 67). 'Sacred' has religious connotations, and he uses the word in a broad sense to include the special importance of human life within the humanist view, which is that human life arises from nature without need for acceptance of a religious origin. Human life is sacred and has intrinsic value from its inception, and he argues that people, including both conservatives and liberals, feel the foetus to have this independent value. People regard great works of art, or the continued existence of a rare animal species, as having a value that is independent of its relation to any particular person, and feel it a shame when it is avoidably destroyed. This is also the case for a foetus. He maintains that liberals accept that abortion is a serious moral decision, at least from the time when the initial organism has successfully implanted in the womb, and that they do not believe abortion is permissible for a trivial reason, such as when it interferes with a planned trip abroad or when it does not have the hoped for gender. Their valuing of the life of the foetus shows in a number of ways, which include recognising the natural physical and emotional bonds that a woman usually has with the foetus. At the same time, he is not taking a conservative position and viewing abortion as wrong in all but the most restricted circumstances.

For Dworkin, recognising the sacredness of life includes not frustrating or thwarting the investment that girls and women have made in their own lives. Where liberals differ from conservatives is in the weight they give to the particular value a woman has invested in her life over the value of continuing with a pregnancy in certain circumstances. It is where she judges that to continue with the pregnancy and have a baby will in a serious way block or hinder her life, in which she has invested time and effort. It is where the loss to her life, in her judgment, would be greater than the loss through ending the life of the foetus. This is considering the foetus as it is, not as it would be if brought into the world, nor as having a right to life, which he does not think can be shown to exist. It is a judgment that a woman has to make within her circumstances and from her recognition of the sacredness of life. It is better, he claims, to see decisions about abortion as reflecting 'more nuanced and individual judgements about how and why human life is sacred' and to see disagreement as 'spiritual'. He believes that to see abortion in this way, rather than as about rights, should prove helpful in bringing the opposed views of conservatives and liberals closer together (1994: 100–1).

Social Policy Aim

Social policy in Ireland is aimed at reducing the number of unplanned and unwanted pregnancies. To this end, the Health Service Executive runs a crisis pregnancy programme, which includes measures relating to sex education, contraception and support for services, as well as research and publications (see www.crisispregnancy.ie/).

EUTHANASIA AND ASSISTED SUICIDE: INTRODUCTION

Much has been written on the ethics of euthanasia and assisted suicide. The literature contains specific arguments both *for* and *against* each practice, along with counter arguments and further probing of particular aspects. Presented here is a summarising account of some of the main arguments put forward on each side, along with arguments made by people who take an intermediary position. The terms 'conservative', 'liberal' and 'intermediary' are used to designate positions on the issue only, as they were in the preceding section on abortion. The arguments are intended to provide a basic understanding for reflection and discussion, as well as a springboard for further study, discussion and debate. Margaret P. Battin's (2003) essay in particular, 'Euthanasia and Physician-Assisted Suicide', gives an overview of the issues along with assessment of the merits of particular arguments and bibliography.

SOME BACKGROUND

Euthanasia

It involves two main elements:

1. The deliberate ending of a person's life on his/her behalf, either at the person's request (voluntary euthanasia) or the request of next of kin where the person does not have the mental capacity to make a decision (non-voluntary).
2. The person is suffering intolerably from an incurable illness or condition in circumstances which are usually terminal, i.e. the illness is progressive, such as certain cancers, and the person is considered likely to die from it within a short period, such as six months. The circumstances may also not be terminal (e.g. paralysis or permanent loss of conscious awareness).

Active euthanasia is where a doctor administers a lethal dose of tranquilising drugs to bring about a peaceful death. Passive is where a doctor either withholds or withdraws life-prolonging treatment, for example, a feeding tube or respirator, and provides for a peaceful death.

Assisted Suicide

This is where a person assists another person who is suffering from an incurable illness or condition to take his/her own life at their request by providing them with the means. The person who has requested assistance performs the final act. While closely related to euthanasia, it is not considered euthanasia because the act, which directly brings about death, is performed by the person who has asked for it and not by anybody else.

Moral and Legal Position

Euthanasia is generally considered morally wrong because it involves taking someone else's life. No one is considered to have the right to do this because of the fundamental value of life. For the same reason, it is generally considered wrong to help people end their own lives in cases of assisted suicide. At the same time, there are those who argue that people have a right to have their life ended when it is their choice, and that next of kin should be allowed to make the choice for them when they have lost the capacity to choose and have minimal or no quality of life arising from their illness or condition. Exit International, for example, is an organisation which campaigns for people to have a right to voluntary euthanasia and assisted suicide.

Both practices are illegal in most countries. In Ireland euthanasia and doctor-assisted suicide are illegal under the Criminal Law (Suicide) Act of 1993. Both practices are legal in Holland subject to conditions providing safeguards, and euthanasia is legal in Belgium. Doctor-assisted suicide is also legal in Switzerland under certain conditions. In Switzerland an organisation called Dignitas provides a service open to people from other countries.

Conservative Arguments

1. Worth of Individual Human Life

This argument holds that it is wrong to end the life of a person. (Killing in necessary self-defence or in a just war is regarded as an exception.) It is wrong primarily because each person's life has intrinsic worth. A person's life has worth of its essence from the fact that s/he is alive. The historical source for the argument that people have intrinsic worth is said to have come from religious cultures in particular (see Kuhse 1993 and Battin 2003). In Ireland this influence has come from the Judeo-Christian tradition and through Roman Catholicism particularly. Part of the religious view includes the belief that each person's life is a gift from God and, as a result, is sacred and carries a duty not to choose to reject the gift through euthanasia or assisted suicide. The view that life has intrinsic worth is not confined to religious belief. It forms the basis for many laws in a secular state where it is seen as necessary for civilised society.

It is also argued that to end a person's life for him/her, or to help him/her end it, goes against nature. It is an argument found in the natural law theory of Thomas Aquinas, from which subsequent writers who defend this view have drawn (Battin 2003: 678). Under Aquinas's theory, as we saw in the chapter on human rights, it is claimed to be self-evident to our reason that it is good that life should always be preserved from the natural human inclination which each person has to preserve his/her life, and also from the natural inclinations which people have to form families and live together in society. It is argued that to allow people to choose to die, even when they find they have lost the will to live and are suffering from an incurable illness, is to allow them to break natural ties to themselves and to others, ties that they continue to have of their nature as persons. To end their lives for them would be killing them as persons.

A related argument is that the various aspects of life that people value, and which others value them for having – their thoughts, emotions, abilities, accomplishments and personality – are inherently bound up with the biological fact of having life. To have *biographical* life requires and presupposes having *biological* life. The two are inseparable. So, even when people consider their *biographical* life no longer worth continuing with and wish to have it ended when they are suffering intolerably and have no appetite for life left, euthanasia and assisted suicide are still wrong because their biological life cannot be considered separate from them as persons. Killing them is still killing a person because personhood belongs to them of their essence (Moreland and Geisler 1990: 72–3).

2. Slippery Slope Argument

If we accept that people have a right to choose to have their life ended under certain conditions, this will create a social climate in which the respect for life that is necessary for civilised society will be weakened. Protecting life against a choice that some want to have is in everybody's interest because it maintains the value of life. To allow people opt for euthanasia would undermine that value. In particular, it is argued that vulnerable people, such as those with particular disabilities or the elderly, may not have their lives valued as fully as they are entitled to. Vellman, for example, argues that allowing for a choice would put pressure on people in vulnerable groups to feel that their lives were of less value than others because of their circumstances. Such pressure might influence them to choose euthanasia if it were legal, something they would not otherwise have considered. For society to allow euthanasia as a choice is to cause harm to people, in that it could interfere with the right of some people to remain living without feeling in any way obliged to consider euthanasia. If it is available as a choice, then to stay alive is something they may feel they have to try and justify rather than take it for granted. It may also give rise to a change in the way some people who are dependant on care are viewed. The burden of justifying why they should still be cared for could come to lie with them, in particular in light of financial costs to families or the state. This can be conveyed in subtle ways by, for example, not encouraging people to continue to live, or by not valuing them enough. To allow for choice will lead to people choosing euthanasia for mistaken reasons or under pressure. In this way Vellman makes the point that we can harm others by giving them choices (2002: 34–7).

A further aspect to the argument is that uncaring relatives of people could put pressure on them to opt for euthanasia in order to be relieved of a burden, financial or otherwise, of caring for them. Relatives who are unscrupulous and abusive may even put pressure on them in order bring forward inheritance. For these reasons, it is seen as too dangerous to allow for euthanasia.

Most writers on euthanasia address the slippery slope argument. Some find it persuasive, others not (see, for example, Hooker 2002: 29–30; Battin 2003: 682–6). The slippery slope argument is seen as having force for policy-makers in particular. It is argued that while we are moved to compassion for people experiencing suffering and who want to die, nevertheless the greater good lies in refusing their requests in order to protect people in society. (See case 2 below.)

3. Damages Doctor–Patient Relationship

The doctor–patient relationship is based on doctors doing whatever they can to save people from dying. If they are permitted to end lives, or assist in people ending it for themselves, then this will radically alter the nature of their role in society. It would conflict with the view central to medical practice, which is that life is intrinsically valuable, and that people should be treated to maintain their health so they can improve the quality of their life, and not to have their lives ended. Also, it would add to the slippery slope argument. For if doctors who are responsible for saving lives are also allowed to end lives, then it would make it more acceptable for people to consider ending their lives, especially people who are vulnerable and may feel they are a burden in the care they require. In addition, from knowing that doctors can also act to end lives, the trust that is essential for patients to have in doctors to look after their medical needs could be weakened. (See Battin 2003: 681–2 for discussion of this argument.)

Liberal Arguments

1. Personal Autonomy or Self-determination

People give meaning and value to their lives by how they choose to live. They value making their own decisions about matters that are important to them. Dying is an extremely significant process for anyone, and death an extremely significant event. So people should be allowed to die on the same basis as they have lived, i.e. on the basis of making their own choice about what they consider of value, and for some this may be to have their life ended to avoid what they see as unnecessary suffering from an incurable illness or condition, in particular when it is diagnosed as terminal. For some conditions and illnesses, suffering can include people feeling the indignity of being dependant on others in whole or in part for their basic needs. Not to allow people this choice is to deprive them of their core sense of self, of their dignity and self-respect, which lies in directing their own lives as rational agents (Brock 1997). In support of this argument, Rachels (1986) draws a distinction between *having a life* made up of aspirations, activities and decision-making, and *being alive* in a biological sense. He argues that society should respect the freedom of choice which some people want when they have lost the capacity to have a life they consider of worth from their illness or condition.

The liberty or autonomy argument is the primary argument made by those in favour of allowing euthanasia and assisted suicide. Brock (1997) adds that the self-determination on which it is based is consistent with the self-determination that is allowed in being able decide whether or not to have, or to continue with, life-sustaining treatment in certain circumstances. For example, people diagnosed with cancer can decide not to undergo chemotherapy or radiation treatment, even when by having the treatment they will most likely live for longer than they would otherwise. However, conservatives argue that there is a significant moral difference between people having a right to refuse treatment, refusal that will lead to their death, and a doctor ending their life, directly in the case of active euthanasia, or indirectly in the case of assisted suicide. In refusing treatment, a person is bringing about their own death by passively allowing their illness or condition take its course, while euthanasia involves actively killing another person and assisted suicide involves giving active assistance, even when done at a person's request and under other legal safeguards.

More broadly, liberal philosophy emphasises the importance of individual autonomy or self-governance and claims people have a right to maximum freedom of action consistent with the freedom of action of others. This means, essentially, that you should be free to do what you like as long as you are not acting in ways that cause others harm. The 'harm principle', as it is known, was expressed by Mill in his essay 'On Liberty'.

The sole end for which mankind is warranted, individually or collectively, in interfering with the liberty of action of any of their members, is self-protection. That is the only purpose for which power can be rightfully exercised over any member of a civilized community against his will, is to prevent harm to others. His own good, either physical or moral is not a sufficient reason.

Mill 2008: 14

Rachels argues that the level of liberty expressed by Mill justifies permitting euthanasia (1986: 180–2). Under the slippery slope argument, there are potential indirect harmful consequences. However, liberals are likely to argue that a law permitting euthanasia could not be held directly responsible for such consequences. It is up to everyone to assert their own autonomy, and for society to protect vulnerable people from harm through its laws, while at the same time ensuring that maximum personal freedom is allowed. Liberals would say Vellman and others who make the slippery slope argument may be underestimating the capacity of people who are considered vulnerable to assert their own autonomy and/or underestimating the capacity of the state to frame effective legal protections.

2. Relief from Suffering Argument

This is the argument that it is cruel and inhumane to refuse a plea from people to have their life ended mercifully when they are suffering intolerably with no prospect of effective relief. They experience suffering to a degree that makes their life no longer worth living and wish to have it brought to a peaceful end. There is a range of conditions that give rise to some people deciding they no longer want to continue with their lives from the suffering it is bringing them, or who if no longer mentally competent to make a decision might want to have it made for them by their next of kin, or by a person appointed to represent their interests. For example, they may experience a lot of severe pain which is difficult to relieve to a degree they find tolerable; they may have dementia to an extent that they no longer recognise themselves or their loved ones; they may not want to live with the restrictions of quadriplegia; or they may be in a later stage of a degenerative disease, such as multiple sclerosis. As a result of these and other conditions, they can feel a loss of dignity and integrity, bodily or mentally or both. This argument stresses that not everyone with these conditions feels this way, and that the lives of people with these conditions remains as important as anyone else's, and it is not a reason for them to be valued any less. But some do feel this way, and have reported on it, and campaigned for euthanasia and assisted suicide to be legal so they can avail of it. They believe a caring society should allow them their choice.

Battin (2003: 686–90) considers points *for* and *against* this argument. One point against, which is commonly made, is that pain management techniques in palliative care have ensured that virtually all physical pain can be relieved, and that if necessary complete sedation is available. Others argue suffering from pain is a subjective matter for individual patients, and some may decide that, despite the best care efforts of doctors, they still find they have an intolerable level of pain. They may also find that the loss of capacity when they require heavy sedation for a terminal illness leaves them with such a small, or no, quality of life that it is not worth continuing to live. There are also conditions in which there may be no physical pain, but people still suffer mentally from severe restriction and/or from facing into a prolonged period before dying, and for which they would like the choice to have their lives discontinued.

Through medical technology and treatments, it is possible to prolong the lives of people who are dying and are close to death. It is accepted, in the conservative as well as the liberal view, that there is no moral obligation, either on patients or on doctors, for a person to be kept alive unnecessarily when death is inevitable and close. A judgment is made on the proportionate or disproportionate benefits of continuing treatment in light of the patient's condition and the quantity and quality of life s/he is likely to gain (Kuhse 1993: 298–9). If the judgment of continuing the treatment is of disproportionate benefit to the patient, then it can be discontinued. This judgment is made with the consent of the patient or, when this is not possible, his/her family. (See also Vatican Declaration on Euthanasia 1980.)

Liberals sometimes argue that, since this is acceptable, it is an example of passive euthanasia, which shows that euthanasia is sometimes permissible, and that this leaves euthanasia open to being justified in other circumstances as well. However, it is debatable whether discontinuing treatment in these circumstances is an example of passive euthanasia. From a conservative view, the *intention* is not to end the life of the patient, even though it is foreseen, but to bring to an end suffering which is having a disproportionate effect on the patient's quality of continued life when death is imminent, and so it does not come within the definition of euthanasia. Instead, even though life-prolonging treatment is withdrawn, it is viewed as acceptance of the human condition and as letting life take its natural course to its end in death. It is sometimes described in terms of 'letting happen' rather than 'making happen'.

A liberal view also makes the point that administering pain-relieving treatment through drugs can contribute to bringing forward a patient's time of death, and, since this makes it part of a process in which ending life for a patient with a terminal illness is occurring, it is consistent with a doctor taking a further step and acting to bring life to an end when it is a patient's choice. However, a conservative argument is that even if administering pain-relieving drugs does contribute to shortening life expectancy, the intention is pain relief, not ending life, and that this makes for a moral difference which rules it out as part of euthanasia. This is another example of the argument from the double effect principle, which we have seen conservatives use in accepting a termination of a pregnancy to save the life of a mother. That is, the main effect, the intended effect, is to relieve pain; the other unintended double effect may be to shorten life. (See Battin 2003: 678–681 on the double effect principle.)

Arguments for Intermediary Position

Best Interests

It is impossible to characterise exactly an intermediary position, as it can relate to different specific circumstances for allowing euthanasia, and not allowing it for other circumstances, across a range of conservative and liberal positions. However, a likely intermediary position is one that accepts the intrinsic-worth-of-life argument and the slippery slope argument. At the same time, it accepts that, on compassionate grounds in particular, euthanasia and assisted suicide should be permitted in certain exceptional circumstances of intolerable suffering, and subject to regulatory safeguards. Vellman (2002), for example, who we have seen is strongly opposed to euthanasia on grounds of protecting people from its abuse, nevertheless accepts it can be justified, and should be allowed, in exceptional cases in which people suffer from intolerable pain and have no prospect of recovery. However, while Vellman supports a view that doctors be given legal permission in certain exceptional cases, he suggests that having 'no policy at all' is 'the best public policy' (2002: 38–9). In exceptional cases, the justification often given is that death is judged to be in a person's best interests. In the first of the two cases described below, a patient's best interests was given as part of the legal reasoning for allowing a woman's feeding tube to be removed given her particular circumstances.

Dworkin also draws in particular from the 'best interests' argument in arguing for euthanasia, and could be considered close to a liberal position. He accepts the intrinsic-worth-of-life argument but argues there are legitimate different interpretations on what the intrinsic worth of life means. For some people, the intrinsic worth of life is demonstrated by people who keep going as best they can even though they have lost physical and mental capacity, and find they have to endure suffering. They value doing this because it is integral to the meaning and value they view their own life as having, and usually also integral to the meaning and value they see human life as having in general. They regard it as being in their own best interests and that of humanity's. Others, however, see the intrinsic worth of life as dependant in particular on 'critical interests' which they have developed in the course of their life (Dworkin 1994: esp. 201–08). Critical interests are different from less important interests, such as an interest in watching sport, gardening or other hobbies. Critical interests have to do with the important decisions people make about the kind of life they value and want to live, and in which they invest time, energy and commitment, and which engages them with a sense of personal responsibility. It might be in a particular career or pursuit, or in a cause, such as social justice, or in having family or other relationships, or in engaging in some particular physical or intellectual activity. They are interests that they find central to the worth of their lives. Dworkin argues that some people find life unbearable when they lose the capacity to be able to maintain critical interests as a result of illness, accident or old age.

He also makes the particular point that people want to see the way they end their life as representing what their life has meant for them, and that it can be devastating for some people that they do not have a choice to have their lives ended for them when they see it as having lost its purpose. It can mean that they have to live out their lives in a way that does not fit in with how they see themselves and would like others to see them. In his approach, Dworkin says, 'the question posed by euthanasia is not whether the sanctity of life should yield to some other value, like humanity or compassion, but how life's sanctity should be understood and respected' (1994: 217).

Two Cases

Passive Non-voluntary

In passive non-voluntary circumstances people cannot make their wishes known because they lack mental capacity, unless they have made an advance health care directive, which we will look at below under social policy. There are a number of conditions that result in loss of mental capacity to make an informed decision, such as advanced Alzheimer's disease, in which patients no longer recognise themselves or their loved ones. The case described here involves what is known as a 'vegetative' state. It is called 'vegetative' from the capacity of a patient's body to continue to grow and develop; however, as a result of brain damage, patients have lost conscious awareness of themselves and of their surroundings and are unable to communicate with their carers, even though they can be awake and have their eyes open. After a certain time, their condition is said to be irreversible, and they are cared for until they die, which may not happen for years or even decades. In rare cases they may regain conscious awareness. (For a UK medical review of the conditions of patients considered to be in persistent and permanent vegetative states and related conditions, see Laureys, Owen and Schiff 2004.)

In 1995 the Irish Supreme Court upheld on appeal the High Court's judgment to remove a feeding tube that had kept a woman, who was described as being in a near persistent vegetative state, alive for over 20 years. The 'Ward of Court (withholding medical treatment)' case, as it is known, was taken by her mother and a committee, and opposed by the hospital in which the woman was receiving care. The Court judgment reflected the autonomy argument, that even though the right to life ranks first in the hierarchy of personal rights, it is nevertheless subject to the citizen's right of autonomy or self-determination or privacy or dignity. This is a right that a person can exercise for himself if competent; if not, then it can be exercised on his/her behalf by agreement between carers and family, as long as they are acting in the patient's best interests. The ruling is also in keeping with the right that people have to decide not to allow or accept treatment which might prolong their life. The judgment was seen to be in the best interests of the woman, given the burden which the artificial means of nourishment was placing on her by keeping her alive when there was no prospect of any improvement in her condition. It also held that the constitutional right to life extends to a right to die a natural death.

Notably, removing the feeding tube was not judged to be an act of euthanasia. The ruling was that death would be from the underlying condition, and not from removing the feeding tube. Since its removal would not be the legal cause of death, it was not setting a precedent for legalising euthanasia. In this way, the Court was reflecting the view that life need not be prolonged unnecessarily when to do so is disproportionate to the benefit to the patient, and that the intention is not to end the patient's life, but to allow her to die. It remains the case that it is against the law for anyone to end the life of a loved one in a vegetative state unless they have first obtained Court approval. (For details of the case and the judgment, see website for the Supreme Court of Ireland, Important Judgments; see also Madden 2005).

Voluntary Active in Assisted Suicide

This is the case of Marie Fleming who died from multiple sclerosis in 2013. She had applied to the Courts for a person to be lawfully allowed to assist her in having a peaceful and dignified death at a time of her choice. She was supported in her application by her partner, Tom Curran, and other family members and friends. In their rulings in 2013, the Courts accepted that she was suffering acutely, with the High Court describing her circumstances as 'harrowing' and the Supreme Court as 'tragic'. However, the Courts rejected her application on two main grounds, which reflect both the intrinsic worth of life of all persons and the slippery slope arguments. Her case was based primarily on the claim that her right to autonomy under the Constitution was interfered with by having a blanket ban on assisted suicide under the law. However, the High Court found that the ban did not interfere disproportionately with her right to autonomy. The State has to value equally the life of all persons, and some people who are categorised as vulnerable would have the protection of their right to life weakened by a legal entitlement to assisted suicide. The Court ruled that even with strict safeguards, it 'would be impossible to ensure the aged, the disabled, the poor, the unwanted, the rejected, the lonely, the impulsive, the financially compromised and emotionally vulnerable would not avail of this option in order to avoid a sense of being a burden on their family and society'. It also found that evidence of risks to abuse in other countries where it is legal were 'all too real'. In upholding the judgment, the Supreme Court ruled that there is no constitutional right to arrange to have one's own life ended at the time of one's choosing. It said judgment in the Ward of Court case (see above) was different in being based on a right to die a natural death, and not a right to terminate a life or have it terminated.

The judgments, however, seemed to recognise her case as having moral justification with legal implications. The High Court said if it could 'tailor-make' a solution to suit her circumstances alone, without affecting the right of others, there might be 'a great deal' to be said for her claim. It also referred to the fact that the Director of Public Prosecutions has discretion not to prosecute and felt the Director would exercise her discretion in a humane and sensitive way 'in this of all cases'. Ms Fleming had also sought that the DPP publish guidelines, as there are in the UK, on the circumstances in which the discretion will be exercised, in order to have legal clarity. However, it was felt this would require a change in the law, which is a matter for the Oireachtas. (For details of case and judgment, see website for the Supreme Court of Ireland, Important Judgments; see also Carolan 2013, January and April; O'Mahony 2013).

SOCIAL POLICY AIM

As mentioned, euthanasia and assisted suicide are illegal in Ireland. Social policy relating to end of life issues and needs is aimed at helping people to cope with difficulties they may have, and where their illness or condition is terminal to enable them in the final stages to have appropriate palliative and nursing care, and for other needs or wishes they may have to be provided for as well as possible. An advance directive is a document in which people can give their views on the health care they would want, and not want, in the event that they become no longer competent to make decisions. It can include people's instructions and preferences regarding life-prolonging treatment, such as being placed on a ventilator or resuscitated, and it enables people to specify forms of treatment they would find unacceptable. Advance directives are in keeping with the right people have to refuse medical treatments and to be involved in decisions regarding their health care. Advance directives have not, as yet, been given a legal footing in Ireland, but the Irish Council for Bioethics and the Law Reform Commission have recommended that they should be. As advance directives stand, they provide a strong ethical basis in autonomy for people's directions to be respected and acted upon by health care professionals, as well as giving guidance (see McCarthy, Donnelly, Dooley, Campbell and Smith 2011:190–5).

To promote interest in getting people to consider how they would wish to be cared for when dying, the Irish Hospice Foundation and the National Council of the Forum on the End of Life in Ireland developed a project called 'Talk Aloud'.

The project has made available an advance directive form which people can use (see website www.talkaloud.ie/).

REVIEW

Abortion, euthanasia and assisted suicide are issues of life and death on which moral arguments have been made in support of the view that it is morally wrong to end life and in support of the view that it is morally permissible in certain circumstances. The considerations in the arguments inform the views which people have and the positions they adopt. Broadly, three positions can be identified: conservative, liberal and intermediary. The considerations also inform, and are part of, public debate and influence legislation and social policy.

FURTHER READING

Abortion

Bryant, J., Baggott la Velle, L. and Searle, J. (2005) *Introduction to Bioethics*, John Wiley & Son, Ltd (Chapter 11).

Harris, J. and Holm, S. (2003) 'Abortion' in *The Oxford Handbook of Practical Ethics*, H. La Follette (ed.) (2003), Oxford University Press.

Vardy, P. and Grosh, P. (1999) *The Puzzle of Ethics*, Fount, HarperCollins (Chapter 12).

Euthanasia and Assisted Suicide

Battin, M. P. (2003) 'Euthanasia and Physician-Assisted Suicide' in *The Oxford Handbook of Practical Ethics*, H. LaFollette (ed.) (2003), Oxford University Press.

Bryant, J., Baggott la Velle, L. and Searle, J. (2005) *Introduction to Bioethics*, John Wiley & Son, Ltd. (Chapter 12).

Hooker, B. (2002) 'Rule-Utilitarianism and Euthanasia' in *The Oxford Handbook of Practical Ethics*, H. LaFollette (ed.) (2003), Oxford University Press.

McCarthy, J., Donnelly, M., Dooley, D., Campbell, L., and Smith, D. (2011) *End-of-Life Care Ethics and Law*, Cork University Press.

Vardy, P. and Grosh, P. (1999) *The Puzzle of Ethics*, Fount, HarperCollins (Chapter 13).

REFERENCES

Abortion

Dworkin, R. D. (1994) *Life's Dominion, An Argument about Abortion, Euthanasia, and Individual Freedom*, Vintage Books.

English, J. (1997) 'Abortion and the Concept of a Person' in *Social Ethics, Morality and Social Policy*, Mappes, T. A. and Zembatty J. S. (eds) (1997), McGraw-Hill.

Grisez, G. (1970) *Abortion, the Myths, the Realities and the Arguments* cited in Mappes, T. A. and Zembatty, J. S. (1997) *Social Ethics, Morality and Social Policy*, McGraw-Hill (p. 4).

Hursthouse, R. (2002) 'Virtue Theory and Abortion' in *Ethics in Practice, An Anthology*, H. LaFollette (ed.) (2002), Blackwell.

Marquis, D. (2002) 'An Argument that Abortion is Wrong' in *Ethics in Practice, An Anthology*, H. LaFollette (ed.) (2002), Blackwell.

Noonan, J. (1968) 'Deciding Who Is Human' *Natural Law Forum 13* (1968): 13 cited in Warren M. A. (2002) 'On the Moral and Legal Status of Abortion' in *Ethics in Practice, An Anthology*, H. LaFollette (ed.) (2002), Blackwell (pps 73 and 75).

Ramsey, P. (1971) 'The Morality of Abortion' in *The Morality of Abortion*, J. Rachels (ed.) (1971) cited in Mappes T. A. and Zembatty J. S. (eds) *Social Ethics: Morality and Social Policy* (p. 19).

Reville, W. (2013) 'A Functional and Essential Debate', *The Irish Times*, 2 May 2013.

Thompson, J. (2002) 'A Defence of Abortion' in *Ethics in Practice, An Anthology*, H. LaFollette (ed.) (2002), Blackwell.

Warren, M. A. (2002) 'On the Moral and Legal Status of Abortion' in *Ethics in Practice, An Anthology*, H. LaFollette (ed.) (2002), Blackwell.

Warren, M. A. (1993) 'Abortion' in *A Companion to Ethics*, P. Singer (ed.) (1993), Blackwell.

Euthanasia and Assisted Suicide

Brock, D. W. (1997) 'Voluntary Active Euthanasia' in *Social Ethics, Morality and Social Policy*, Mappes, T. A. and Zembatty, J. S. (eds), McGraw-Hill.

Carolan, M. (2013) 'Assisted Suicide Ban Cannot Be Diluted Even in "Harrowing" Case of MS Sufferer', *Ther Irish Times*, 11 January 2013.

Carolan, M. (2013) 'Supreme Court Rejects Fleming Case but Says Ruling Does Not Preclude Legislation', *The Irish Times*, 30 April 2013.

Kuhse, H. (1993) 'Euthanasia' in *A Companion to Ethics*, P. Singer (ed.), Blackwell.

Laureys, S., Owen, A. M and Schiff, D. (2004) 'Brain Function in Coma, Vegetative State, and Related Disorders', *The Lancet*, Vol. 3, September.

Madden, D. (2005) 'Allowing Beloved to Die Is Not Killing', *The Irish Times*, 31 March 2005.

Mill, J. S. (2008) *On Liberty and Other Essays*, Oxford World Classics.

Moreland, J. and Geisler, N. (1990) *The Life and Death Debate: Moral Issues of Our Time*, New York Praeger.

O'Mahony, C. (2013) 'DPP Needs Clear Protocols after Assisted Suicide Ruling', *The Irish Times*, 15 January 2013.

Rachels, J. (1986) *The End of Life, Euthanasia and Morality*, Oxford University Press.

Vatican Declaration on Euthanasia (1980), available at www.euthanasia.com/vatican.ie (accessed 28 August 2013).

Vellman, J. D. (2002) 'Against the Right to Die' in *Ethics in Practice, An Anthology*, H. LaFollette (ed.), Blackwell.

13
Conclusion

We have seen that a number of values and principles can be considered to inform and guide social care practice, and to provide justification for decisions. They provide bearings for managing cases of individual need, for having an informed viewpoint on issues and for developing a more caring society. Gilligan summed up values and principles as belonging to either one of two categories: detached or engaged (see Banks 2004: 90). By 'detached' is meant the values agree with the reasoning side of our nature. These values include treating people as equals and with respect, human rights, the greatest happiness principle, social contract ethics and social justice. By 'engaged' is meant the values agree with our emotional side. The more engaged values include care, empathy and being virtuous toward others for their good. At the same time, there is not a clear distinction between values that agree with reason and those that agree more with emotion. For example, as we have seen, reasons also provide justification for why care, empathy and acting for the well-being of others are values. Also, a sense of social justice is a powerful natural emotion which gives rise to efforts to establish how it should be understood by rational arguments.

In practice in social care, the relevance of one value or principle more than another will depend on the issue and its context. Traditionally, values from both detached and engaged categories have been part of social work practice and ethos. They can be looked upon as two sides of the same coin (Banks 2004: 93; 186–70). From different angles, each shines a light on an aspect of what is understood as morally good. The aspects can be similar, as with well-being and care, or they can be different, as in conflicting views on social justice and on issues such as abortion or euthanasia.

We have seen also that the philosophical justification for values and principles is open to critical evaluation. Valid criticisms can be made of the arguments on which they are based. But this is not to say that faults or weaknesses found in philosophical arguments prove that the values and principles are false or lack worth. It is to recognise that, in so far as human understanding can grasp the basis for values, the basis is open to questioning and further exploration and discussion.

Our engagement with our moral sensibility through values can be considered to have deep and powerful roots which cannot be clearly or fully understood. For Iris

Murdoch, our sense of morality is what makes us 'uniquely human'. For example, it is our human moral sense that makes us want to help famine and disaster victims. It is why we condemn the torture of prisoners and demand that governments who allow for it end the practice. It is what makes us think that for anyone to have to sleep rough in the streets at night is 'not right'.

For Iris Murdoch, it is as if our moral sensibility 'came to us from elsewhere'. She sees it as giving us 'an intimation of "something higher"' (1992: 26). By 'something higher' she means a 'transcendent' dimension. By 'transcendent' is meant having a sense of belonging to something larger than us, which at the same time is seen to have independent value. Traditionally, this dimension has been the province of religious belief. But whether people take their morals from religious belief or from values without the backing of religious belief, she believes there is still some ultimate guide at work (1992: 511). She sees evidence for a transcendent moral guide in art and describes a work of art as like 'a picture of goodness itself' (1992: 9).

> The art-object, transcendent, clarified, self-contained, alone secure and time-resistant, shedding light upon the miserable human scene, prompting compassion and just judgment, seems like a picture of goodness itself, a sort of semi-sensory image of a spiritual ideal.
>
> Murdoch 1992: 9

In a similar vein, Seamus Heaney sees that our engagement with transcendent experience in art brings us in touch with a moral guide, with 'our need for an ultimate court of appeal'. For him, 'poetry is the ratification of the impulse towards transcendence'. Poetry provides us with a court, as do the other arts, in which we can experience and learn about what is of ultimate value without it having to be symbolised by belief in God (O'Driscoll 2008: 470).

How can our experience of art give us access to a transcendent moral guide? To understand this we need to try and see what makes for a work of art, and then try and see how it might also have a bearing on our moral impulse or sensibility. Asked what poetry had taught him, Seamus Heaney said that 'poetry itself has virtue'. It has virtue 'in the sense of possessing a quality of moral excellence'. For Aristotle, as we have seen, a virtue is an excellence or a power. From reading a great poem we can get a sense of its excellence or power. We can also sense in it particular moral virtues, for example, honesty and trustworthiness. For Seamus Heaney, a great poem has virtue 'in the sense also of possessing inherent strength' through three qualities: wholeness, harmony and radiance. These three qualities are the marks of a work of art which Aquinas originally identified, and Seamus Heaney cites them in their original Latin (O' Driscoll 2008: 467). The English translation is the one given by James Joyce in a passage in his novel A *Portrait of the Artist as a Young Man* where the character of Stephen Dedalus analyses their meaning

(2001: 163–5). Wolterstorff also identifies a work of art by its possession of a similar set of three qualities: unity of completeness and coherence, internal richness of parts, and as giving a sense of intensity or brightness (1980: 164–8).

But how does an artwork with these qualities give us moral guidance? In their loftiness in high art the qualities seem far removed from ordinary experience. The answer would seem to be that by having these qualities art keeps itself together in an illuminating way. There is a sense in which both art and ethical values share a capacity to meet a deep need that we have to keep ourselves together, both as individuals and as a society (see also Heaney 2002/3). If we had no moral values, or art in any form, to guide us in our lives, our sense of our self as person would not only be impoverished but also lost in not knowing how to behave or what to value. We would flounder in inconsistency and fragmentation. The quality in art of wholeness or completeness acts, in particular, as a model for the moral quality of integrity, and for the integration of values into behaviour and character.

Charles Taylor also writes about art providing us with a means of having a transcendent experience which gives us access to a guide for our moral sensibility. It does so through enabling us to experience an epiphany. An epiphany can be described as a spiritually uplifting and revealing experience in which we get a sense of wholeness coming from something of ultimate meaning and value, but which does not have a specific content that can be identified. From engaging with art, Taylor suggests we experience 'epiphanies' of fulfilment, however brief and fleeting, in which we can sense the very source of morality (1989: 477; 431; 428; 425).

In having an ultimate source in qualities of wholeness, harmony and brightness, values are not given to us already established, in a clear form, for putting into practice. In their expression in words and actions, in a variety of different and changing contexts, they challenge us, like the way making a piece of art challenges an artist, in having to be made and re-made from lines of thought and behaviour which try to be adequate to human experience in an open and uncertain world. An open and uncertain world gives them their edge and vitality and tests their adequacy.

We can draw moral nourishment and guidance from art in a general way. But what about having a specific account of morality which would draw from the guidance and source felt to be accessible through art? Tony Judt wrote in his book on the roots of the international financial crisis, *Ill Fares the Land*, that we need a new 'moral narrative' in which people can share. He points to a breakdown in acceptance of the traditional understanding of values, inherited from the philosophers of classical Greece and the Enlightenment period, as well as from religion. He sees the traditional understanding of values as no longer convincing. The breakdown shows in political debates, in particular, where the choice between a policy or decision and another is essentially ethical, yet the debates are confined to immediate practical matters, such as budgets and economic requirements.

Instead of an overall shared ethical understanding or vision of what is good for society, there is assertion and counter-assertion about how to meet people's material interests. He sees this as having led to public scepticism and lack of trust in politics, while the moral impulse remains indisputable (2010: 178–184; 164). In Chapter 9 on social well-being we saw how Alasdair MacIntyre also wrote about a crisis in ethics; how he sees it as showing the relevance of reviving Aristotle's ethics in which we recognise the need for virtuous behaviour, such as honesty and consideration for others, in order to benefit from social practices, such as business and family life.

Perhaps a new, shared moral narrative will emerge which will be more capable than the traditional one to engage interest and provide direction. If it does, Judt recognises that it will have to be based on a transcendent dimension to human experience and not on some new form of pragmatism which seeks to satisfy everybody's particular interests. 'What we lack is a moral narrative: an internally coherent account that ascribes purpose to our actions in a way that transcends them' (2010: 183). But it is hard to envisage what a new, publicly-convincing moral account based on a transcendent dimension would contain, in particular in democratic society where there is a diversity of views about what is of ultimate value. It would seem to need in the first place broad recognition of the way in which art can provide for an experience of a transcendent moral source. It would then somehow have to be able to give this experience practical expression in a shared coherent account.

Even if such a new account is developed, it will still come down to how well it is put into practice. Martha Nussbaum (1990) has explored this aspect of ethics through looking at how well or badly characters in novels manage the opportunities, challenges, adversities and setbacks in the very particular circumstances of their lives, having regard to their human nature and forces outside their control. In a practical way, literary fiction can draw us into the circumstances of other people's lives which we can relate to in our own lives and circumstances. As we read, we can find ourselves experiencing a shifting undercurrent which is tuning and fine-tuning our moral sensibility within the light of the novel itself as an artwork, giving us access to a transcendent moral source.

As a guide for taking better care of others and ourselves, ethics will continue to be about managing the gap between the values we aspire to have and our actual behaviour. Finally, while philosophical understanding of traditional values and principles continues to provide guidance, ethics in practice is, as Aristotle recognised, an art, the art of living.

REFERENCES

Banks, S. (2004) *Ethics, Accountability and the Social Professions*, Palgrave.

Heaney, S. (2002/2003) 'Reality and Justice: On Translating Horace' in *Irish Pages*, *A Journal of Contemporary Writing*, *The Justice Issue*, Vol. 1., No. 2 (pp. 50–3).

Joyce, J. (2001) *A Portrait of the Artist as a Young Man*, Wordsworth Classics (see also note 418 to the text for Aquinas reference).

Judt, T. (2010) *Ill Fares the Land*, Penguin Books.

Murdoch, I. (1992) *Metaphysics as a Guide to Morals*, Chatto & Windus.

Nussbauum, M. C. (1990) *Love's Knowledge, Essays on Philosophy and Literature*, Oxford University Press.

O'Driscoll, D. (2008) *Stepping Stones, Interviews with Seamus Heaney*, Faber and Faber.

Taylor, C. (1989) *Sources of the Self, The Making of the Modern Identity*, Harvard University Press.

Wolterstorff, N. (1980) *Art in Action*, William B. Eedermans Pubishing Company.

Appendix

GUIDE TO WRITING AN ETHICS ESSAY

Aim to Convince

As a subject, ethics is part of philosophy. Philosophical writing aims to convince the reader with the strength of arguments made. It tries to show why something can be considered true or valid on the basis of rational arguments as distinct from opinion or feeling.

Argument

An argument is a connected series of statements containing evidence about some central claim (or conclusion) which the writer is trying to support.

Evidence

Evidence can be of different kinds: ideas and insights that have explanatory power; examples that illustrate and support a point; factual data such as survey results; and logical connections – material that can rationally be regarded as supporting a claim or conclusion. Distinguish between evidence and unsupported opinions or views. For example, we might say that a particular philosopher holds a certain view, but this of itself does not make the view valid. We need to show the evidence s/he gives us for his/her view.

Aim for Explanatory Depth

There can be a tendency to flag or name-check a philosopher's views and leave it at that, but they need to be explained to communicate to your reader that you understand them. For example, 'rights' or 'human rights' are frequently mentioned in ethics. You might write the following sentence: 'It is wrong for Mary to be treated in this way because it goes against her human rights' or 'Mary has a right to better treatment'. But why does Mary have the right being claimed for her?

Where does it come from? Can her particular case of need be linked to a human rights theory, such as natural law, from which you can claim her right ultimately comes? Then there is the further question about how valid the theory is. Does it have a weakness? If you think it does, how does the weakness affect the claim you are making that Mary has a right?

In a similar way, we might claim that racism is wrong because it goes against Kant's categorical imperative to treat all people as equal. But what exactly is Kant's imperative, and how does it explain why racism is morally wrong?

To take another example, we might write that we should look out for the well-being of others because, as Aristotle says, we are social beings. True, but go a bit further: why exactly does Aristotle think we are social beings? It is because, he argues, the existence of family, friends and community has come about naturally as the means that provide for human well-being. Human interdependency and well-being are inseparable. We are all dependant on others to survive and prosper.

Explain what You Mean

This is important to avoid your reader thinking you mean by a word or term something different to the meaning you intend. For example, there are different senses to the meaning of the world 'liberty': freedom to live as you choose within the law; freedom from absolute poverty in the developing world; and civil and political freedoms in democracies. 'Poverty', too, is a word that can be used either in the sense of absolute poverty; consistent poverty; and being at risk of poverty. People who are homeless could mean those who have to sleep rough in the streets; those in temporary (or long-term) sheltered accommodation; or people on local authority waiting lists for an apartment or house.

The precise meaning may be clear from the context, but it may not be, in which case it should be made explicit.

Note, too, that what you mean by 'equality' needs to be specified. Is it equality of moral status? Is it income equality or equality of wealth? And if you mean by equality, 'greater equality' or 'more equality', i.e. a reduction in the gap between those who have a lot and those who have less, rather than actual equality, this needs to be made clear.

State Your Purpose

If there is a particular essay title, it will indicate the purpose. However, sometimes an assignment topic can be quite open, and it is then largely up to you to define your purpose.

Defining the purpose of your essay in an introduction is central to its success. Your purpose is your personal statement of intent: you set out what you want to achieve and what you intend to show or prove. In addition to your purpose, include an outline of the ground you intend to cover. That is, give the reader an indication of the scope of your essay, how wide-ranging or narrow you intend it to be. Mention specific aspects you intend to cover. Your purpose might be to defend a particular point of view, to compare two ideas, or to present research findings and draw conclusions from the evidence.

Aim to keep your purpose within achievable limits. There is a tendency to try to achieve too much by choosing a big topic and having a broad scope. The tighter you can define your purpose and your approach, the better.

Develop Your Argument

Whatever your purpose, it is essential to keep it clearly in mind while you write and not lose sight of it. See yourself as following a particular line along which you are making a succession of related points toward a conclusion. If you do go off on a tangent, which you consider interesting and relevant, make clear to your reader that this is what you are doing, and explain why you feel it is necessary and relevant. But always come back to your central point. You need to connect up your material around your purpose. In particular, refer back to your purpose in your conclusion and draw together in summary form the main points that have borne it out.

Show a Grasp of Material

Aim to show you have grasped material by giving your own account of it in your own words and integrating it with its sources for which you provide references. Some essays can lack a sufficiently strong sense of the student providing his/her guiding narrative thread through the material; source material is presented either in quotation or in paraphrase without comment on its significance, relevance or implications; and a reader learns about particular source material but not enough about why it is being included and where the student is going with it, or what the student thinks about it. The difficulty is, then, that a reader gets little sense of the student's understanding of the material. Try to get on top of your source material so you can show you are using it for your purpose, while at the same time expressing it accurately. What you make of your sources counts a lot in demonstrating your level of understanding. So, include also critical evaluation of material, explaining why you think it has strengths and weaknesses.

Make Good Arguments

1. Guard Against Generalisations

A generalisation is a sweeping statement or oversimplification. It involves an assertion that something is true of everyone or everything belonging to a particular class or group. It may be true of most people or things in a group or class, but 'most' or 'many' or 'some' is not the same as 'all'.

Sometimes a generalisation expresses a prejudice against a whole group of people, such as politicians, business people, asylum seekers or prisoners. Or it is made to avoid giving a matter due thought, i.e. to come to a quick conclusion to avoid having to think about a situation that is more complex and requires making distinctions.

2. Think Points Through

Examine points you make to see if they stand up. For example, if you are arguing for a general rule, is there an example of an exception to the rule which someone could argue is justified. If so, should the rule fall because of the exception, or should the exception be accommodated alongside the rule as a qualification to it? In either case, there will be implications, and these need to be brought out and weighed up.

3. Avoid Suppressing Evidence

If your evidence does not fit the conclusion you were hoping to make, so be it. Modify your conclusion to account for the evidence you have discovered. You may, as a result, have a less dramatic conclusion, but your qualified one in which you highlight limiting factors will be all the stronger for having been based on evidence that is not simple or neat but takes account of complex facts or circumstances.

4. Show Understanding of Counter Arguments

In arguing for a conclusion, if you know there is another possible view supported by other arguments, it will strengthen your essay if you can include it. Of course it will depend on your purpose and on word count requirements. You may want to make dealing with an opposing view central to the purpose of your essay. In this case you will need to address the opposing arguments to show why you think they are flawed or inadequate compared to the view you are taking. Alternatively, you can summarise an opposing view to show you are aware of it as a contrast.

5. Avoid Jumping to Conclusions

Build your argument toward your conclusion, and let the argument indicate what your conclusion will be. If you have a pet theory or viewpoint, you need to avoid letting it rule your understanding.

6. Keep an Open Mind

Usually the argument will not point to a clear and definite conclusion. The conclusion will be valid subject to qualifications. It is important, then, to show the limitations of the conclusion by including the qualifications and explaining why they are relevant. The argument may point to two or more possible conclusions or courses or actions, with each having advantages and disadvantages. When this happens it can be hard to opt for one conclusion without compromising the weight that needs to be given to factors not covered by it. You can then spell out the implications of each conclusion as a basis for deciding between them, or as a basis for further consideration or research.

Provide a Strong Conclusion

Your conclusion is always of particular importance. Draw together and restate your main points and findings and develop your considered viewpoint/judgment on them. In particular, spell out the implications that you see follow from your conclusion. Make as much as you can from your conclusion that is consistent with it. Look on it as your opportunity to contribute further to the understanding of the subject.

Index